Managing Business Finance

D0551795

University of Worcester
ILS, Peirson Building
Henwick Grove, Worcester WR2 6AJ

A1088480

We work with leading authors to develop the
strongest educational materials in business and finance,
bringing cutting-edge thinking and best learning
practice to a global market.

Under a range of well-known imprints, including
Financial Times Prentice Hall, we craft high quality print
and electronic publications which help readers to understand and apply their content, whether studying or
at work.

To find out about the complete range of our
publishing please visit us on the World Wide Web at:

www.pearsoneduc.com

Paul FURNISS

Managing Business Finance

D R MYDDELTON

FINANCIAL TIMES
Prentice Hall

An imprint of **Pearson Education**

Harlow, England · London · New York · Reading, Massachusetts · San Francisco · Toronto · Don Mills, Ontario · Sydney
Tokyo · Singapore · Hong Kong · Seoul · Taipei · Cape Town · Madrid · Mexico City · Amsterdam · Munich · Paris · Milan

University of Worcester
ILS, Pe... Building   A 1088480
Henwick Grove, Worcester WR2 6AJ

658. 15
MYD

Pearson Education Limited
Edinburgh Gate
Harlow
Essex CM20 2JE
England

and Associated Companies around the world

Visit us on the World Wide Web at:
www.pearsoneduc.com

First published 2000

© Pearson Education Limited 2000

The right of D R Myddelton to be identified as the author
of this Work has been asserted by him in accordance with the
Copyright, Designs and Patents Act 1988.

All rights reserved. No part of this publication may be reproduced, stored
in a retrieval system, or transmitted in any form or by any means, electronic,
mechanical, photocopying, recording or otherwise, without either the prior
written permission of the publisher or a licence permitting restricted copying
in the United Kingdom issued by the Copyright Licensing Agency Ltd,
90 Tottenham Court Road, London W1P 0LP.

ISBN 0 273 64645 1

British Library Cataloguing-in-Publication Data
A catalogue record for this book can be obtained from the British Library

Library of Congress Cataloging-in-Publication Data
Myddelton, David Roderic.
  Managing business finance / D.R. Myddelton.
    p. cm.
  Includes bibliographical references and index.
  ISBN 0-273-64645-1 (pbk.)
    1. Business enterprises–Finance. 2. Corporations–Finance. I. Title.

  HG4026.M932 2000
  658.15–dc21   99-089251

10 9 8 7 6 5 4 3 2 1
04 03 02 01 00

Typeset by 60
Printed in Great Britain by Henry Ling Ltd., at the Dorset Press, Dorchester, Dorset

CONTENTS

Look at Risk. ⭜

5.3. Measuring profit over time 55
5.4. Net present value and variants 59
5.5. Internal rate of return 63
5.6. Summary 66
Problems 67

6 More on capital projects **70**
6.1. Working capital 70
6.2. Taxation 71
6.3. Capital disinvestment 73
6.4. Inflation 75
6.5. Capital budgeting 77
Problems 80

7 Mergers and acquisitions **82**
7.1. Reasons for acquisitions 82
7.2. The process of merging 85
7.3. Accounting 88
Problems 90

8 Risk and uncertainty **93**
8.1. Risk 93
8.2. Uncertainty 96
8. Both Risk & Uncertainty 98
8. 101

9 Borrowing **104**
WHOLE CHAPTER 104
sk 107
9.3. Other types of debt 108
9.4. Valuing debt 111
Problems 114

10 Ordinary share capital **115**
10.1. Shareholders' funds 115
10.2. The stock exchange 116
10.3. Stock market indices 120
10.4. Issuing equity shares 123
Problems 127

11 Cost of capital **129**
WHOLE CHAPTER 129
) 130

LIST OF FIGURES

LIST OF TABLES

PREFACE

Managing Business Finance is based on *The Essence of Financial Management* (Prentice Hall, 1995), which was part of the now discontinued Essence series of books. The general flavour and aims of the book remain unchanged, but developing the text outside the confines of the series has allowed more scope for the inclusion of new material and improved pedagogical features.

The book has been thoroughly revised and updated. Some of the descriptive material has been dropped and the treatment of inflation reduced, in favour of the addition of new sections on financial regulation, efficient markets, the equity risk premium, accounting for acquisitions and mergers and foreign exchange risk.

More international material has been added in several of the chapters, and problems (and solutions) provided where appropriate.

Financial management is largely about *matching* or *balancing*:

- the maturities of liabilities with the lives of assets
- the currencies of borrowing with those of operations; and
- the required rate of return on investments with their risk.

So, as shown below, this book 'matches' five asset chapters (3 to 7) with five finance ones (9 to 13). The other four chapters cover both assets and finance: the introduction (Chapter 1), interest rates (Chapter 2), risk and uncertainty (Chapter 8) and valuing companies (Chapter 14).

1. Introduction

2. Interest rates

ASSETS	FINANCE
3. Cash	9. Borrowing
4. Working capital	10. Ordinary share capital
5. Basic capital project appraisal	11. Cost of capital
6. More on capital projects	12. Capital structure
7. Mergers and acquisitions	13. Restructuring

8. Risk and uncertainty

14. Valuing companies

This book probably does contain rather more on assets (and therefore rather less on finance) than most textbooks on financial management. There may not be much financial theory relating to working capital, but in many firms current assets represent the bulk of total assets. Managing them properly is thus important, both at the margin and in aggregate. It is critical, for instance, for marketing managers to appreciate the key variables in extending credit to customers, and for production managers to understand the total costs, as well as the benefits, of holding stock. It is no coincidence that management consultants often concentrate first on the management of working capital. They recognize that many firms are weak in this area – not so much because it is difficult, but because it requires continual vigilance.

Capital project appraisal is familiar territory in textbooks. This book explains discounted cash flow methods by first referring to the Net Terminal Value method, before moving on to Net Present Value. The reason for this approach is the more explicit discussion of what the interest rate (or discount rate) actually means – it is an 'opportunity cost', representing what else the firm (or its shareholders) could have done with the money. It is more important to appreciate what the interest rate means than to be the world's leading expert on calculating it to three places of decimals. In general, people – by no means just 'students' – tend to be absurdly credulous in the accuracy of the information they sometimes assume a company will have available. I have chosen to treat mergers and acquisitions as a form of capital investment project, which seems logical.

The chapter on borrowing looks at this form of finance both from the lender's and from the borrower's point of view; and also distinguishes shorter-term from long-term borrowing. The chapter on ordinary share capital also discusses stock exchanges and global market capitalization.

Then follow two chapters on the core of corporate finance – cost of capital and capital structure. The book looks in detail at two approaches to calculating the cost of equity capital – the Capital Asset Pricing Model and the Dividend Growth Model. Each has its pros and cons; and each approach has an underlying logic But precision in practical calculations is elusive. The book also discusses how to estimate the Weighted Average Cost of Capital by combining the cost of equity and the cost of debt by suitable 'weighting'.

As to capital structure, I follow the traditional view that over a wide range, capital structure is probably not a critical issue. At least there is fairly widespread agreement that in general it matters more in which assets a firm invests than how it finances them. In particular, it is a mistake to think that brilliant financing can somehow redeem an indifferent project. Even if one answers the question: 'How much debt should a company have in its capital structure' with the apparently glib response: 'Not too little and not too much!', one still ought to provide some clues about how to tell whether one has 'too little' or 'too much' debt. The section on 'The corporate life cycle' (as in the *Essence of Financial Management*) is largely based on *Corporate Financial Strategy* (John Wiley, 1993) by my colleague Professor Keith Ward.

The chapter on restructuring looks at forms of business (partnerships, limited companies), as well as briefly considering privatization. It also deals briefly with financial distress and with liquidation. Finally, there is a separate chapter on valuing companies, which brings together much of the material from earlier chapters. As throughout the book, I try to keep my feet on the ground, in discussing how people in the real world think about such matters.

This book is intended for general management students, not for finance specialists nor for academics. Thus I try to deal with important basic questions, such as: what do interest rates consist of? is cash or profit more important? how can one tell whether a capital investment project is worthwhile? how should a company decide on its dividend policy? how are shares in companies valued?

But the book does not attempt to cover in much detail peripheral, more specialized or less important questions, for example: how frequently should a business re-order stock? coping with capital rationing by linear programming; details of derivatives trading; fine distinctions between types of borrowing; detailed derivation of the CAPM formula.

I have tried to make the Glossary as useful as possible. It is more extensive than in many textbooks; and I have included a number of accounting terms as well as American equivalents of English terminology.

Finally, it may be helpful to say a few words about the problems and solutions. I believe the inclusion of problems (which *The Essence of Financial Management* omitted due to lack of space) is a big improvement. Students quite reasonably like to have the chance to manipulate numbers for themselves to make sure they have got the hang of the techniques discussed in the text. In some ways, though, I would prefer to label these 'problems' as being 'exercises'. I do not want to pretend that most of them reflect reality. Mostly the problems assume that all necessary variables are known, and it is simply a question of working through the logic to develop the correct answer. That is fine as far as exercises are concerned (and all the correct 'answers' are given at the back of the book). But I have deliberately not tried to incorporate too much extraneous detail by way of 'reality' – it would take up too much space, without simulating realistic business problems.

I envisage the book being used either by individuals who want to grasp the basics of financial management in a fairly straightforward way or on courses where much of the learning will involve discussion of 'real' business cases (not necessarily focussed entirely on *financial* management). This is how we use the book at Cranfield on our general management MBA and other programmes.

I would like to take this opportunity to thank my academic colleagues at Cranfield, especially Ruth Bender and Lance Moir, for detailed comments on early outlines of this book. I am grateful to those MBA students at the Cranfield School of Management who were kind enough to comment on the original book, either in draft form or as published as *The Essence of Financial Management*. I would also like to thank the anonymous referees who took a good deal of trouble to provide constructive criticism. I have followed their advice where I agree with it.

Finally, I should like to thank my secretary Sheila Hart for all her help and support, which I have come almost to take for granted whenever I produce another book. She has, as usual, been a tower of strength. On this occasion I should also like to express my thanks to Diane Billing for helping someone who must have seemed almost beyond redemption to come to terms with word processing on a computer. Oddly enough, the key lesson seems to be the same as in financial management, namely: 'don't panic'. It is due to Diane's patience and expert guidance that I have learned that lesson.

CHAPTER 1

Introduction

1.1. Business finance

Financial objectives of a business

The main **financial objective** of a business enterprise is to maximize the **wealth** of its owners, that is to say shareholder value. This means nearly the same as maximizing **profits** but allows for their timing. Thus companies try to make profits and to avoid losses and over time the profit and loss account reports success or failure in this respect.

Why are profits ever possible, above a 'normal' rate of interest on capital invested? Mainly because of ignorance. If people dealing on markets (both as buyers and as sellers) had complete knowledge, the prices of products would already fully reflect consumers' valuations. This **arbitrage** view of profit stresses the information content of price signals in the market. (Hence price controls are damaging because they distort the signals.)

In order to succeed in the longer term, a business must survive in the short term. Among other things, this means being able to pay its bills in cash when they become due. So financial managers must arrange to have enough cash at the right time.

v. relevant

The market system

Businesses aim to make a profit by satisfying customers. It is a mistake to regard managers and workers as the two 'sides' of industry or commerce. The real distinction is between consumers on the one hand and producers – owners, managers and workers – on the other. (Hence consumers may welcome the competition from foreign producers which domestic producers deplore.)

The market system is not a zero-sum game. In normal markets both buyer and seller can expect to gain from a voluntary market exchange, because they differ in their subjective valuation of the goods or services. (The Greek word for 'exchange' [*catalassein*] also means 'to change from enmity into friendship'.)

Consumers will not pay more than they think goods or services are worth (to them), which puts a ceiling on producers' total costs. The 'profit motive' gives producers an incentive to discover how much goods or services *are* worth to consumers – and

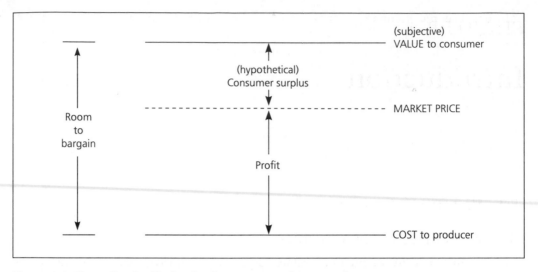

Figure 1.1 The split of added value between producers and consumers

to find ways either to add more value or to reduce costs. Figure 1.1 shows how producers and consumers share the total value added: consumer valuations minus producers' costs.

There are three main kinds of market: financial markets, labour markets and product markets, both industrial and retail. These markets deal with money, people and goods and services.

The market system is not static: it is a dynamic process, always having to adapt to changing conditions. The market may tend towards equilibrium, but never reaches it, as new disturbing features keep on appearing. The 'gale of creative destruction' means long-term competition from new goods and services, new technologies, new sources of supply, or new types of organization. This makes business management a difficult task, full of pressures and risks.

Owners and managers

The directors of the largest UK companies between them own less than one-tenth of 1 per cent of the equity **shares** in their firms. With very few exceptions they are professional managers not owners. This gives rise to **agency problems**. How can **principals** (owners) monitor the actions of their agents (the managers) and induce them to act in the **shareholders**' interests? Especially when the managers usually know a lot more about the business than the owners.

Managers build careers on their track record of success in business. The most important function of annual company **accounts**, subject to **audit** by independent accountants, is to record the **stewardship** of managers. It is always open to the owners to dismiss poor managers and hire others they hope will do better. This happens to football club managers: it happens to corporate managers too.

It has become common to reward managers partly by means of share option schemes or profit-related bonuses. But share option schemes do *not* 'align the interests' of managers who are already heavily committed to the success of their firms with those of well-diversified shareholders. How could they? And bonus schemes linked to current reported profits may encourage creative (dishonest) accounting and **short-termism**.

In contrast, owner/managers of small businesses suffer from no such potential conflict of interest. But they may not always aim to maximize their business profits. For example, the owner/manager of a small shop may prefer to close early, or not open on Saturdays, in order to enjoy more leisure. As a sole owner he is perfectly entitled to do this if he thinks it will maximize his own psychic well-being. But it would hardly please the shareholders of a large company if its managers chose not to maximize profits in order to enjoy more leisure! A competitive market would (sooner or later) replace such managers with others who *would* try to maximize the owners' wealth.

Most **limited companies** are private not public ('ltd' not 'plc'). They may be too small or too new to meet the minimum requirements for listing on a stock exchange. They may not need to raise more **equity** capital and their main shareholders may not wish to sell any of their shares. The owner/managers may prefer to remain private, to retain control and avoid the risk of takeover by others. They may not relish the pressures of public **listing** – both the stock exchange rules and the demands of outside investors.

1.2. The financial environment

Financial markets

There are four main kinds of financial markets:

1. Money markets which deal in short-term finance.
2. Foreign exchange markets, which deal in currencies (either on a spot or a forward basis).
3. **Capital markets**, which deal in long-term finance, both **debt** (e.g. the Eurobond market) and equity (international stock exchanges).
4. **Derivatives** markets, dealing in **options** and futures.

These markets are normally open twenty-four hours a day, based on the three major centres of London, New York and Tokyo.

Financial institutions

The main private sector financial institutions are banks, building societies, pension funds and insurance companies. Banks are the main source of short-term and medium-term loans for businesses; while for larger firms, pension funds and insurance companies are the main source of long-term external finance (both debt and equity).

3

Table 1.1 Shareholdings in ordinary shares of UK listed companies 1963–93

	1963	1969	1975	1981	1989	1993
Personal	56.1	49.5	39.8	30.4	23.3	19.3
Companies	5.1	5.4	3.0	5.1	3.6	1.5
Financial institutions						
Pension funds	6.4	9.1	16.8	26.7	30.4	34.2
Insurance companies	10.0	12.2	15.9	20.5	18.4	17.3
Unit trusts, investment trusts etc.	13.9	14.7	15.3	10.7	10.0	10.3
	30.3	36.0	48.0	57.9	58.8	61.8
Public sector	1.5	2.6	3.6	3.0	2.0	1.3
Overseas	7.0	6.6	5.6	3.6	12.4	16.1
Total	**100.0**	**100.0**	**100.0**	**100.0**	**100.0**	**100.0**

Table 1.1 shows the spread of shareholding in ordinary shares of listed UK companies at six dates between 1963 and 1993. The main long-term trend is that over the thirty years there has been a massive switch away from personal ownership of shares (down from 56 per cent to 19 per cent) towards pension funds (up from 6 per cent to 34 per cent). The same trend has occurred in the United States, to a somewhat lesser extent.

The clearing banks provide for debt settlement through their system of clearing cheques and direct debits. They are also important financial **intermediaries**, receiving small amounts of savings from a large number of people and then lending them out again to individuals and businesses.

Building societies used to operate mainly by receiving deposits of savings and lending them out to enable people to buy houses and flats. (The UK's rented housing sector is smaller than in the rest of Europe, while housing ownership is higher.) But since the 1980s, building societies now offer a complete range of retail banking services, and several have legally become banks.

Merchant (wholesale) banks arrange finance for companies (both debt and equity), and give financial advice, for example, on **acquisitions**. They also manage the investment assets of the larger pension funds, insurance companies and **investment trusts** and **unit trusts**.

Life insurance companies and pension funds receive long-term savings from people during their working lives, which they pay out again, together with interest, during retirement (pensions) or on death (life assurance). Partly for tax reasons and partly for **portfolio** reasons, pension funds have become the main owners of UK equities. (The state pension scheme is not 'funded': it runs on a 'pay-as-you-go' basis from current tax revenue. This is a huge problem for some EU countries, such as Germany, France and Italy, where private pension funds are much less widespread than in the UK.)

In the public sector, the key financial institution is the **Bank of England**, which was founded in 1694, nationalized in 1946 and made 'independent' in 1997. The Bank has several important functions:

1. It is the government's banker, taking in tax revenues and making payments, and managing the national debt.
2. It advises on and operates the government's monetary policy, issues bank notes and coins, and holds the country's foreign currency reserves. All these functions would transfer to the European Central Bank if the UK were to join Economic and Monetary Union (the 'single currency') within the EU.
3. It acts as banker for the clearing banks, and acts as 'lender of last resort' to the financial system.

Financial regulation

Between providers and retail purchasers of many kinds of financial services there can be a large difference in their relative knowledge (**'asymmetric information'**). (The same is also true for doctors and garages and their customers.) It is hard for an investor to find out which providers are both honest and competent (search costs are high). Mistakes could cause disastrous loss, and where there are few repeat purchases (as, for instance, with one-off purchasing of pensions), the normal competitive safeguard of reputation and 'brand names' may not work. Hence there may well be some need for regulation; but what sort and how much?

The tradition of British self-regulation has advantages. It is cheap and flexible, though this 'club' approach may risk being not strict enough in dealing with offenders and can tend to maintain excessive barriers to entry. In place of the previous, less formal, system, recent changes have imposed much more statutory control. Figure 1.2 outlines the scope of the new **Financial Services Authority** (FSA), which regulates most financial services with extensive powers.

As well as banks and various professional bodies, the FSA oversees SROs such as SFA, IMRO and PIA, and RIEs such as LSE, **LIFFE** and LCE. Whether the benefit from all this alphabet soup outweighs the costs is hard to say. The begetter of the whole system,

FINANCIAL SERVICES AUTHORITY (FSA)		
Self-Regulatory Organizations (SROs)	Recognized Investment Exchanges (RIEs)	Recognized Professional Bodies (RPBs)
Securities and Futures Authority (SFA)	London Stock Exchange (LSE)	Accounting bodies
Investment Management Regulatory Organization (IMRO)	London International Financial and Futures Options Exchange (LIFFE)	Law societies
Personal Investment Authority (PIA)	London Commodities Exchange (LCE)	

Figure 1.2 The Financial Services Authority

the late Professor Gower, rejected any sort of cost-benefit analysis: he was not competent to undertake it and he was sceptical about its use. Such a casual approach gives the powers-that-be an incentive to over-regulate, since their aim will be the absence of scandals at almost any cost. (When a scandal does occur, by the way, 'despite' the existence of extensive controls, the 'solution' proposed is nearly always still *more* regulation!)

Another important area concerns company accounts, which must give **'a true and fair view'** of performance for the past year and of the financial position at the end of it. Two main sources of rules instructing accountants (and auditors) how to achieve this are company law and **accounting standards**. The Companies Act 1985 (amended in 1989) takes fifty pages to cover the form and content of company accounts. And UK accounting standards (listed in Appendix 1, page 199) contain even more detailed instructions about disclosure and measurement in accounts. Together with notes they now comprise more than 1200 pages.

1.3. Accounting

Balance sheet

The accounts of a company (or group of companies) consist of three main financial statements: balance sheet, profit and loss account and **cash flow** statement (see Chapter 3) – together with notes to the accounts and the auditors' report.

The **balance sheet** shows a firm's financial position at the end of an accounting period. It distinguishes **assets** (*uses* of funds) from **liabilities** (*sources* of funds). Table 1.2 sets out a simple example.

An asset is a valuable resource which a business controls. Accounts normally show assets at their original (**'historical'**) money cost, less any deductions to allow for subsequent using-up or erosion of value. **Fixed assets** are long-term resources: firms use them to provide goods or services, rather than to sell in the normal course of business. They include land, buildings, equipment, etc. **Current assets (stocks, debtors,** cash) are short-term resources likely to turn into cash within twelve months after the balance sheet date, if not already **liquid.**

A liability is what a business owes to others. **Current liabilities** are due for settlement within twelve months after the balance sheet date. UK balance sheets deduct them from current assets, to show **working capital** (= **net current assets**). **Long-term liabilities** are amounts due more than twelve months after the balance sheet date. Regular interest payments are due on amounts borrowed.

Shareholders' funds (**'capital** and **reserves'**) are amounts which the owners of the business have provided – either directly (by subscribing cash for **ordinary shares**) or indirectly (by means of **retained profits** or in other ways). In a sense they are ultimate liabilities of a company to its shareholders; though the actual amount payable would vary depending on how much remains after selling all the firm's assets and paying off all the other liabilities. Thus the amount of shareholders' funds in the balance sheet does *not* represent what the owners' interests are 'worth'. (So the American expression

Table 1.2 Hardstaff Products plc: Balance sheet at 31 March 2000

	£ million	£ million
Fixed assets		
Intangible		20
Tangible		55
Investments		10
		85
Current assets		
Stocks	45	
Debtors	40	
Cash	15	
	100	
Less: Current liabilities	35	
Working Capital		65
Total assets less current liabilities		150
Less: Long-term borrowing	25	
Provisions	5	
		30
		120
Shareholders' funds		
Called-up ordinary share capital		50
Retained profits		70
		120

'net worth' is highly misleading!) As long as a company continues in business, no amounts are legally due to shareholders unless the directors decide to distribute **dividends** out of profits.

The amount of long-term sources of funds must always equal long-term net uses of funds. Each amounts to £150 million for Hardstaff Products. Hence balance sheets always balance! This is the principle of **double-entry** accounting.

Profit and loss account

The **profit and loss account** (P & L account) summarizes a firm's income and expenses for an accounting period (normally a year). It shows how much of a period's profit ('earnings') the firm has paid in dividends to shareholders, and how much it has retained in the business. (The latter amount represents the *link* with the balance sheet.)

Profit is **sales revenue** (**turnover**) less total **expenses** for a period; and a **loss** is simply a negative profit. As Table 1.3 shows, much of the detail in a profit and loss account consists of a classified list of the various expenses, with subtotals at intervals.

A published profit and loss account would normally show details of operating expenses in the notes to the accounts. To help run the business, however, internal ('management') accounts would show much more detail, both for the balance sheet and for the profit and loss account. For example:

Table 1.3 Hardstaff Products plc: Profit and loss account for the year ended 31 March 2000

	£ million	£ million
Turnover		240
Cost of sales:		
Materials	50	
Labour	80	
Depreciation	15	
Other production overheads	25	
		170
Gross profit		70
Selling and distribution	17	
Administrative expenses	29	
		46
Operating profit		24
Interest payable		4
Profit before tax		20
Tax		5
Profit after tax		15
Ordinary dividends		6
Retained profit for the year		9

1. Results for periods shorter than a year, often one month (or four weeks).
2. Results analyzed by product groups and geographically. (The published accounts also show these in the notes.)
3. **Budgets** for future periods, as well as past results.
4. Much more detailed analysis for income and expenses and for assets and liabilities.

Basic accounting concepts

Four basic accounting concepts underlie the numbers in any set of accounts:

1. The **going concern** concept assumes that an enterprise will continue in business. This normally means accounts showing assets at (recoverable) **cost**. Cost may be recovered either out of the proceeds of trading sales revenue or from ultimate resale of fixed assets. If one assumed that the company was about to be **liquidated** (**wound up**), it would then be prudent to show assets at the amount they would realize on immediate sale (**net realizable value**), which might be much less than cost.
2. The **accruals concept** where possible **matches** expenses against revenues: firms recognize revenues as they earn them and expenses as they incur them in transactions. It would normally be less realistic for a firm to recognize transactions only when it received or paid *cash*. The British government's recent switch from cash accounting to accrual ('resource') accounting represents a change of emphasis – away from

authorization and honesty (though both are still required!) towards performance and efficiency.

3. The **consistency** concept requires the same accounting treatment for similar items from one period to another, to allow readers to compare results between periods and establish reliable trends over time. When there is a change in accounting treatment, for some good reason, company accounts disclose the fact and try to quantify the effect. This concept does *not* mean that one company has to use the same accounting treatment as another company. Hence comparing the results of different companies remains difficult, despite the existence of accounting standards laying down detailed rules.

4. The **prudence** (conservatism) concept means that accounts include revenues and profits only when they are **realized**, either in cash or in the form of assets whose ultimate proceeds are fairly certain. In contrast, accounts provide in full for all 'expected' losses and expenses.

The basic purpose of accounts, in reporting on the stewardship of the directors, is to give 'a true and fair view' of a company's profit or loss for the accounting period and of its financial position at the end of it. This means following a number of accounting conventions which have grown up over the years (and which may evolve in future). Normal accounts leave out many important commercial assets, especially internally-generated assets such as business know-how and **goodwill**.

1.4. Business performance

Return on investment

A common measure of operating performance is **return on investment** in **net assets**. This has a number of names:

- Return on investment (ROI)
- **Return on net assets** (RONA)
- **Return on capital employed** (ROCE)
- **Return on funds employed** (ROFE)

This important measure expresses operating profit (**profit before interest and tax – PBIT**) as a percentage of long-term net operating assets, either for the whole group or for parts of it. In principle a company can compare how well it manages to employ its assets against the returns available from other possible uses of scarce capital funds (after allowing for **risk**).

For Hardstaff Products plc., the return on net assets for the year ended 31 March 2000 was 16.0 per cent:

$$\frac{\text{Operating profit}}{\text{Net assets}} \quad \frac{24}{150} = 16.0 \text{ per cent}$$

One can also express this as: **profit margin** (10.0 per cent) × net asset turnover (1.6 times):

$$\frac{\text{Operating profit}}{\text{Sales}} \quad \frac{24}{240} = 10.0 \text{ per cent}$$

$$\frac{\text{Sales}}{\text{Net assets}} \quad \frac{240}{150} = 1.6 \text{ times}$$

Another useful way to analyze a company's rate of return on net assets is to set out the main items of profit and of net assets in a diagram such as in Figure 1.3.

The main components of profit (sales revenue, cost of materials, cost of labour, etc.) can each be analyzed between quantity and price; and this basic approach will often give clues to possible improvement.

In general, to improve its rate of return on investment, a company can either increase its profit for a given amount of net assets, or maintain its profit while reducing the amount of net assets. In the latter case, it can then invest any surplus capital to earn a return, and thus increase total profits. (This is the **opportunity cost** of the investment in net operating assets.)

A different way to view return on investment is to deduct from the 'return' a charge to represent interest on all capital employed (equity as well as debt). What is left is then close to true economic profit: it has various names, such as **residual income** or **economic value added (EVA)**.

If Hardstaff Products, for example, used a capital charge of 12 per cent (before tax), the amount of residual income would be £6 million:

	£m
Operating profit	24
less: Capital charge: 12 per cent × £150 m	18
Residual income	+6

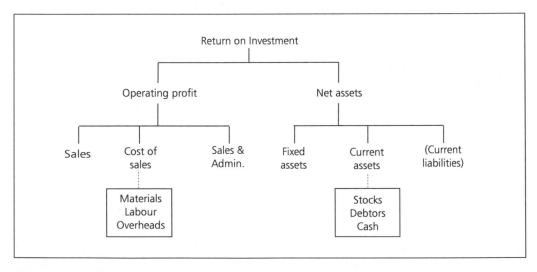

Figure 1.3 Analysis of 'Return on Investment'

Clearly it would be possible for companies reporting a positive accounting profit to show a negative residual income (an economic *loss*) if their accounting profit was not large enough to cover the capital charge.

Other aspects of performance

Most measures of performance should be looked at over a period of several years. This is partly to give an idea of 'trends' over time, and partly to allow for any particular year's results being atypical.

One important measure is growth rate in sales. This needs to allow for **inflation**; and may also require adjustment if there have been significant acquisitions or disposals during the period.

Operating profit margin (on sales) is another measure which matters. Profit margins can vary widely between different industries: food retailers might have a margin not much above 5 per cent; while a pharmaceuticals company might have a profit margin of 20 per cent or more.

Both the above measures may be looked at in aggregate for a group; but it will normally be more useful to have regard to segment analysis, and examine the results separately for each of the various business sectors in which the company operates.

Problems

Problems 1.1 to 1.5 are based on the accounts of Bulldog plc, which are set out below:

Balance sheet at 30 June 2000

	£m	£m
Fixed assets		175
Current assets		
Stocks	20	
Debtors	50	
Cash	10	
	80	
Current liabilities		
Short-term borrowing	15	
Other creditors	45	
Net working capital		20
'Net assets'		195
Less: Long-term borrowing		75
Shareholders' funds		
Paid-up ordinary 25p shares	20	
Retained profits	100	
		120

Profit and loss account: year ended 30 June 2000

	£m	£m
Turnover		190
Cost of sales	130	
Selling and Admin. expenses	30	
		160
Operating profit (PBIT)		30
Interest payable		6
		24
Tax		6
Profit after tax		18
Ordinary dividends		12
Retained profits for the year		6

Please calculate the following financial ratios. (Use the glossary if you need to.)

Problem 1.1.

a. Return on net assets
b. Profit margin
c. Net asset turnover
d. Residual income, assuming a 12% after-tax capital charge on equity.

Problem 1.2.

a. Stock turnover
b. **Days' sales in debtors**
c. Current ratio
d. Acid test ratio

Problem 1.3.

a. Debt ratio
b. **Interest cover**

For the following ratios, where necessary assume a market price per share of 270p.

Problem 1.4.

a. Dividend payout ratio
b. Dividend cover
c. Dividend yield

Problem 1.5.

a. Earnings per share
b. Earnings yield
c. Price/earnings ratio

CHAPTER 2

Interest rates

2.1. Time

Pure time preference

Interest rates can allow us to compare money amounts at different points in time. This is crucial in business (and in economics). The interest rate comprises three component parts: preference, inflation premium, and risk premium.

The difference between the near and distant future is important in finance, as in other areas of business. Long-term investments may promise returns only after many years; while long-term borrowing provides funds which are safe precisely because they need not be repaid for a long time.

A business may often choose to forgo a smaller profit soon in the hope of a larger profit later: for example, pricing low with a new product in order to build up market share. People used to talk about firms trying to 'maximize profits'; but modern finance theory talks about 'maximizing wealth'. This requires some way to compare profits in different future periods. For this purpose the rate of interest functions, in effect, as an 'exchange rate through time'.

Pure **time preference** refers to the ratio between how consumers value present goods as against the same goods in future. If consumers did not in general prefer present goods to future goods, why would they ever consume anything? The convention is to quote the ratio as an annual rate. (This may call for special care when looking at periods of less than a year.) In effect, a pure interest rate represents the 'price of time'. It need not relate to *money*, though it often does.

In general, firms often try to **match the maturities** of their liabilities (sources of finance) with those of their assets (uses of funds). So do financial institutions. 'Borrowing short and lending long' can clearly be dangerous: a firm might then have to repay the borrowings at short notice without being able to demand repayment of its own long-term investments.

Compound interest is a very powerful concept, and can easily deceive the unwary who think the annual rate looks quite low. For example, if someone aged 20 put aside £1,000 a year, and reinvested it at a real rate of return of 5 per cent a year, by the time that person was 70 years old (ignoring tax) the fund would amount to more than £200,000.

The term structure of interest rates

The different redemption rates of government **bonds** reveal the **term structure** of interest rates. That means how annual rates of interest vary depending on the length of time until a loan **matures** (falls due for repayment). Charting interest yields against the time to maturity may show at least three different shapes, reading from left to right, as in Figure 2.1.

According to the expectations theory, the term structure will be upwards-sloping (as it normally is) if investors expect that interest rates will rise, but downwards-sloping if they expect interest rates to fall. An important influence may be expected future rates of *inflation* (see below).

The liquidity preference theory argues that most lenders want to lend short-term, while most borrowers want to borrow long-term. Hence borrowers have to offer lenders a premium to induce them to lend long, which implies an upwards-sloping term structure. This may reflect an aspect of *risk* (see below).

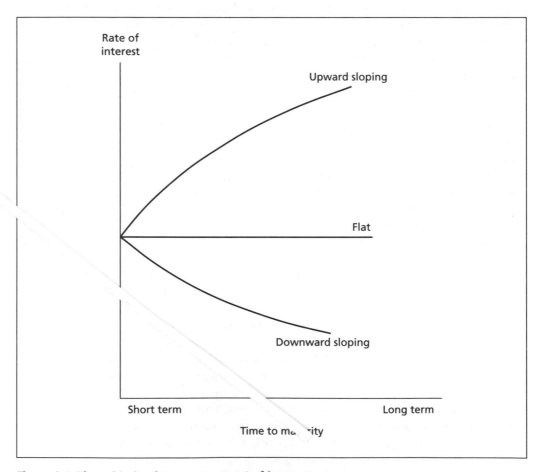

Figure 2.1 Three kinds of 'term structure' of interest rates

Index-linked gilts

British government bonds are known as **'gilt-edged' securities**, or simply 'gilts'. In 1981 the government started issuing **index-linked** gilts which it guaranteed against inflation by indexing both the interest and the **principal**.

Government stocks are normally regarded as **risk-free**, in that a government which controls the printing presses is almost certain to be willing and able to repay when due any money that it has borrowed. (The **inflation premium** which lenders may demand reflects the likelihood that the purchasing power of the money may have fallen between the date of the loan and its repayment.) Under EMU arrangements, the money supply is under the control of the European Central Bank, *not* of national governments. Hence French or German bonds are no longer 'risk-free'.

The **yield** on index-linked gilts thus provides a direct market measure of 'pure' time preference (without either an inflation premium or a risk premium). At the time of writing, in June 1999 (varying slightly, depending on the term), index-linked gilts yielded about 2 per cent. This is rather lower than the yield on gilts throughout most of the nineteenth century. (In those days, on the gold standard, people didn't expect permanent inflation; hence nominal yields on risk-free gilts were the same as 'real' yields.)

The rate of pure time preference, like other market prices, can vary over time; though much more important reasons for nominal interest rates to vary are inflation and risk, to which we turn below.

2.2. Inflation

Post-war UK inflation

Over the whole 52-year period from 1947 to 1998, the average rate of inflation in the UK has been more than 6 per cent a year. Prices in the post-war period have multiplied more than twenty-fold. There have been four main inflation episodes:

1. 1947–67 (21 years): moderate, averaging about 4 per cent a year;
2. 1968–81 (14 years): high, averaging about 12 per cent a year;
3. 1982–90 (9 years): fairly high, averaging about 6 per cent a year;
4. 1991–98 (8 years): moderate, averaging about 3 per cent a year.

The famous issue of 'Dalton's' 2½ per cent Consolidated Stock was made at par in 1946. By 1999 each £100 nominal of stock was worth only about £2.20 (in terms of 1946 purchasing power) – a real loss of capital of over 97½ per cent. This highlights two points: even so-called 'risk-free' securities are not completely free from risk of loss if there is unanticipated inflation; and even an inflation rate averaging 'only' 6 per cent a year can be cumulatively devastating.

Figure 2.2 shows the 15-year average annual rate of inflation in the UK between 1967 and 1998. Until after the Second World War the 15-year annual average rate of inflation had never exceeded 2 per cent a year in peacetime. Indeed, as far as one can tell,

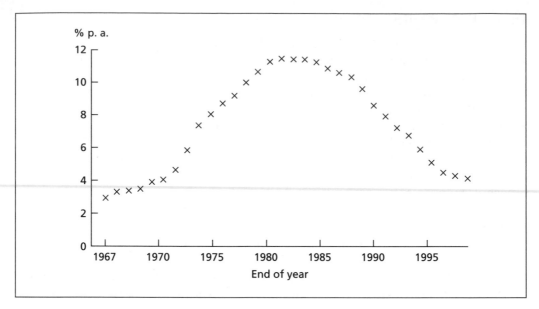

Figure 2.2 15 year average annual rates of UK inflation 1952–67 to 1983–98

the purchasing power of the pound was much the same on the outbreak of the First World War in 1914 as it had been on the Restoration of Charles II in 1660. In other words, over a quarter of a millennium the UK currency's purchasing power was virtually constant.

This background helps one understand that the double-digit rates of inflation common world-wide during the 1970s were completely unprecedented in the UK. It is therefore perhaps not surprising that some important financial aspects of business life (for instance, the tax system and accounting practice) reacted slowly.

Problems of inflation

Inflation causes financial problems which are both important and complex; and any rate above 3 or 4 per cent a year is serious. Inflation affects the following:

1. The required rate of return on new investments.
2. Valuing assets.
3. Managing working capital.
4. The extent and type of borrowing.
5. Foreign exchange rates.
6. Accounts using money as the unit of measurement.
7. **Taxation**.

In discussing financial numbers, we must distinguish between 'money' ('nominal') amounts and 'real' amounts. In general, the best way to avoid being fooled by inflation – especially its cumulative effect over a number of years – is to reckon in **'real' terms** of **constant purchasing power**.

Another critical question is whether or not people expect the actual rate of inflation. Most people now seem to expect inflation which is low in the context of recent decades – between 1 per cent and 3 per cent a year in most OECD countries. So if inflation actually turns out to be much higher than that, most of it will have been unanticipated – and therefore, perhaps, especially damaging.

The inflation premium

Rates of interest on money include an inflation premium which allows for the expected future rate of inflation. Thus interest rates are higher in Brazil than in Switzerland because people expect higher inflation in Brazil so there is a higher inflation premium.

If the interest rate would be 3 per cent a year in the absence of inflation, and if both borrower and lender expect future inflation of 5 per cent a year, then the nominal money rate of interest will be about 8 per cent a year. (Strictly it should be not $3 + 5 = 8$ per cent, but $1.03 \times 1.05 = 1.0815$, or 8.15 per cent; but where the annual inflation rate is in single figures this refinement is hardly worthwhile.)

Of course people may be wrong in what they expect the future rate of inflation to be. In the 1970s, nominal interest rates were much lower than the rate of inflation turned out to be. (It was unanticipated.) So, for several years running, 'real' interest rates (nominal money interest rates minus actual rates of inflation) were **negative**.

In June 1999, for 15-year maturities, money gilts yielded about 5 per cent and index-linked gilts about 2 per cent. Hence the market seemed to be expecting UK inflation over the next 15 years to average about 3 per cent a year.

Inflation and the term structure

Long-term inflation expectations may be slow to change. Just before sterling left the European exchange rate mechanism (ERM) in September 1992, the short-term UK interest rate stood at about 10 per cent a year. This may have seemed rather high in the depth of a recession, with inflation at 3½ per cent a year and falling. But the rate aimed to keep sterling's exchange rate within the agreed ERM band. High UK interest rates had to match high German interest rates which were needed to control German inflation following reunification.

When it proved impossible to keep sterling within the ERM, UK short-term interest rates soon fell to around 6 per cent. This level was more suitable for the domestic UK economy when sterling was no longer tied at a fixed rate to the Deutschmark. Longer-term UK interest rates, however, scarcely moved. So a downward-sloping term structure at the end of August 1992 (expecting future interest rates to fall from their high short-term level) was replaced by an upward-sloping term structure at the end of September (now expecting future interest rates to rise from their much-reduced short-term level).

In late 1999 UK short-term interest rates are much higher than euro rates: about 5 per cent versus 3 per cent. But 10-year interest rates are about the same: 5 per cent. Hence the pound's term structure is flat or slightly downward-sloping, the euro's upward-sloping.

2.3. Risk

The risk premium

The third component in most interest rates on business loans is a **risk premium**. Smaller businesses often have to pay a higher rate of interest than large ones because lending to them is usually 'riskier'. This means that smaller firms in general are more likely to default on interest or principal repayments. Rather than require an extremely high risk premium, a bank which thinks the risk very large in a specific case may simply refuse to lend at all.

Risk may relate to the nature of the business rather than its size. For example, food retailing is fairly stable, whereas drilling for oil is very risky. Or the risk may relate to the managers: someone with an established track record will be regarded as less risky to lend to than someone with no business experience.

Modern portfolio theory (see Chapter 11) suggests a straight-line relationship between the risk premium demanded in calculating the total required rate of return and the level of risk perceived. The capital market line in Figure 2.3 shows this.

Even at *zero* risk, there is still a positive interest rate of 5 per cent. This is the 'risk-free' rate of return, which comprises pure time preference of 2 per cent plus an inflation premium of 3 per cent. Thus the yield on 'risk-free' UK government stocks would be 2 per cent on index-linked gilts and 5 per cent on ordinary money gilts (we ignore taxation here).

Thereafter as risk increases (reading from left to right along the horizontal axis) so does the rate of return required (on the vertical axis). Corporate bonds would normally carry a small risk premium, while an equity investment involving 'average risk' requires a risk premium of perhaps 8 per cent. (Chapter 11 explains where this comes from.)

Thus the total required rate of return for an average-risk equity investment is 13 per cent, made up as follows:

	%
Pure time preference	2
Inflation premium	3
Risk premium	8
Total required rate of return	13

It will be obvious that the required money rate of return could be very different for a low risk or a high risk; for investing in bonds rather than in an equity project; or for an investment in a foreign currency where inflation expectations were different. Even the rate of pure time preference can vary, though usually fairly slowly, and not by very dramatic amounts.

Credit agencies, such as Standard and Poor's or Moody's, assess the risk attaching to specific bonds or borrowers: the highest rating is AAA then AA, A, BBB, and so on.

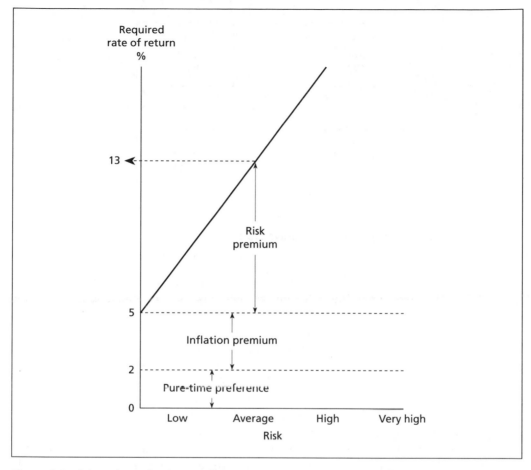

Figure 2.3 Risk and required rate of return

Bonds rated BBB and above are of 'investment grade', while bonds rated BB or below are 'speculative grade' (or '**junk bonds**'). Bonds with low ratings tend to have high interest rates due to high risk premiums: a bond rated BBB is likely to have a yield at least 100 **basis points** above one rated AAA. Corporate managers may desire the highest credit rating, almost as a status symbol; but minimizing risk to lenders may not always maximize value for shareholders.

2.4. Foreign currencies

Foreign exchange rates

One can regard interest rates (pure time preference) as 'exchange rates over time', between one date and another (see Chapter 5) In the same way, foreign exchange

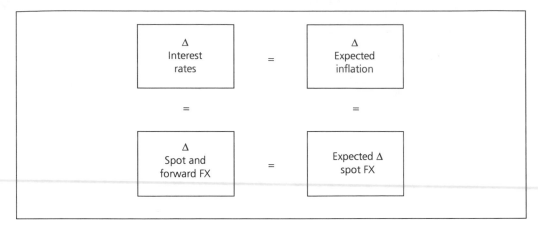

Figure 2.4 Four-way Foreign Exchange equivalence

rates represent 'exchange rates' between one currency and another. The first words of a famous novel expressed this thought nicely: 'The past is a foreign country ...' (Of course, so is the *future*!)

The **purchasing power parity (PPP) theorem** states that – in the long run – foreign exchange rates will adjust to reflect the relative rates of inflation of the currencies concerned. This explains, for example, why the pound fell so much (about 80 per cent) against the Swiss franc between about 1965 and 1995.

Figure 2.4 sets out a model of four-way equivalence between interest rates, expected inflation, and spot and forward foreign exchange rates. Turning the purchasing power parity theorem around helps explain some of the tensions within Europe's Economic and Monetary Union (and before that, in the Exchange Rate Mechanism). If there is to be a single currency, in effect 'foreign' exchange rates must be fixed. It follows that long-term rates of inflation must be the same in all EMU countries. But this implies an EMU-wide economic policy, which of course has major political implications.

The European 'single' currency, the euro, affects the eleven countries in EMU. For other countries it makes little difference in principle, it is just another foreign currency. Thus there is a foreign exchange rate between the pound sterling and the euro, just as there is between the pound and the US dollar. As a matter of fact, the pound has tended to move more in line with the dollar than with European currencies. The 'starting rate' for the euro was £1 = 1.41 euros; at the time of writing the exchange rate is £1 = 1.54 euros. (Apparently the European Commission prefers the euro to be quoted in terms of UK pence: 65 pence = 1 euro. Because the pound is a 'heavy' currency, we normally quote foreign exchange rates the other way round.)

Problems

Problem 2.1.

A 15-year indexed government bond yields 3.0 per cent a year, while a 15-year ordinary (non-indexed) government bond yields 7.5 per cent a year. What is the implied inflation premium over the period, approximately? *Precisely?*

Problem 2.2.

If people's expectations of inflation in future were to increase, what would you expect to happen to the yields:

a. on indexed bonds?
b. on non-indexed bonds?

Why, in each case?

Problem 2.3.

Assuming that everyone is agreed on the future rate of inflation that they expect, what would be the likely effect of introducing 'usury' laws putting a ceiling on the maximum rate of interest which could legally be charged to borrowers? What sort of borrowers might be affected, and what sort would probably not be?

Problem 2.4.

Under what circumstances might money interest rates be negative *ex ante* (in advance)?

Problem 2.5.

Under what circumstances might real interest rates be negative *ex post* (after the event)?

CHAPTER 3

Cash

3.1. Money

What is money?

Money is any generally accepted medium of exchange. Its main function is to act as a means of payment. If there were no money people would have to exchange goods and services by means of barter. This is a cumbersome process where two people must each want precisely what the other has got.

Centuries ago, gold or silver came to serve as money, being relatively scarce, stable, durable, divisible, and easy to recognize. The ruler's seal on a coin stated and guaranteed its weight (and implied its fineness); this avoided the need to assay or weigh the metal at each payment, and made such coins acceptable 'at face value'. Eventually milled edges prevented coin-clipping; but rulers of nations themselves often 'debased' the currency by adding base metal to the precious metal.

Bankers held money (gold) in safe-keeping and issued paper notes (receipts) to the owners (depositors). These banknotes represented a promise to pay the holder on demand a certain amount (weight) of gold, and most people found them more convenient to use for payments than gold itself. Soon, therefore, bankers saw no need to 'back' each paper note with equivalent gold in their vaults. In practice a bank could issue about ten times more 'paper money' than the gold it held, and lend out the extra money at interest to borrowers.

Some loans would be for long periods; so if every holder of a bank's paper notes were to demand instant repayment in gold (a 'run on the bank'), the bank would be unable by a wide margin to meet its legal obligations Hence prudent banks had to take great care to avoid any public loss of confidence in their **solvency.** They did this partly by matching the maturities of their assets and liabilities and partly by very cautious attitudes towards risk. As a result the paper notes of a reliable bank were reckoned to be 'as good as gold'.

In time central banks evolved, to serve as banker to the government as well as to the commercial banks. They often became the sole issuer of paper notes and 'lenders of last resort'. Eventually most governments nationalized their central banks and withdrew people's right to convert paper banknotes into gold. That made it easy (and tempting) for governments to go on printing more and more notes, thus inflating the supply of paper ('fiat') currency. Few governments were able to resist this modern version of **currency debasement**.

The quantity theory of money, in its simplest form, says that the larger the money supply, the less the value (**purchasing power**) of each unit of currency. Keynes accepted that in the long run this was probably true; but famously said that 'in the long run we are all dead'. One of the main practical problems of business management is balancing the short term and the long term.

A stable money can represent a store of wealth. More important, as long as the purchasing power of money is reasonably stable, it can represent a **unit of account**. This allows economic calculation in terms of money. If money loses purchasing power fast, however, it becomes less useful as a unit of account; hence pressures in modern times for a system of **inflation accounting.**

Why do firms need cash?

Most people carry some cash around with them to cover various day-to-day trans-actions, such as paying for a haircut or buying a newspaper. In the same way, firms may need large sums of money, for example, to pay wages or, from time to time, to pay for new equipment, to settle tax bills, or to repay borrowing.

But carrying too much cash can be risky. There are sometimes reports of mysterious tourists carrying £250,000 around London in used notes of small denomi-nations who stop for a cup of coffee and when they emerge find their taxi has disappeared with their cash in a bag on the back seat. Banknotes – being anonymous – are subject to the risk of loss; but this does not apply to cash held in a bank account.

Most countries now have laws against 'money laundering', which oblige bankers and others to report to the authorities any suspicious transactions in cash, even for fairly small amounts (say, £5,000). It would nowadays be foolish for anyone to suppose that even a 'private' bank account is really immune from government snooping. And credit cards make it possible to discover a great deal about the persons using them: their patterns of spending, their whereabouts on any date, etc.

Strictly speaking what one needs is not so much cash itself as the 'ability to pay'. Thus many individuals now carry credit cards to let them make day-to-day purchases for which they might once have needed cash. In the same way, a firm which has arranged **bank overdraft** facilities may not need to hold any positive cash balance with its bank: it can simply continue to draw cheques (instructions to the bank to pay amounts to some-one else) up to the extent of its agreed borrowing limit.

Many retail shops hold quite large sums of cash in their tills. This is not to cover cash purchases (for which they would use other sources); nor is it merely a result of cash tak-ings from sales (which they would promptly bank). The main function of till cash is to enable shops to offer change to customers paying in cash. An old cartoon joke shows a passenger apologizing to a bus conductor as he offers a £50 note in payment of a £1 bus fare: 'I'm afraid I haven't got any change.' The conductor pours 490 10p coins into his lap and replies: 'Well you have now!'

The pattern of weekly cash receipts and payments in most businesses will fluctuate somewhat. For example, bad weather may affect cash sales of a department store. A firm may choose to hold some extra cash as a precaution to be on the safe side, so that even if things go slightly wrong, it will still be able to make ends meet. The amount of the cash safety margin will depend on how business managers feel about the risks of running out of cash (both how likely it is and how much it would matter). The rate of interest might also be relevant. A firm may also happen to hold cash as a result of errors in forecasts of the timing or amount of cash receipts or payments. Thus improving a firm's forecasting skills may allow it to hold less cash.

Finally, the speculative motive is ever-present in business, for example, where firms expect prices of supplies to change. Stock exchange investors may increase their cash holdings by selling shares whose price they expect to fall. To succeed (in making a profit) they must guess not just the *direction* in which the market is going to move, but also the *timing*. One far-sighted investor I knew realized as early as 1938 that the fixed $35 per ounce price of gold would have to increase sooner or later as a result of cumulative American inflation. In the end he was proved 'correct' – but only in 1968, thirty years later!

In a firm's balance sheet, 'cash' (sometimes '**liquid resources**') normally comprises three items:

1. Cash in hand, which consists of notes and coins. Accountants call it 'petty cash', and in most businesses the amount is small.
2. Current accounts with banks (demand deposits), available to make payments by cheque or to draw out in cash. Such accounts may not earn interest.
3. Deposit accounts with banks (time deposits), which do earn interest; and can be converted into cash on short notice (often seven days).

Another current asset is 'marketable securities' which, for practical purposes, may be very similar to cash.

International money

Most countries have their own national currencies. The eleven European countries which adopted a single currency (the euro) in January 1999 are an exception; and it is too soon to tell whether those countries will remain independent or whether the high-risk euro project will collapse. Multinational companies may need to deal in several currencies, reflecting world-wide operations, investment and financing. Chapter 8 section 4 discusses the special risks this may involve, such as exchange restrictions and exchange rate changes.

Table 3.1 shows exchange rates at 9 July 1999 between some of the main world currencies:

Table 3.1 Exchange rates between main world currencies, 9 July 1999

	£1 =	$1 =	€1 =	Y1000 =
Pound sterling	*	0.64	0.66	190
US dollar	1.55	*	1.02	122
Euro	1.52	0.98	*	1.25
Japanese yen ('000)	5.26	8.17	8.02	*

3.2. Cash flows

Flows of cash in business

A firm gets money from three main sources:

1. Owners (shareholders), who start the business with equity share capital (and some-times contribute further share capital later).
2. Lenders (banks and others), who provide long-term or short-term funds.
3. Customers, in respect of goods or services sold to them.

Funds deriving from sales to customers are sometimes referred to as **internal finance**, funds directly from owners or lenders as **external finance**.

A business spends money on four main categories:

1. Long-term ('fixed') assets, such as buildings and equipment.
2. Short-term ('current') assets, such as stocks of goods.
3. Wages, overheads, and other current expenses.
4. Taxes paid to government.

Figure 3.1 shows the main sources and uses of funds in business, including the payment of interest to lenders and dividends to shareholders.

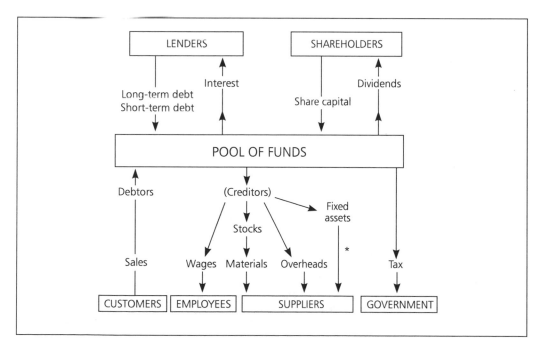

Figure 3.1 Main flows of funds in business

Cash flow statement

In addition to the profit and loss account and the balance sheet (Chapter 1), all but small companies must also publish a cash flow statement showing the firm's cash receipts and payments over the past year. ('Small' companies are roughly those with annual turnover under £2 million or total assets under £1 million or fewer than 50 employees.)

Table 3.2 shows, somewhat simplified, the format of the cash flow statement. There are three main headings, showing cash flows arising from Operating, Investing and Financing. Many companies will show a net cash inflow from Operations and a net cash outflow on Investment. A growing company will often have a net deficit of cash before external Financing (as Investment would normally exceed net cash inflow from Operations.) The opposite might be true with a mature or declining company. The final balancing item represents the change in cash during the period.

A steady-state company should be able to finance replacement of tangible fixed assets out of net cash inflows from its ongoing business. In the absence of any inflation, one might expect net spending on tangible fixed assets roughly to equal the provision for **depreciation**.

Table 3.2 Hardstaff Products plc: Cash flow statement for the year ended 31 March 2000

	£ million	£ million
Operations		
Operating profit before tax and interest		24
Add: Depreciation		15
		39
Less: Increase in working capital		
Debtors up	4	
Stocks up	3	
Creditors up	1	6
Cash generated from operations	=	33
Less: Interest paid	4	
Tax paid	4	
Dividends paid	5	
		13
Net cash from operations	=	20
Investing		
Purchase of tangible fixed assets	13	
Proceeds from sale of tangible fixed assets	1	
Acquisition of subsidiary	7	
		19
Surplus before financing		1
Financing		
Proceeds from issuing ordinary shares	1	
Net proceeds from long-term borrowing	4	
		5
Net increase in cash		6

'Free cash flow' represents the excess of net cash generated above the level of reinvestment needed to maintain the scale of the business in future. In practice it is often difficult to measure precisely how much spending on fixed assets is for 'replacement' and how much represents 'expansion'; hence it is hard to determine the amount of 'free cash flow' accurately.

Clearly the dividend policy represents an important area of discretion when firms are managing their long-term cash inflows and outflows. (See Chapter 12.)

3.3. Cash and profit

Cash and profit are different

Cash and profit are two of the main concerns of the financial manager. Both are important, but they are different. Cash is a liquid asset owned by a business, a means of payment enabling it to buy goods or services. A firm's cash balance can be either too large (earning a low rate of return) or too small (risky).

Profit is an accounting measure of improvement in well-being, the surplus earned after deducting all business expenses from sales revenues and other income for a period. In general, the larger the profit the better.

Table 3.3 lists and classifies some of the main differences between cash and profit. It shows that most of these differences disappear sooner or later. Most items relate to the

Table 3.3 Why profit and cash may differ

Difference	Balance sheet effect
P & L expense, not cash payment	**Profit *down***
• Purchase on credit	• Creditors up
• Tax charge not yet paid	• Tax liability up
• Write off bad debt or stock	• Debtors or stock down
• Depreciation of fixed asset	• Net fixed asset down
Cash payment, not P & L expense	**Cash *down***
• Purchase of stock for cash	• Stock up
• Payment of creditor	• Liability down
• Purchase of fixed asset for cash	• Fixed asset up
• Pay dividend, buy back shares	• Equity down
P & L income, not cash receipt	**Profit *up***
• Sale on credit	• Debtors up
• Reduce provision for expense	• Provisions (liabilities) down
• Share of subsidiary/associate profit	• Fixed asset investment up
Cash receipt, not P & L income	**Cash *up***
• Credit customers pay	• Debtors down
• Sale of fixed asset for cash	• Fixed asset down
• Borrow long term	• Long-term liability up
• Issue share capital for cash	• Equity up

short run (such as amounts owing for credit sales); some relate to the medium-term (depreciation of fixed assets, and borrowing and repaying loans); and only a few items remain different through much of a company's life (non-depreciable fixed assets such as land, and new issues or buy-backs of share capital).

In accrual accounting, the amount of expenses charged in a period will usually not equal the amount of cash paid out. Where a firm acquires tangible fixed assets for cash, it does not deduct the whole cost from profit in the same accounting period. Instead the firm's accounts charge only a fraction of the cost as depreciation expense in each period of the asset's life.

If a firm sells goods for more than they have cost, it has made a profit. But until the customers have paid for the goods, it may have no cash. In contrast, when a business borrows money, the immediate result is to increase its cash balance. But no company would dream of treating the amount borrowed as a profit! It will have to repay the loan in due course.

Are cash flows less open to 'creative accounting' than reported profits? Probably not: in the short run firms can manipulate cash flows even more easily than accrual accounting numbers by means of 'leads and lags'. For instance, they can delay many cash payments for a while (or cash receipts). The accounting principle requiring consistency of treatment over time is an important safeguard for readers of accounts. In the long run it can be much more difficult to affect cash flows, but the same is true of accounting profits.

Cash flow and depreciation

The financial press often uses the term '**cash flow**' to mean 'retained profits plus depreciation' for a period. The point is that depreciation is merely an accounting entry in the period in which it appears as an expense. The only cash payment is for the purchase of a fixed asset at the start of its life. So since the accounts have deducted depreciation expense from turnover in measuring profit, it needs to be 'added back' in order to translate the figure for profit into an estimate of 'cash flow' for the period. (Depreciation is not the only item in the profit and loss account which may not represent cash – see Table 3.3 – but it may often be the most important such item.)

If depreciation were really a 'source' of funds – instead of simply not being a use of funds – it would be possible for a company to increase its cash balance merely by increasing its charge for depreciation expense in the profit and loss account! But doing this, of course, would reduce reported profit to exactly the same extent. Thus there would be no effect on cash flow. (Nor would changing depreciation expense make any difference to the tax bill, since the **Inland Revenue** have their own rules for '**writing-down allowances**'.)

Example 3.1

Suppose Hardstaff Products plc increased its £15 million depreciation expense in the year ended 31 March 2000 (see Table 1.3) by 40 per cent, to £21 million. As Table 3.4 shows, the figure for 'cash flow' would remain unchanged.

Table 3.4 Cash flow and depreciation

£ million	Original Accounts	Depreciation up by 40%
Profit before depreciation	35	35
Depreciation expense	15	21
Profit before tax	20	14
Tax on profit (unchanged)	5	5
Profit after tax	15	9
Dividends payable	6	6
Retained profits	9	3
'Add back' depreciation	15	21
= Internally generated cash flow	24	24

Cash or profit: which matters more?

Both cash and profit matter, but people sometimes wonder whether one matters more than the other. A firm which discovers a profit opportunity *ought* to be able to raise enough money to finance the project, if capital markets are working properly. On that view, profit matters more than cash. Someone who can identify (potential) profit can get cash finance and thus earn the profit. But someone who only has cash will merely get in return the going risk-free rate of interest – but *no* profit.

Is it profit (earnings per share) or cash flow that drives share prices? Since profit and cash often tend to move together, it can be hard to tell. Some years ago, US tax rules allowed companies to switch from **first in, first out (FIFO)** to **last in, first out (LIFO)** in valuing stock. This would reduce reported profits, but it would also reduce tax payable and thus *increase* cash. Shares in companies which made the change performed better than shares in companies which chose not to. Conclusion: where earnings per share and cash flow moved in opposite directions, cash mattered more than profits.

It is wrong to suppose that the stock market attaches a constant **price/earnings ratio** to whatever amount a company reports as earnings per share. If that were so, increasing reported earnings – even through a one-off change in accounting policy – should increase the share price pro rata. But *quality* of earnings matters as well as quantity. In fact, what matters more than current results is expectations about future results; and that applies to cash as much as to earnings.

Still, 'creative' accounting may sometimes fool readers of accounts into making wrong estimates of the future, which can then affect share prices. And managers may be very concerned about the amount of earnings their companies report if their pay partly depends on it. (Which suggests a poorly-designed executive pay scheme.)

One item, often large, about which there is sometimes a question, is purchased goodwill arising when one company (A) acquires another (B). If A pays £180 million cash and the fair value of B's tangible net assets is £120 million, then the surplus, £60 million, is 'goodwill'. Company A must normally write it off as an expense over a maximum of 20 years (see Chapter 7).

In the profit and loss account such **amortization** of goodwill is a 'non-cash' item. (It has no effect on tax.) But that is only because companies publish annual accounts and goodwill lasts longer than one year. If Company A were to prepare 20 year accounts, goodwill *would* then appear simply as a cash expense. Some people argue that goodwill doesn't really count because it is 'only a book-keeping adjustment'. In logic they ought to say the same about the purchase and depreciation of tangible fixed assets too; but they don't.

3.4. Cash planning

Forecasting cash receipts from sales

No company wants to run out of cash. Creditors a company was unable to pay might force it into liquidation (see Chapter 13); or at least it might have to raise funds at a very high cost, and subject to burdensome conditions. A company's cash balance should be high enough to protect against any serious chance of running out, but not so high as to tie up excess funds in low-yielding uses. Financial managers of a business must decide what cash levels to aim at. Then they need to forecast the amount and timing of likely future sources and uses of cash.

Careful forecasting of the amount and timing of future cash receipts and payments has the following benefits:

1. It tests the financial results of plans in advance, before making firm commitments.
2. It reveals possible future needs to raise more capital, which may take time to arrange.
3. It helps avoid piling up non-interest-bearing cash.

The most critical single estimate is very often the forecast of sales turnover, since this nearly always represents a firm's main source of cash receipts. Forecasting cash receipts from sales may be subject to a large margin of error, since it depends on three different estimates, each of which may vary:

1. The physical volume of sales.
2. The average selling price per unit.
3. The average delay in payment (credit period taken) by customers.

Example 3.2

A financial manager is preparing a six-month cash forecast beginning in January. He decides to start by estimating cash receipts from sales, with the following basic assumptions:

- Sales revenue will be £200,000 a month for the first three months, rising to £250,000 for April and May, and to £300,000 in June.
- He expects 10 per cent in value of the sales to be for cash; the rest on credit terms resulting in the collection of cash on average one month after the date of the credit sale.
- At the beginning of the period debtors amount to £185,000.

Table 3.5 Cash receipts from sales: January to June (£'000)

£'000	January	February	March	April	May	June	=	Total
Underlying data								
Total sales	200	200	200	250	250	300		1,400
Credit sales 90%	180	180	180	225	225	270		1,260
Cash receipts								
From debtors	185	180	180	180	225	225		1,175
Cash sales 10%	20	20	20	25	25	30		140
Total	205	200	200	205	250	255		1,315

Table 3.5 translates these assumptions into a schedule of expected cash receipts from sales, month by month. Cash received in the period differs from the value of goods sold, due to credit.

Over the whole six months the totals are as follows:

	£'000
Opening debtors	185
Add: Total sales	1,400
	1,585
Less: Closing debtors	270
= Cash received in period	1,315

As compared with total sales of £1,400,000, there is an £85,000 shortfall of cash received (at only £1,315,000). This results in an £85,000 increase in debtors between the start and end of the period (from £185,000 to £270,000).

Forecasting other cash inflows and outflows

Cash payments for operating expenses often relate fairly closely to sales volume, after allowing for time-lags. Though stocks of materials may vary for a number of reasons (see Chapter 4), purchases of materials normally vary more or less with expected future sales. Suppliers will probably allow a credit period, so payment of cash in respect of purchases may occur at about the same time as sales are made (though somewhat before they are paid for).

Short-term sales fluctuations may not much affect some other expenses. The labour force, for example, may be fairly stable in the short term. And many overhead expenses, such as office rent, utilities, etc. may be more or less 'fixed' (both in amount and in timing) in the short term. It may be more difficult to forecast discretionary expenses, such as advertising, staff training or **research and development**. These can be subject to change at short notice.

An overall cash forecast needs to include various other cash payments and receipts, even if there is no direct link with day-to-day operations. Payments other than for normal expenses may include: taxation; interest; dividends; acquiring fixed assets. In addition there may be capital transactions, such as repayment of loans or buying back shares.

Cash receipts may stem from a number of sources other than sales: from disposing of old equipment; from interest or dividends on investments. And again there may be capital transactions, such as borrowing or issuing new share capital. Many of these forecasts are not easy to make with precision.

Pro forma balance sheets

The projected (pro forma) balance sheet method of forecasting funds requirements involves a forecast of *all* balance sheet items (not just cash) at a definite future date. It involves four major steps:

1. Forecasting the net total amount for each of the assets.
2. Listing the liabilities:
   a. that will occur without special negotiation (such as trade creditors and taxation);
   b. that have to be specifically arranged (such as bank overdrafts).
3. Estimating profits for the period, less dividend payments. Since profit is a residual between two much larger amounts (sales turnover less total expenses), this may be subject to a wide margin of error.
4. Totalling the estimates of assets, liabilities and shareholders' funds, to reveal whether there remains a surplus or shortage of funds on the date chosen. Any surplus would somehow be invested, and a projected shortage might be covered by raising more money, or in some other way (such as reducing one or more assets).

The pro forma balance sheet method forecasts all the balance sheet items, not just cash. It can forecast certain financial ratios, such as return on net assets (or, indeed, it may be based on the assumption that certain financial ratios remain constant). It can also make rough – but often helpful – forecasts where forward plans may not yet exist in sufficient detail to allow cash flow forecasting.

The method forecasts balance sheet amounts only at the end of the period, not during the interim. It will therefore reveal maximum needs for funds only if the balance sheet date represents a moment of maximum strain. (If there is doubt about the most suitable date to choose, one can always make several projections at different dates.)

It is often worth noting in writing the key assumptions which underlie the forecasts; and it can be useful to try to assess the rough margin of error in the key items. Modern data-processing equipment makes it easy to prepare detailed forecasts, and to test them by varying the assumptions (**sensitivity analysis**).

Using the same assumptions, the projected balance sheet method and the detailed cash flow forecast approach should (of course) produce the same estimate for the end-of-period cash balance. The pro forma balance sheet method forces an explicit assumption about fixed assets and the components of working capital. These may be very important; yet they can be surprisingly easy to overlook in a cash flow forecast.

Problems

Problem 3.1.

A company is set up with £200,000 cash; and during its first six months the following events and transactions occur:

January: machinery is bought for £100,000 cash.
February: goods are bought for £50,000 cash.
March: the same goods are sold for £150,000 cash.
April: further goods are bought for £200,000 cash.
May: the goods are sold, on two months' credit, for £300,000.
June: valuers reckon the machinery is now worth £80,000.

Calculate:

a. profit for the six-month period;
b. cash flow from operations for the period;
c. the end-of-June cash balance.

Problem 3.2.

A firm buys a machine for £200,000, expecting it to last for ten years.

a. What depreciation would you suggest is charged each year as an expense against profits?
b. Assuming that annual pre-depreciation profits amount to £50,000, what would the annual post-depreciation profits be?
c. Would your answer to (a) change if annual pre-depreciation profits of only £15,000 were expected next year? Why or why not?
d. Soon after buying the machine, the firm decides it would be sensible to rely on only five years' useful life from the machine. What effect, if any, would this have on:

   (i) the annual depreciation charge? (ii) profits? (iii) cash flow?

Problem 3.3.

Spanner Ltd., a civil engineering company, accepts a government contract to build a road bridge for £8 million. The job should take two years. Earth-moving machinery must be purchased for £1.2 million, which can be sold for £200,000 at the end of the contract. Labour costs will be £300,000 quarterly in the first year and £400,000 quarterly in the second year. After three months, materials will be needed; and over the next four quarters, weekly deliveries will be made at a rate of £500,000 worth per quarter. Other costs (administration, petrol, etc.) are expected to be about £200,000 per quarter over the whole contract. Assuming progress accords with an agreed plan, 'progress' payments will be made to Spanner under the contract, starting from the second quarter, amounting to £700,000 per quarter. The balance of the £8 million outstanding will then be payable on the completion of the contract.

Making (and stating) any further assumptions you think necessary:

a. prepare a quarter-by-quarter table of cash receipts and payments for the two years of the contract;
b. show what is the maximum cash 'investment' the contract requires and when it arises;
c. calculate the expected profit or loss on the contract.

Problem 3.4.

Gordon Bennett has asked for overdraft facilities to start up a new business and the bank has asked for information to assist them in assessing his requirements. Assuming that the business commences on 1st July, and that Mr. Bennett provides £12,000 initial cash capital on 1st July and a further £8,000 on 1st October, it is expected that:

a. Rent will be £200 per month, payable on the first day of each month in arrears.
b. Materials will be bought during July to a value of £4,800. In subsequent months, purchases will be such as to maintain the stock of materials at £3,200. Payment for these materials will be made at the end of the month following that of purchase.
c. Wages will be £1,000 in July and £5,000 per month from August onwards.
d. It is anticipated that a salesperson will be engaged from 1st August at a salary of £1,200 per month.
e. Production will be 100 units in July and 500 units per month thereafter. Each unit uses £8 of raw material and £10 of labour.
f. Sales will be nil in July and August, but are expected to be 200 units in September, 400 units in October and then 500 units each month. The selling price will be £36 per unit, payable at the end of the second following month.
g. Sundry expenses will be £600 per month and Mr. Bennett expects to draw £400 per month for private purposes.
h. Machinery costing £20,000 will be bought on hire purchase; a deposit of £2,000 will be paid in July and instalments of £1,000 in each month thereafter.

Required:

A cash budget for the period from 1 July to 31 January inclusive, showing the estimated bank overdraft outstanding at the end of each month. (Ignore interest thereon!)

Problem 3.5.

Mrs. Congreve decides to start a business making and selling soft toys. She has only $4,000 to invest. This sum of money she places in the business account at the bank on 1st January. She also finds a small workshop which she rents at $160 a month payable on the last day of each month. She employs one person to work for her at the beginning. That employee is paid $400 a month. As sales begin to improve she employs a second person at the same salary from 1st April. That second person helps to double output and sales.

Other costs are:

Materials: $1,000 in January and thereafter $400 per month.
Other production costs: $100 a month.
Delivery van: on hire purchase at $1,000 payable in January, thereafter at $200 per month.

The soft toys are sold for cash at a standard price of $40 each. The number of toys sold during the first six months was: January none; February 5; March 20; April 30; May 60; June 60.

Required:

a. Prepare a cash flow statement for the six months January to June. Show the amount of money in hand or requiring overdraft facilities at the end of each month.
b. Calculate how much profit or loss the business made during the first six months of operation.

Problem 3.6.

How is it possible:

    a. for a profitable firm to run out of cash?
or b. for a cash-rich firm to be unprofitable?

CHAPTER 4

Working capital

4.1. Working capital as a whole

The working capital cycle

Working capital is the excess of current assets over current liabilities. The two main items are stocks and debtors: they represent a firm's investment in goods which are unfinished, unsold or unpaid for. Together these amount to nearly half the total assets of UK listed companies.

In view of its size, working capital is clearly important to many firms, large and small. (A useful ratio to calculate is working capital as a percentage of annual sales turnover – defining working capital as: stocks plus debtors plus a minimum level of cash, minus trade creditors and accruals.)

A firm needs to determine a suitable level of investment in working capital – and then carry out the policy. Managers may 'decide', for example, that debtors should average no more than one month's credit sales; but someone still needs to make sure that the customers owe no more than that. In other words, working capital does need to be 'managed'.

Figure 4.1 shows the working capital cycle of a manufacturing business. The business first buys **raw materials** on credit, then uses labour and capital equipment (in various proportions in different industries) to convert them into **finished goods**. Often there are intermediate stages of partly-completed goods, known as work-in-progress.

On sale of the finished goods, legal title passes to the customer; and it is at this point that accounts recognize the sale and the profit thereon. The customer either pays cash or buys on credit. If the latter, when the debtor finally pays cash to settle his account he completes the transaction. Where the customer orders goods which then have to be made, the sale is recognized when manufacture is completed and the goods are delivered.

Thus the working capital cycle involves using cash to acquire raw materials, to pay for overheads and to pay labour wages to convert materials over time into finished goods, which the firm then sells to customers who finally pay for them. A profitable business should receive more cash at the end than it pays out ('invests') during the working capital cycle. This is in order to pay at least the following: (a) taxes on profits; (b) interest on borrowing; (c) dividends to shareholders; and (d) to replace capital assets.

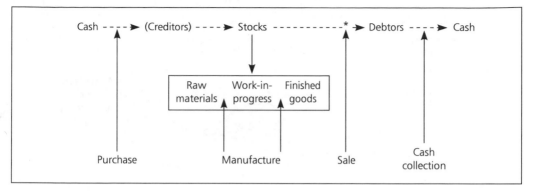

Figure 4.1 The working capital cycle

In times of inflation, merely increasing the money amount of assets may not represent 'real' growth. This serious accounting problem affects both planning cash flows and measuring profit or loss. It is a worrying sign if a company can only maintain its existing level of business by raising more long-term capital. A healthy firm ought to be able at least to maintain its present real size out of internally generated cash flow, though it may have to raise new long-term capital in order to finance real expansion.

Financing current assets

A hotel may always be full even though no single person is permanently resident. In the same way, each item in working capital may be 'current' (since individual items of stock and debtors are continually turning into cash), but the net total may in effect represent a long-term investment requiring long-term finance to support it.

Some companies' current assets may fluctuate during the year, perhaps because of seasonal sales or production patterns. For example, garden equipment sales may be highest during the spring and early summer, whereas toy sales may tend to peak towards Christmas. Figure 4.2 shows two approaches to financing short-term peaks.

A cautious company may aim to finance its maximum need by long-term funds. This low-risk policy will leave surplus cash to invest (at a fairly low rate of return) during the off-peak period. A more aggressive company, in contrast, may finance only its minimum level of net current assets with long-term funds. It will be in the riskier position of needing short-term finance during the seasonal peak; but by restricting its financing to what it needs it may hope for higher returns for shareholders. (In either case, the net accounting total of 'working capital' may actually be fairly constant – since short-term surplus cash or short-term borrowing (negative cash) would both themselves count as part of the net 'working capital' amount.)

Liquidity

Liquidity means the ease with which an owner can turn an asset into cash: both the speed and the certainty of net proceeds. In a perfect capital market this would not matter, since

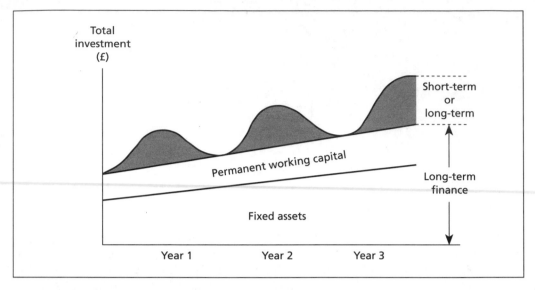

Figure 4.2 Financing seasonal current assets

an asset's owner would always be able to borrow its full value. But in the real world it may often be easier to turn cash into assets than assets into cash.

As usual, managers need to seek a balance. Having too little liquidity might lead to problems in paying bills; while having too much might result in a low rate of return (on nearly risk-free assets).

Accounting ratios based on aggregates need to be interpreted with caution. Table 4.1, for example, sets out Tesco's February 1999 working capital figures (slightly simplified and rounded). At first sight they may seem somewhat alarming. The **current ratio** is 0.37 and the **acid test ratio** only 0.16. Thus current liabilities (now required to be

Table 4.1 Tesco plc: working capital at 27 February 1999 (£m)

Current assets	
Stocks: goods held for resale	595
development property	72
Prepayments and other debtors	151
Cash etc	328
	1146
Creditors: falling due within one year	
Bank loans, overdrafts, etc.	830
Trade and other creditors & accruals	1815
Corporation tax	236
Proposed final dividend	194
	3075

called 'creditors: falling due within one year') are more than double current assets, and net working capital is over £1,900 million *negative*! What is going on? Is Tesco going bankrupt, despite annual sales (excluding VAT) of £17,000 million?

In all financial and accounting work an essential rule to bear in mind is: don't panic! If a particular number looks odd, it is worth spending a little time thinking why the number works out as it does.

The £595 million stock (at cost) at 27 February 1999 (all ready for sale in retail stores) represents less than two weeks' sales. So we could expect all of it to have turned into cash (at selling prices) by mid-March. Indeed Tesco's stock is a good deal more 'liquid' than most companies' debtors! Clearly the acid test ratio (which omits stock) gives much too gloomy a view for this type of retailer. In fact Tesco's sales in the month of March will probably yield about £1,500 million cash.

Not all the current liabilities are due for payment within the next month or so. Tesco won't pay the proposed final dividend until early July. And most of the £236 million corporation tax bill is not due for some months. There is little doubt, too, that the bank loans and overdrafts could mostly be rolled over if necessary.

So even if we assumed that all other creditors of £1,815 million were due within the next month and a half, we could expect the company to have more than £2,000 million cash available from one and a half month's sales. The firm could replace its stock on credit. Thus Tesco's liquid position seems perfectly adequate.

The truth is that a balance sheet gives only rather a crude idea of the real position, and we need to know a good deal about a specific business before we start to draw reliable conclusions. Accounting ratios based on aggregates are a very useful device to develop worthwhile questions – but they rarely provide all the answers.

4.2. Stocks

Types of stock

Money invested in stocks ties up financial resources which a firm could have used elsewhere. This represents a real opportunity cost.

A manufacturing company holds three main types of stock (**inventory**): raw materials, work-in-progress and finished goods. Most firms also hold stationery and maintenance supplies for use in the course of business. (They are usually included with raw materials stocks.)

Stocks are normally stated in accounts 'at cost' (or net realizable value if lower). The 'cost' of bringing a product to its present location and condition includes production overheads, based on the normal level of activity.

What determines stock levels? In general, the level of sales volume; the relationship between production and sales; the nature of the production process; and the cost of holding stocks. Service industries tend to have low stocks because they usually cannot 'store' their products in finished form. The same may be true of some 'manufacturing' companies, such as newspaper publishers.

Table 4.2 Stocks held in different industries

£ million	Rio Tinto Mining	Br. Aerospace Aerospace	B.A.T. Tobacco	Tesco Food retailing
Raw materials	148	124	1,550	
Consumables	137			
Work-in-progress	142	1,009	495	
Long term contracts		1,067		
Finished goods	350	108		
Goods for resale			120	595
(progress payments)		(905)		
Dev'pt. properties		39		72
	777	1,442	2,165	667
% COGS	23%	23%	36%	4%
% assets	8%	16%	29%	8%

Table 4.2 shows the proportion of various types of stocks held by four different businesses. The table also shows total stocks for each company related to annual cost of sales and to total assets.

For British Aerospace, work-in-progress is very large, though mainly offset by progress payments. British American Tobacco has very high raw tobacco stocks. Rio Tinto's finished goods stocks are the largest single category. All three firms' stocks in total represent a significant proportion of annual **cost of goods sold**, though stocks as a proportion of each firm's total assets varies from Rio Tinto's 8 per cent to British American Tobacco's 29 per cent. Tesco's stocks are rather different: they virtually all comprise 'finished goods' available for resale; and they represent only a small proportion both of annual cost of goods sold and of total assets. Evidently the problems of managing stock vary in different industries.

Raw materials stocks represent a buffer between outside suppliers and the demands of the production process. The level depends mainly on buying aspects: the nature of the goods (whether they are perishable, bulky, expensive); possible interruptions to supplies (for example, from crop failures); how quickly suppliers can deliver more supplies of components (some Japanese car makers fly in supplies of components several times a day as part of their 'just in time' approach); the economics of bulk purchasing; and expected changes in future prices and in sales volume.

Work-in-progress depends largely on the method of production (such as batch versus flow); the importance of set-up costs; the length of the process (bakeries will have lower work-in-progress than shipyards); and whether subcontracting is possible. Managing the process is likely to be important, for example, trying to eliminate bottlenecks.

Finished goods stocks represent a buffer between customers' demand and possibly intermittent supply from the purchasing or manufacturing side of the business. The level depends mainly on selling aspects: whether the firm is making goods to order; the reliability of sales forecasts; the number of product lines and the range of choice for customers; policy on the risk of stock-outs; and expected changes in sales volume.

Costs of holding stocks will vary for different industries, and may include such items as handling costs, storage costs, insurance and obsolescence, as well as interest on the money amount tied up. Average stockholding costs may total as much as 25 per cent of book value a year, hence there is a clear need to balance the benefits from holding stocks at any given time against the costs. Too little stock may delay the production process or fail to satisfy customers; too much may be very expensive.

Managing stock

Forecasting whether a change in sales volume is temporary or more permanent can be crucial in deciding whether to change the rate of production or of purchasing. A wrong decision could mean either piling up unwanted stocks or else running out of stock and thus losing potential sales. Either could be very expensive. The essence of business is judging the direction, extent and timing of changes in market conditions in the uncertain future.

In managing stocks, as in many other areas of business management, a useful control device can be 'ABC analysis' (Figure 4.3). This assumes that a small proportion (say 20 per cent) of the total *number* of items will usually account for a large proportion (say 80 per cent) of the total *value* of all items. (It is sometimes called the '80/20' rule.)

The implication for management is fairly obvious. Rather than pay equal attention to all items, it may make better commercial sense to look first at the few Class A items which account for most of the value, then at Class B items, and only at the end consider the many small Class C items.

Another useful tool is to calculate the rate of **stock turnover** in a period, by dividing the cost of goods sold in a period by the amount of stock held. From a financial point of view, both production managers and sales managers may have reasons for preferring high levels of stock (that is, low rates of stock turnover). In practice, therefore, it is

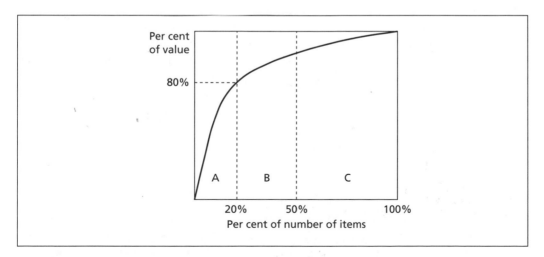

Figure 4.3 ABC analysis

important to hold managers responsible for *all* the costs of holding stock, including imputed interest.

In theory one can develop 'economic order quantity' (EOQ) models to determine the optimum pattern of re-ordering stocks. Such models attempt to balance the cost of holding stock against the cost of reordering, in the context of annual usage. In practice there is often so much variation and uncertainty that commercial judgement is likely to be more important.

4.3. Debtors

Components of 'debtors'

The current asset heading 'debtors' may include a number of items other than amounts due from trade customers, as listed in Table 4.3. Trade debtors themselves are shown net of any provision for doubtful or **bad debts**. UK accounts don't usually show the amount of such provisions. There may be proceeds due from sale of fixed assets or of business units. Nearly always there will be some **prepayments**, for insurance, rent, etc. There may be amounts due in respect of tax recoverable. Often there are miscellaneous 'other' debtors. And, confusingly, there may be included in 'current' assets, under debtors, amounts in respect of 'long-term' debtors, not due for more than one year. (This is because such long-term debtors are not included under 'fixed assets' according to Companies Act definitions.)

Individual customer credit

There are normally two decisions to make in advance about individual credit customers: whether to extend credit at all; and, if so, up to what maximum amount? There are several ways to check the creditworthiness of potential new customers: credit bureau reports, past financial statements, bank references, trade references from other suppliers, and perhaps even the views of the selling firm's own sales people.

The credit control system should include a regular review of all customers, to ensure that they are not exceeding their maximum credit limits (either in amount or in time). But one must be realistic: people will tend to ignore unduly low credit limits (just as motorists tend to ignore unduly low speed limits on the roads).

Table 4.3 Typical items included in 'debtors'

Trade debtors
    less provision for bad or doubtful debts
Proceeds due from disposal of fixed assets
Prepayments
Tax recoverable
Other debtors
Debtors due after one year

Some customers ignore credit terms blatantly, either the total amount of credit or the period of credit taken. Ultimately there is an implied threat of legal action against customers who fail to pay amounts according to the credit terms agreed. But it is probably better to avoid this if possible: the supplier wants his money, but dislikes the trouble and expense of taking formal legal action against debtors.

One useful way to get money from overdue debtors can be simply to telephone and ask directly why they haven't paid. Some companies even telephone large customers *during* the credit period to confirm that they can expect to receive the amount owed on the due date. This also enables them to sort out any queries in good time. Such behaviour is not 'unsporting'; it is merely businesslike.

In the end, however, a seller may prefer not to do business with a customer who takes too long to pay. Recently one of the UK's biggest book publishers closed the credit account of a large book retailer 'because of persistent late payments over an extended period'. Publishers need retail outlets for their books; but the outlets also need suppliers.

Overall credit control

A powerful simple tool for measuring debtors is to calculate the average number of days' sales still owing at the end of a period.

Example 4.1

Sales for the past calendar year amounted to £180,000, and debtors at the end of December totalled £30,000. So (ignoring VAT for the moment), 61 days' sales were outstanding:

$$\frac{£30,000}{£180,000} \times 365 = 61 \text{ days}$$

Or we could do the sum in two stages:

Daily sales $\qquad \dfrac{180,000}{365} = £493$

Outstanding $\qquad \dfrac{£30,000}{£493} = 61 \text{ days}$

In terms of *months*, average sales = £15,000 per month; so £30,000 outstanding equals 2.0 months.

If December sales were £25,000 and November sales £15,000, a more accurate estimate, relating to actual sales month by month rather than to averages, could suggest an average credit period outstanding of 41 days. We assume that customers pay in date order. Then total end-December debtors of £30,000 include all of December's £25,000 sales (= 31 days) plus £5,000 of November's £15,000 sales (= 10 days).

Unfortunately **value added tax (VAT)** complicates the position, as the 'sales' or 'turnover' figure reported in accounts excludes VAT, while the amount owed by debtors includes it. In the above example, assuming all credit sales are subject to VAT at $17\frac{1}{2}$ per cent, sales *including*

VAT are £180,000 × 1.175 = £211,500. Hence the actual number of days' sales outstanding in debtors is:

$$\frac{£30,000}{£211,500} \times 365 = 51.8 \text{ days}$$

(This is the same as 61.0 days ÷ 1.175.)

The amount invested in debtors (or '**accounts receivable**') depends partly on the volume of credit sales. Since most firms want to increase sales volume, the main way of trying to control total credit outstanding is to limit the average period of credit taken by customers. This depends both on the credit terms offered and on the effectiveness of the seller's collection procedures.

Example 4.2

Over four years, one major company reduced its average credit period from 137 days to 92 days. With sales of £600 million a month, the saving of 45 days' credit amounted to saving an investment in debtors of £900 million! As interest rates at the time were in double figures, the interest saved exceeded £100 million a year. Such a potential prize would certainly make the employment of a few competent credit controllers seem very worthwhile.

Good credit managers are quick to respond to changes in the overall pattern of debtors. They also tend to operate with specific targets, either in absolute money amounts or in terms of average days' sales outstanding. Of course, proper management of debtors requires continual vigilance throughout the year.

If the average credit period which customers are taking is too high, or increasing beyond target, management must find out why. Has **trade credit** policy changed? Or the mix of customers (e.g. between domestic and export)? Is the company giving priority attention to the largest customers? Sending out invoices and statements promptly? Chasing up slow payers urgently enough?

Risk and return from debtors

Selling for cash avoids any need to 'invest' in debtors by (in effect) lending them money. But most companies want to offer terms at least nearly as attractive as their competitors, as a marketing device. The two main risks in extending trade credit are that the customer will either take too long to pay, or else fail to pay at all (bad debts).

In practice opportunity losses due to debtors taking too long to pay tend to be far more important than losses — sometimes dramatic — due to bad debts. For example, some large companies or government departments are very bad debtors, in that they sometimes take a long time to pay, even though their accounts may be most unlikely to end up literally as 'bad debts'. Being 'important' customers (and knowing it), they often take much longer to pay than the official credit terms offered. Yet nobody doubts that they will pay all right *in the end*. In that sense they are 'good' debts, but often very slow. Time is money ... The big company which succeeded in reducing by 1½ months the average credit period taken by its customers was notorious for taking a very long time to pay its own bills. (Hence the Latin tag: *Bis dat qui cito dat* – 'He gives twice who gives quickly'.)

One way of viewing the opportunity cost of credit is to recognize the true cost of allowing a **cash discount** to customers who pay promptly. If customers on average take 45 days after invoice date before paying, then a 2 per cent discount for payment of cash within 10 days would cost 2 per cent for 35 days credit saved. This amounts to an annual rate of over 20 per cent a year ($2 \times 365/35 = 20.9$ per cent). What matters here is the 45 days' credit which customers *actually* take on average, not the company's official credit terms of (say) 30 days.

There are two problems in practice with offering cash discounts for early payment, apart from the fact that they may need to amount to a high interest rate in order to be attractive. First, debtors who cannot pay soon enough to claim the cash discount may then choose to pay very late. Second, it can be tricky withdrawing the cash discount at a later date if the firm wants to change the policy.

Another possible approach would be to charge interest on overdue accounts, but this is not popular nor easy to implement (though threatening to charge interest may hurry some debtors up). The Late Payment Act, enacted in 1998, allows small companies to charge large companies interest at 8 per cent above base rate on bills unpaid after 30 days. It is not yet clear whether this legislation is working as hoped. It seems that many companies, both small and large, are ignoring it.

The 'return' from extending credit to customers consists of the marginal **contribution** to profit from the extra sales made (assuming that there would have been no sale without offering credit). Trade credit policy has to balance the possible return against the risk. Incurring *no* bad debts at all suggests that a firm is probably taking too few credit risks. In view of the likely returns foregone, it makes little sense to refrain from making sales on credit to 99 customers on the off-chance that the 100th customer may fail to pay the whole amount due. In this respect commercial companies, normally having much larger contribution margins, can well afford to take larger credit risks than can banks (which merely make a 'turn' of a few per cent rate of interest).

Some firms reduce the amount of working capital tied up in debtors by using **factors**. The factoring company buys some or all of a firm's debts, at full value less a factoring charge, and then undertakes to collect them. Sometimes any bad debts remain to be borne by the firm itself not by the factor (which affects the charges). Most factoring arrangements allow the factor to reject some customers, perhaps on grounds of poor creditworthiness. The factoring service may also include sales ledger administration (for an extra fee).

4.4. Spontaneous creditors

Components of 'creditors'

The amount of current liabilities (creditors due within one year) to deduct from current assets determines the extent to which net working capital needs long-term funds to

Table 4.4 Typical items included in 'creditors'

Trade creditors
Accrued charges
Social security and other taxes
Other creditors
Corporation tax: UK and overseas
Dividends proposed
Deferred income
Short-term borrowings

finance it. Certain items of short-term finance, such as bank overdrafts and short-term loans, carry interest and firms have to negotiate them specially. We discuss them in Chapter 9 as part of corporate debt. Table 4.4 sets out a typical list of other items of creditors which occur more or less spontaneously.

Trade creditors

Suppliers often sell goods and services on credit rather than for cash, with a time lag of up to 3 months between supply and payment. Unlike bank overdrafts, trade credit usually needs little formal negotiation (except perhaps for new firms); yet for many companies it can be an important 'permanent' source of finance.

Purchasers should be aware of any cash discounts which suppliers are offering for prompt payment. The implied annual rate of interest can be high, so if financial resources permit it is often worthwhile taking advantage of them. Otherwise, at least purchasers should take the maximum credit period available.

At the other end of the payment scale, it may seem almost cost-free to take extended credit from those suppliers that permit it. But the obvious risk is that the supply of goods or services may eventually stop, possibly at a most inconvenient time. Also if supplies are ever short for some reason, good payers may well receive preference.

The average period of credit a firm allows to customers is often similar to that which suppliers allow the firm itself, though the periods can vary in different industries. But the total *amount* of debtors may often be larger than the total for trade **creditors** ('**accounts payable**'). The difference comes from the profit margin, and also from certain cash expenses such as wages and from depreciation. Firms with high value-added will tend to have low trade creditors, since a high proportion of their costs will comprise wages rather than raw materials or bought-in parts.

Some other non-cash expenses, such as depreciation, will not appear in trade creditors; which may, however, include amounts for purchases of fixed assets not yet paid for. Indeed, separate disclosure seems a good idea. For example, Thames Water plc discloses: trade creditors – operating £65 million; capital £85 million.

Accrued charges consist of costs incurred for goods and services which suppliers have not yet invoiced. Typical examples might be utility charges, rent and business rates, or audit fees. The total of accrued charges can be surprisingly large.

Amounts owing for social security and other taxes include **income tax** (PAYE) and social security taxes deducted from employees' wages, as well as employers' social security 'contributions'. Amounts due for Value Added Tax are also included under this item.

Tax on profits

Corporation tax payable on profits appears under a separate heading both in the profit and loss account and in the balance sheet. It includes UK tax on UK profits, and foreign taxes on profits earned overseas. Tax on the current year's profits (other than '**deferred tax**': see Chapter 9) is normally payable within less than twelve months from the end of the **financial year**. Indeed payments on account are due even before the year end in most cases.

There are special rules for computing tax on profits, so **taxable profit**, to which the rate of corporation tax applies, is not the same as reported profit before tax in the accounts. For instance, Inland Revenue writing-down allowances replace the depreciation expense in the accounts. Thus a UK company cannot reduce its tax bill by increasing its book depreciation charge. Moreover the tax rules may completely disallow certain legal, capital and other items of expense; or there may be timing differences both for **revenues** and for expenses.

Proposed dividends

Most UK companies pay an **interim dividend** on ordinary shares during the financial year (if they are 'listed' on a stock exchange), and propose to pay a **final dividend** after the year end. The balance sheet shows the proposed final dividend as a current liability, on the assumption that shareholders will approve it at the company's annual general meeting. The profit and loss account shows the total of interim and final dividends as an 'appropriation' of profit (not as an expense charged against it).

In some countries the practice is to include ordinary dividends as a separate item in the accounts only when companies have actually declared them to be payable so that they have become a legal debt. In such cases, the end-of-year balance sheet will normally show no current liability in respect of a final dividend. Instead there will be a larger addition to shareholders' funds for 'retained profits' for the year. Logically this makes good sense.

Deferred income

Some kinds of enterprise, for example, magazine publishers or schools, regularly receive significant amounts of income in advance of providing services. This is called 'income received in advance' or 'deferred income'. Any such amounts not yet fully earned by the end of a financial year obviously cannot be shown as revenue in that year's profit and loss account. Instead they appear as a separate item of current liabilities in the balance sheet. Strictly the current liability is to provide the service in future (normally within twelve months of the balance sheet date), not to pay money. But if, for some reason, the service were never provided, there would probably be a legal liability to repay at least a proportion of the amount received in advance.

Problems

Problem 4.1.

A newsagent sells £500 worth of newspapers on credit each week. He only sends out bills to credit customers once a quarter; and on average they take two weeks to pay.

a. What is the newsagent's average level of debtors? (Assume one month = four and one-third weeks.)
b. What will the newsagent's average level of debtors amount to if he changes to sending out bills once a month? (Assume customers still take two weeks to pay.)
c. How much would such a change save him each year, if interest rates are 12 per cent a year?

Problem 4.2.

A company with current liabilities of £120,000 has the following current assets: stock £80,000; debtors £60,000; and cash £40,000.

a. What is the current ratio?
b. What is the acid test ratio?
c. What is the amount of working capital?

Problem 4.3.

Paterson's credit sales in a year are £150,000; and end-of-year debtors amount to £40,000. Terms are settlement within one month after invoice. Sales in the last four months of the year are as follows: September £20,000; October £15,000; November £12,000; December £8,000. Ignoring VAT, how many days' sales are outstanding in debtors:

a. using the annual sales figures?
b. using the monthly sales figures?
c. Using monthly sales figures, but assuming the pattern of sales for the last four months of the year was: September £8,000; October £12,000; November £15,000; December £20,000?

Problem 4.4.

Refer to problem 4.3 above. Assuming that nobody has paid before the due date, both for parts (b) and (c) in problem 4.3 above, what proportion of total debtors at 31 December represents amounts that are:

a. overdue?
b. at least one month overdue?
c. more than two months overdue?

Problem 4.5.

Centaur's balance sheet contains the following items: stocks £55,000 (raw materials £15,000, work-in-progress £15,000, finished goods £25,000); debtors £48,000; creditors (for materials) £18,000. Annual sales amount to £180,000; and cost of goods sold represents two thirds of sales (of which materials amounts to one third of sales).

Assuming that work-in-progress represents on average goods that are half-finished, (and ignoring liquid resources and current liabilities other than creditors) how many days' operations does net working capital represent?

Problem 4.6.

Describe two alternative approaches towards financing seasonal working capital needs. What are the pros and cons of each?

Problem 4.7.

In what circumstances may it be acceptable for working capital to be negative?

Problem 4.8.

Why may it be undesirable for a company which sells on credit to have zero bad debts?

CHAPTER 5

Basic capital project appraisal

5.1. Background

The capital investment process

Capital investment means spending money (or resources) now in the hope of getting more back later. But this need not appear in the balance sheet as a fixed asset: examples of 'revenue investments' might be research projects or promotion of brands. 'Investment' as such is not worthwhile: it needs to yield a profit. This applies even (perhaps especially) to so-called 'strategic' investments – though *measuring* profit can be very difficult.

There are several key stages in the investment process, as Table 5.1 shows. Probably the most important step is the first – finding worthwhile ideas for capital investments. They may stem from spotting opportunities or from responding to problems in all areas of the business. This requires alertness, imagination and a commercial way of thinking.

Another aspect of finding worthwhile projects is to identify parts of the business that don't generate a profit. Then – if you can't find a way to make them profitable – simply *stop doing them*. Reducing losses is a good way to increase net profits; and there may sometimes also be cash receipts from disposing of assets.

To analyze a project may require data about customers, competitors, technology, and so on. One must also explore alternative ways to achieve the aim of a project. Most companies try to screen some alternatives out before spending too much time on them.

Capital investment may encompass the whole range of strategy, R&D, marketing, production, as well as finance. There will be a need for detailed market forecasts, engineering estimates, political assessments, and so on. Hence large projects involve groups of people from many parts of the business.

Later sections of this chapter and the next deal with the *financial* details of appraising capital projects. But other aspects may be more important. For example, sometimes projects contain 'strategic options' which can be difficult to quantify (see Chapter 8).

Even after the decision to commit funds to a project, it still remains to implement that decision. This vital process may take many months, and mistakes here can be very costly. Delays can easily lead to large cost over-runs or loss of market share to competitors. Where conditions have changed, the actual project may not be quite the

Table 5.1 Key steps in the capital investment process

1. Generate ideas: opportunities and solutions to problems.
2. Search out relevant information.
3. Identify possible alternatives.
4. Determine specific project details.
5. Evaluate financial consequences.
6. Assess 'non-financial' consequences.
7. Make a decision.
   If to proceed:
8. Implement and control project.
9. Monitor results.

same as the one that management approved. This may be revealed by **post-project audits** (see Chapter 6).

Estimating net benefits

It can be hard to estimate a project's net benefits in future. What consumers will want in a few years' time, what competitors will be up to, how production methods and technology may change – all are uncertain. Yet they may affect the project's life, sales, selling prices, costs. And even in so-called market economies, firms have to cope with extensive and often changing government interference – from regional government, from national government, or from the European Union in Brussels.

Three main kinds of capital project are: replacing equipment, to reduce costs or improve quality; expanding productive capacity, to meet growing demand; or providing new facilities, to make new products. An expansion or new-product project may promise to increase sales revenue by more than operating costs and thus increase profits. A cost reduction project, in contrast, may not affect sales revenue at all: the net benefit of the project is lower future operating costs than would otherwise occur (see Figure 5.1).

In projecting how much net improvement will result from a project, the forecast of sales revenue is often critical. For example, publishers may be able to calculate production costs quite closely, with a fixed selling price, but sales volume may be very uncertain; or petrol companies may be fairly sure how much petrol they will sell, but not what the selling prices will be. On the other hand, ship-building on a fixed-price contract would provide almost certain sales revenue, but uncertain costs and timing.

Reaching a sensible answer may depend on asking the right questions. For example, for a capital project the choice may be:

1. Whether or not to buy machine H.
2. Whether to buy machine H or machine J.
3. Whether to buy machine H now or later.
4. How many machine Hs to buy.

We shall not deal in this chapter with how to *finance* capital projects (for example, whether to buy or lease machine H). As a rule it is best to separate the question whether

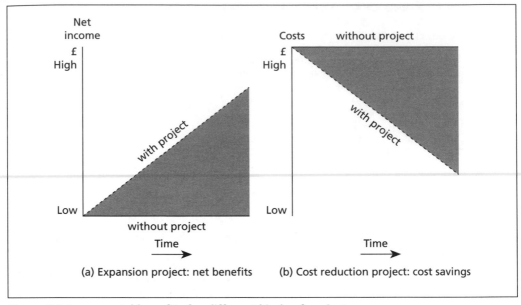

Figure 5.1 Incremental benefits for different kinds of project

a project is worthwhile from the (usually less important) question of how to finance it. Often companies, in effect, have a pool of funds from which they can finance all worthwhile projects.

In general we want to know what difference a project will make, so we take into account only the incremental capital costs, revenues and expenses. These are often **incremental cash flows** that will occur if the project goes ahead but not otherwise. But we may also need to be aware of opportunity costs. For example, if we go ahead with a project we shall use some spare land we already own; but if not we shall sell the land for £400,000. Then if the project goes ahead there is a 'cash outflow' of £400,000 – being the *loss* of the £400,000 cash *inflow* that would occur if the project did *not* go ahead.

5.2. Simple appraisal methods

Average accounting return on investment

Profitability is often expressed as an annual rate of return on investment (ROI).

Example 5.1

Table 5.2 shows two rival capital projects, each lasting for three years. Project A requires an initial investment of £9,000, Project B of £15,000. Project A will produce cash receipts of

Table 5.2 Project A versus Project B

£'000		Project A		Project B	
Investment outflow	Year 0		− 9		− 15
Cash receipts	Year 1	+ 3		+ 6	
	Year 2	+ 4		+ 8	
	Year 3	+ 8		+10	
		+15		+24	
Net profit (3 years)		+ 6		+ 9	
Average annual profit		+ 2		+ 3	
$\dfrac{\text{Average annual profit}}{\text{Initial investment}}$		$\dfrac{2}{9}$ =	22%	$\dfrac{3}{15}$ =	20%

£3,000 in Year 1, £4,000 in Year 2, and £8,000 in Year 3; while Project B will produce cash receipts of £6,000 in Year 1, £8,000 in Year 2, and £10,000 in Year 3.

When we deduct the initial investment from total cash receipts (in effect charging depreciation), Project B yields a larger total profit (9 versus 6). The projects have the same life (three years), so Project B also yields a larger average annual profit than Project A (3 versus 2). But if we divide the average annual profit by the initial amount invested, Project A produces a higher annual rate of return on investment than Project B (22 per cent versus 20 per cent); so using this method we would say that Project A is (slightly) better.

The average rate of return on investment (normally in terms of an annual percentage) does tell us something about a capital project's estimated profitability. But the averaging process cuts out relevant data about the *timing* of the returns.

Example 5.2

Suppose we now compare Project B (as before) with a new Project C which also requires £15,000 initial investment. Project B's expected profits (NB: not its cash inflows) are £1,000, £3,000, and £5,000 in Years 1, 2 and 3; while Project C's expected profits, let us suppose, are £5,000, £3,000, and £1,000 (in the reverse order to Project B).

The average annual rate of return on investment is the same for the two projects: 20 per cent per year (£3,000/£15,000). The only difference is that Project C gives a profit £4,000 larger than Project B in Year 1, but £4,000 smaller in Year 3. (This is actually a cash inflow difference of £4,000 as well.) In total, over the whole three-year life of the projects, this difference balances out; but the larger cash inflow in Year 1 under Project C can be invested for two years to yield a positive *extra* return. In view of this, Project C is better than Project B; but the average rate of return on investment method, which ignores the timing of the returns, conceals this relevant point.

Where the returns happen to be the same in each year of a project's life (like an **annuity**), this timing objection matters less. But the use of average accounting rate of return on investment also raises some tricky questions. For example: What do we

Table 5.3 Cash flows for Project B and Project C

		Project B £'000	Project C £'000
Initial investment	Year 0	−15	−15
Cash receipts*	Year 1	+ 6	+10
	Year 2	+ 8	+ 8
	Year 3	+10	+ 6

* Profits + £5,000 each year

mean by 'return' and by 'investment'? How do we handle tax and inflation? How do we estimate the life of the project? What about capital recovery? How can we determine the minimum acceptable rate of return?

Payback

Even more widely used than accounting rate of return on investment is the **payback** method. This shows how many years it will take before a capital project 'pays back' the amount invested (that is, before the total net cash receipts exceed the initial investment). The shorter the payback period the better. To calculate the payback period we look at after-tax cash receipts from a project, rather than accounting profits. Thus we only deduct cash expenses from sales receipts, not depreciation.

Example 5.3

Let us now look again at Project B and Project C, each costing £15,000, assuming that they generate cash evenly throughout each year (see Table 5.3).

The payback period for Project B is easy to calculate. £6,000 is repaid in Year 1, £8,000 in Year 2, and £10,000 in Year 3. Thus Project B's payback period is 2.1 years (two years totalling £14,000 plus one-tenth of Year 3 @ £10,000 equals the initial investment of £15,000). In a similar way we can calculate Project C's payback period as being only 1.6 years (Year 1 £10,000 plus 5/8ths of Year 2's £8,000). Figure 5.2 shows a graphical picture of the payback periods.

The payback method of project appraisal has one clear advantage over the average rate of return on investment method: it takes timing into account, at least to some extent. It is also simple to calculate and easy to understand, which may explain why so many companies still use it. But the payback method has a serious disadvantage: it totally ignores cash receipts *after* payback. This is vital since there can be no profit unless we get back *more* than the original investment.

Example 5.4

Suppose that in Year 4 Project B produces a cash inflow of £20,000 while Project C produces only £1,000. According to the payback method, that would *not* change the relative merits

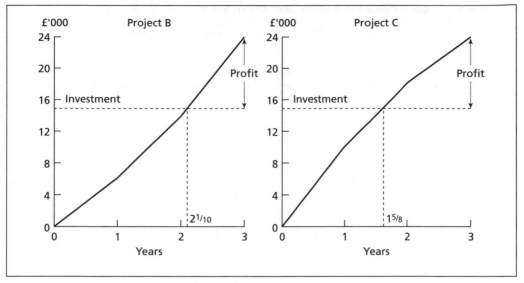

Figure 5.2 Payback periods for Project B and Project C

of the two projects: Project C would still be 'better' than Project B because of its shorter payback period. This clearly does not make business sense!

While it may be a useful relative measure of risk (faster payback means less risk), the payback method does not measure profit. Nor is it clear how to determine a suitable minimum payback period. After all, some very successful drugs have taken more than ten years to pay back all the investment in research and development. And you can get the best possible payback – instantaneous! – by not investing at all!

In practice companies often use payback as a rough screening device, especially for simple projects at lower levels of the firm. And where the return happens to be the same in each year, then the payback method may rank projects in the same order as more accurate methods of assessing whether capital projects will yield a profit – to which we now turn.

5.3. Measuring profit over time

The 'time value' of money

Capital investment involves spending money (or resources) now in the hope of getting back more later. To tell whether the returns are large enough, we need a way to compare returns in the future with investment now – to compare money amounts over time.

A given amount of money now is worth more than the same amount of money in future. Why? Because we can invest the money today to yield a return.

Interest rates do not merely reflect inflation: they also allow for time preference and risk (see Chapter 2). Some types of financial investment (in the stock market) are more

Table 5.4 Future Values of '£1000 now' at 8 per cent a year

	End of Year 0 (now) £	End of Year 1 £	End of Year 2 £	End of Year 3 £
Future values	1000 ⟶	1080 ⟶	1166 ⟶	1260
Present values	1000 ⟵	1080		
	1000 ⟵		1166	
	1000 ⟵			1260

risky than others (bank deposits). They require a higher return to compensate for the higher risks.

Let us suppose that we can invest money today to yield 8 per cent a year. Then £1,000 invested today will grow (compounding once a year) to the following amounts:

In 1 year's time to £1,000 × 1.08 = £1,000 × 1.080 = £1,080

In 2 years' time to £1,000 × $(1.08)^2$ = £1,000 × 1.166 = £1,166

In 3 years' time to £1,000 × $(1.08)^3$ = £1,000 × 1.260 = £1,260

Thus using an interest rate of 8 per cent a year, the future value of '£1,000 now' is £1,260 at the end of three years. Or looking at it the other way round, the **present value** of '£1,260 one expects to receive at the end of three years' is £1,000 now (see Table 5.4).

What then is the present value of '£1,000 one expects to receive at the end of three years'? Clearly it must be £794, as follows:

$$\frac{£1,000}{(1.08)^3} = \frac{£1,000}{£1.260} = £794$$

We can prove this by showing what would happen if we invested £794 today at 8 per cent a year. Each year the effect of compound interest is to add 8 per cent of the start-of-year cumulative amount invested, as follows:

After 1 year the amount becomes: £794 + £63 = £857

After 2 years the amount becomes: £857 + £69 = £926

After 3 years the amount becomes: £926 + £74 = £1,000

Thus we can see the present value of £1,000 one expects to receive at any future date (see Table 5.5).

Assuming an interest rate of 8 per cent a year, the present value of any amount (call it 'a') one expects to receive at the end of three years is 0.794a. Thus 0.794 is the **discount factor** for three years at 8 per cent a year: $1/(1.08)^3$. (We shall normally use discount factors correct to three decimal places. This is quite accurate enough for most practical purposes, though it can cause minor 'rounding' problems.)

Table 5.5 Present values of '£1000 in future' at 8 per cent a year

	End of Year 0 (now) £	End of Year 1 £	End of Year 2 £	End of Year 3 £
Future values	794 ⟶	857 ⟶	926 ⟶	1000
Present values				
$= \dfrac{1000}{1080} \times 1000$	926 ⟵	1000		
$= \dfrac{1000}{1166} \times 1000$	857 ⟵		1000	
$= \dfrac{1000}{1260} \times 1000$	794 ⟵			1000

In effect this gives us an 'exchange rate over time'. Just as compound factors tell us the future values of present-day money amounts, so discount factors tell us the present value of future money amounts.

Appendix B (pages 201 to 203) shows tables of discount factors for annual interest rates between 1 per cent and 50 per cent and for 1 to 50 years hence. Table 1 shows the present value of £1 to be received at a future date for a range of **discount rates**. Thus looking across to the 8% column, and looking down to Year 3, we see the factor of 0.794 which we have been discussing.

Table 2 in Appendix B shows the present value of annuities, that is £1 *per year* to be received for a number of future years for a range of discount rates. Thus again using the 8% column, when we look down to Year 3 we see a factor of 2.577. This represents the present value of £1 received at the end of Year 1 (0.926) plus the present value of £1 received at the end of Year 2 (0.857) plus the present value of £1 received at the end of Year 3 (0.794). Thus Table 2 is a *cumulative* version of Table 1. (2.577 = 0.926 + 0.857 + 0.794.)

Net Terminal Value

If money yields 8 per cent a year, then that is the minimum required rate of return on a capital investment project (sometimes called the '**hurdle rate**'). Why invest in a capital project expected to yield *less* than 8 per cent a year? We need to get a higher return from capital projects for the investment to be worthwhile. (At this stage we ignore tax and possible differences in riskiness.)

Example 5.5

Nellam Ltd. is thinking of expanding its fleet of vehicles by one 20-ton truck costing £52,000. It would operate the truck for four years and then scrap it. The company expects net cash inflows from the extra business to be £12,000, £14,000, £16,000 and £18,000 in Years 1 to 4,

Table 5.6 Net terminal value for Nellam's new truck project

End of year	Cash flow £	Compound factor @ 8% a year	Terminal value £	TV total £
0 (now)	−52,000	$(1.08)^4 = 1.3605$		−70,746
1	+12,000	$(1.08)^3 = 1.2597$	+15,116	
2	+14,000	$(1.08)^2 = 1.1664$	+16,330	
3	+16,000	$(1.08)^1 = 1.0800$	+17,280	
4	+18,000	$(1.08)^0 = 1.0000$	+18,000	
				+66,726
Net terminal value			=	−4,020

which we assume to occur at the *end* of each year. (These amounts are cash flows: they do not deduct **straight-line depreciation** on the truck of £13,000 a year.)

Should Nellam acquire the extra truck? We can compare the two choices as follows:

1. Invest £52,000 in buying the truck and receive the resulting cash inflows.
2. Do not buy the truck – in which case Nellam will merely earn the going rate of interest of 8 per cent a year on the £52,000.

Table 5.6 sets out the expected financial results from the project.

Since we are looking at a project with a four-year life, we need to allow for Nellam to reinvest any cash received before the end of Year 4. We assume the company can do this to earn the going rate of 8 per cent a year. Thus, for instance, Nellam can invest the £16,000 cash received at the end of Year 3 to earn 8 per cent interest in Year 4, making the amount of cash £17,280 by the end of Year 4. Similarly for other cash receipts in earlier years.

Clearly the investment in the truck is *not* worthwhile. Its **net terminal value** is negative (−£4,020). Rather than buying the truck (which provides only £66,726 by the end of Year 4) Nellam would be better off earning 8 per cent a year on the £52,000 for four years. That would accumulate to £70,746 by the end of Year 4.

The net terminal value (NTV) method compounds a project's cash inflows to the terminal (**horizon**) date using the 'opportunity cost' of capital – the rate money can be invested at if *not* used for the particular project. It then compares the project's cumulative amount at the horizon date with the result from simply investing the initial amount at that rate for the project's life. Because the assumed rate of interest – in this case 8 per cent a year – is the *minimum* rate that needs to be earned on the project itself, it is also called the hurdle rate (or **'required rate of return'**).

A variant, called the **compounding to horizon** (CH) method, determines *what is* the compound rate of interest needed on the initial investment to produce the same cash amount by the horizon date as the project itself will produce. In Nellam's truck project, an annual rate of 6.4 per cent a year will compound £52,000 to £66,726 by the end of Year 4. Since this is less than the going interest rate of 8.0 per cent, the project is not good enough to justify going ahead with it. (This method is sometimes called the 'modified internal rate of return' method: it differs from the usual **'internal rate of**

return' method, which we shall discuss below, in making a different reinvestment assumption for the project.)

5.4. Net present value

Net present value

The **net present value** (NPV) method of investment appraisal (like the net terminal value method: see above) calculates a project's profit by comparing cash payments and cash receipts at the same point in time. Rather than looking at the *end* of a project's life, however, it looks at the *start*. It does so by *discounting* expected future cash flows back to the present (that is, back to the 'end of Year 0'). It then compares the total 'present value' (= End of Year 0 value) of the future cash receipts with the initial capital investment in the project.

The NPV method multiplies future cash flows by a suitable discounting factor. (This is the same as dividing by a suitable compounding factor.) The discounting factor depends on two things: the discount rate (or interest rate); and how far ahead in time the cash flow arises.

Example 5.6

Looking again at the Nellam truck project, we see that its net present value (as set out in Table 5.7) is negative. Hence the project is not worthwhile. The cost of investing in the project is £52,000 now, while the present value of the expected future cash receipts (discounted at 8 per cent a year) is only £49,045. That is hardly smart business: it represents a loss (in present value terms) of £2,955.

The principles used to calculate net present value are *exactly the same* as for net terminal value. In particular, the meaning of the interest rate is exactly the same whether it is used for discounting (as in NPV) or for compounding (as in NTV): it represents the 'opportunity cost' of capital, the rate of interest that one could earn if money was *not* invested in the project. Hence both NPV and NTV *always* give the same signal about

Table 5.7 Net present value for Nellam's new truck project

End of year	Cash flow £	Discount factor @ 8% a year	Present value £	PV total £
0 (now)	−52,000	×1.000	= −52,000	−52,000
1	+12,000	×0.9259	= +11,111	
2	+14,000	×0.8573	= +12,002	
3	+16,000	×0.7939	= +12,702	
4	+18,000	×0.7350	= +13,230	
				+49,045
		NPV	=	−2,955

whether or not a project is worthwhile. The only difference is that NPV compares amounts at the start of the project, NTV at the end.

The numbers from the Nellam truck project show that NPV is exactly equivalent to NTV:

$$\text{NPV(EOY 0)}: \quad -£2,955 \times 1.3605 = \text{NTV(EOY 4)}: \quad -£4,020$$

and

$$\text{NTV(EOY 4)}: \quad -£4,020 \times 0.7350 = \text{NPV(EOY 0)}: \quad -£2,955$$

In computing net present value (and net terminal value) we have been assuming that cash flows arise only at year ends. In practice they may occur more or less evenly throughout the year, but our assumption (which is common) is simpler and unlikely to change the decision. Remember that nearly all the numbers we use are only estimates. (For obvious reasons, we do make a different assumption when calculating payback periods.)

Notice that we round all numbers to the nearest pound. There is no advantage in spurious accuracy. Figures for cash flows are usually no more than estimates; their precise timing is often uncertain; and determining the 'correct' discount rate to use is not at all easy. The only reason why in this case we used discount factors to 4 decimal places – rather than 3 – was to avoid minor 'rounding errors' when showing that NPV and NTV methods were precisely equivalent.

In practice, firms use net present value rather than net terminal value. Managers prefer to think in terms of present values rather than in terms of future values. Also NPV enables them to compare different projects at the same point in time (EOY 0); whereas projects with different lives would have different terminal dates, which would make it hard to compare NTVs directly.

The great advantage of the net terminal value method, at least in a textbook, is to clarify the precise meaning of the interest rate used in **discounted cash flow** methods. The compounding approach of the NTV method makes quite explicit the opportunity cost nature of the interest rate.

The NPV method, as we have seen, compares cash receipts and payments expected to result from a capital project. It multiplies them by discounting factors to translate all expected future cash flows from a project into present values (that is, into EOY 0 money terms). Figure 5.3 pictures this approach.

Discounted cash flow (DCF) methods involve forecasting both the amount and the timing of incremental cash flows which will occur if a firm undertakes a project, but not otherwise. Note that DCF methods deal with cash flows and *not* with accounting profits, income and expenses. Hence in listing future cash flows we ignore non-cash items such as depreciation. To tell whether we expect a project to be worthwhile, we simply see whether or not the present value of the project's discounted net receipts exceed the present value of the cash investment.

In other words, we first *value* the project (by estimating the net present value of the cash receipts expected in future), and then compare that amount with the project's cost. If the project's value is more than its cost, it will have a positive net present value after deducting the cost from the total present value. It is then worth undertaking on financial

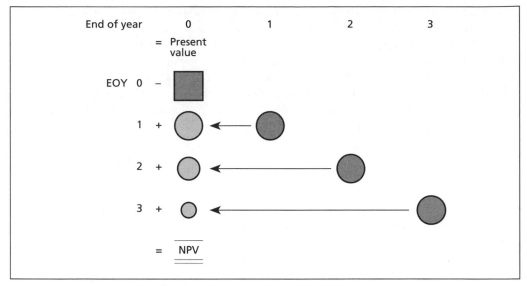

Figure 5.3 The discounting process in net present value (NPV)

grounds: it will increase wealth. Figure 5.4 shows a way to picture this valuation process. The project's cost may simply be the amount of the initial cash investment, as in the Nellam truck project. But sometimes projects consist of several cash payments spread out over time, which themselves need to be discounted back to present value terms. It is not always easy to tell what discount rate to use for such 'deferred' investments – the same discount rate as for future cash receipts or some lower-risk discount rate.

The NPV method, in theory, will always give the correct answer if one assumes all three of the following:

1. One can correctly forecast the amounts and the timing of all the future cash flows.
2. One can correctly estimate the risk-adjusted opportunity cost of capital.
3. There are no relevant non-quantifiable aspects to a capital project.

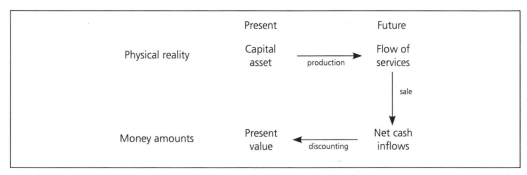

Figure 5.4 Valuing a capital asset

The sweeping and unrealistic nature of these three points makes it clear that in practice no method, however theoretically satisfactory, can guarantee to give a precisely 'correct' answer. The business world is much too uncertain for that.

Should a company go ahead with a project which promises a sufficient positive net present value, but which may result in losses for accounting purposes in the first year or two of its life? In general the answer is 'Yes'. Unless the project is so large that it threatens to swamp the rest of the company's business, one can usually count on poor accounting results for one project being offset by good accounting results for others.

Profitability index

Companies sometimes may choose to 'ration' capital, for strategic or other reasons. A variant of the net present value method may then be useful, called the **profitability index (PI)**. This method divides the present value of a project's cash inflows by the present value of the investment. In the Nellam truck project this is £49,055/ £52,000 = 0.94. Clearly if the index exceeds 1.00, the signal from the numbers is 'go ahead' – just like a positive net present value. (Sometimes the index is multiplied by 100, which would give a figure of 94 here.)

Where there is **capital rationing** (see Chapter 6), companies may use the profitability index to rank projects. Where not all projects with a positive net present value can go ahead, a company may prefer those with higher PIs (rather than those with higher absolute NPVs). One problem with PIs, however, may be how to interpret the meaning of the discount rate if it does not really represent the opportunity cost of capital.

Another use for the profitability index may be to indicate the margin of safety for a project. If, for example, the PI is above 1.00 but not more than (say) 1.20, then the estimates of future cash flows don't have to be much out before the PI may fall below 1.00. On the other hand, where the PI exceeds 1.50, there is quite a large margin of error before the project fails to seem worthwhile.

Annualized cost

The net present value method 'capitalizes' future cash inflows, and compares their discounted present value total with the initial investment. Where cash flows are the same each year ('annuities'), it may sometimes be easier to 'annualize' the initial investment, and compare that with the (equal) annual cash inflows. (A similar approach can help to compare projects with different lives.)

Suppose the Nellam truck project were expected to produce equal cash inflows each year. The **annualized cost** of the £52,000 initial investment over 4 years @ 8 per cent a year is £52,000/3.312 = £15,700. Hence the project would be acceptable only if the annual cash inflows exceeded £15,700. [From Appendix B, Table 2: 3.312 = 0.926 + 0.857 + 0.794 + 0.735 (from Table 1), the discount factors for Years 1 to 4 at 8 per cent a year.]

Table 5.8 Net present value of Project B, using an 8 per cent discount rate

End of year	Cash flow £	Discount factor at 8%	Present value £
0	−15,000	1.000	−15,000
1	+ 6,000	.926	+ 5,556
2	+ 8,000	.857	+ 6,856
3	+10,000	.794	+ 7,940
	Net present value		+ 5,352

Discounted payback

The payback period which we discussed earlier can also use discounted cash flows, to give a **discounted payback** period. Table 5.8 shows the result of discounting Project B's cash inflows of £6,000, £8,000 and £10,000 in Years 1, 2 and 3 at 8 per cent a year.

The net present value would be £5,352, and the *discounted* payback period would be 2.33 years. (This is £12,412 pv received by the end of year 2 – assuming for this purpose cash received evenly throughout the year – plus £2,588/£7,940 = 0.33 of Year 3.) This compares with the simple payback period calculated above of 2.10 years.

It should be obvious why using *discounted* cash flows will always lengthen the payback period. This refinement does not overcome the main drawback of the payback method (namely, that it does not measure profitability); though if there is a finite period within which discounted pay back is expected to be achieved at least that implies that the net present value is positive.

5.5. Internal rates of return

Internal rate of return

Another widely-used method of discounting cash flows is the internal rate of return (IRR) method (also called the DCF yield method).

The net present value method lists the amount and the timing of all the expected incremental future cash flows from a project; and the internal rate of return method does the same. The NPV method then applies a pre-selected discount rate to see whether the net total of all the discounted cash flows is positive or negative. If the NPV is positive, then the project is worthwhile (from a financial point of view); if the NPV is negative, it is not.

In contrast, the IRR method determines, by trial and error, what is the (unknown) discount rate which, when applied to the same cash flows, will produce a net present value of exactly zero. That discount rate is the project's 'internal rate of return'. To see whether or not a project is worthwhile, the firm must compare its IRR with the hurdle rate (or criterion rate) – which, of course, is the pre-selected discount rate used in the NPV method.

Example 5.7

In Table 5.7, using an 8 per cent discount rate, we found an NPV of −£2,955 for Nellam's new truck project. The project's IRR must therefore be less than 8 per cent, since in order to produce an NPV of zero, we need to discount the project's future cash inflows rather less. In Table 5.9 we calculate the NPV again, using discount rates of 6 per cent and 4 per cent. Since one result is positive and the other is negative, it is evident that the IRR must lie somewhere between 4 per cent and 6 per cent (closer to 6 per cent, since that NPV was closer to zero).

We can estimate the approximate IRR as follows:

$$IRR = 6\% - \left(\left[\frac{526}{2108 + 528} \right] \times 2\% \right)$$

$$= 6\% - \frac{1056}{2636}$$

$$= 6\% - 0.40\% = 5.60\%$$

Or we could start from the other end, with 4%, as follows:

$$IRR = 4\% + \left(\left[\frac{2108}{2108 + 528} \right] \times 2\% \right)$$

$$= 4\% + \frac{4216}{2636}$$

$$= 4\% + 1.60\% = 5.60\%$$

Nellam would need to compare the IRR of 5.6 per cent with the required minimum hurdle rate. If that hurdle rate is 8 per cent, clearly 5.6 per cent is not acceptable. Figure 5.5 shows what the truck project's net present value amounts to for a whole range of discount rates.

Three values are worth noting:

1. Using a 0 per cent discount rate, the NPV is +£8,000.
2. The net present value is zero at a discount rate of 5.6 per cent; this is the internal rate of return.
3. Using an 8 per cent discount rate (the hurdle rate), the NPV is −£2,955.

A project with a higher internal rate of return may not always be 'better' than a project with a lower IRR, even on financial grounds. This is for two main reasons. First, the amount invested may be different. Is a 40 per cent IRR better than 15 per

Table 5.9 Calculating IRR by trial and error: Nellam truck project

| | | Discount factor | | Present value | |
| | Cash flow | | | 4% | 6% |
End of year	£	4%	6%	£	£
0	−52,000	1.000	1.000	−52,000	−52,000
1	+12,000	.962	.943	+11,544	+11,316
2	+14,000	.925	.890	+12,950	+12,460
3	+16,000	.889	.840	+14,224	+13,440
4	+18,000	.855	.792	+15,390	+14,256
	+60,000			+54,108	+51,472
				+2,108	−528

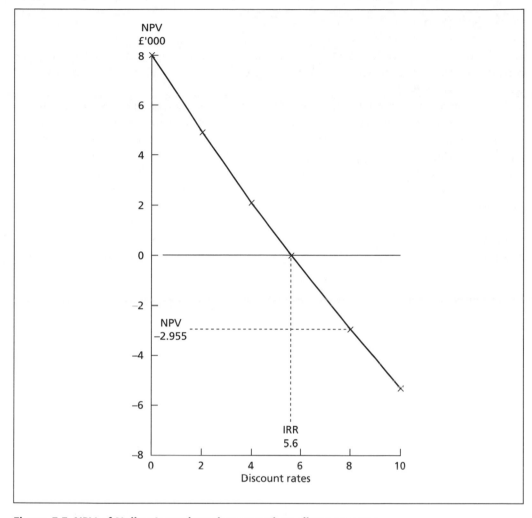

Figure 5.5 NPV of Nellam's truck project at various discount rates

cent? Perhaps not, if one earns the 40 per cent return on an investment of £100, but the 15 per cent on an investment of £10,000. The *scale* of the investment may be relevant.

The second reason is that IRR, in effect, assumes **reinvestment** (of cash inflows) at the project's own internal rate of return. But this is unlikely to be the actual opportunity cost of capital; which makes it hard to compare two different projects. In contrast, the NPV method (like the NTV method) always assumes that a firm can reinvest its cash inflows at the *same* interest rate.

The IRR method is also subject to certain other technical problems: for example, if there are negative cash flows during the project's life. And it is not so versatile and robust as the NPV method in some respects: for instance, NPV can use different discount rates for different kinds of cash flows, or for different periods, which IRR cannot.

5.6. Summary

In this chapter we have looked at several discounted cash flow methods, which Table 5.10 summarizes. The two most widely used are Net Present Value (NPV) and Internal Rate of Return (IRR).

Even where one of the DCF methods appears to show that a project is worthwhile, it is still important for managers to satisfy themselves about the business case for it. In other words, *why* should a particular project make a profit? If there seems to be no specific reason, then the apparent result of the financial assessment must be open to doubt. All experienced managers know how easy it is for optimistic assumptions to make a project look good. That is why it is sensible to try to identify which are the key assumptions underpinning a project.

It cannot be too strongly stressed that financial estimates are nearly always just that – estimates. Often with a very large margin of error. It might not be going too far to call them guesses, as a rule. In making good business decisions, judgement about the uncertain business future is likely to be far more important than technical expertise with discounted cash flows.

Table 5.11 summarizes the results of Pike's 1992 survey of capital investment evaluation methods used by 100 large UK firms. It shows that those that use discounted cash flow methods may also use one or both of the simpler methods. In particular the payback method is still widespread.

Table 5.10 Summary of various DCF methods

	Pre-selected interest rate	Reinvestment assumption	Trial-and-error procedure	Rate-of-return solution
Net terminal value (NTV)	Yes	Yes	No	No
Net present value (NPV)	Yes	Yes	No	No
Profitability index (PI)	Yes	Yes	No	No
Annualized cost (AC)	Yes	Yes	No	No
Discounted payback	Yes	n/a	No	No
Compounding to horizon (CH)	Yes	implicit	Yes	Yes
Internal rate of return (IRR)	No	implicit	Yes	Yes

Table 5.11 Popular capital appraisal methods

	Frequency of use in 1992 in 100 large UK firms				
Percentages	Total	Always	Mostly	Often	Rarely
Payback	94	62	14	12	6
Internal rate of return	81	54	7	13	7
Net present value	74	33	14	16	11
Accounting rate of return	56	21	5	13	17

Problems

Problem 5.1.

a. What compound rate of interest is required to double a sum of money in five years? In ten years?

b. The Retail Prices Index, based on January 1974 = 100, reached 395 by January 1987, when the new series was started. What annual average rate of inflation does this imply?

c. The Retail Prices Index started at 100 in January 1987, had reached 165 by January 1999. What annual average rate of inflation does this imply?

Problem 5.2.

Calculate the *present value* of the following future cash flows at the given annual rate of interest (r) in each case:

a. £550 1 year away, $r = 10\%$.

b. £1,728 3 years away, $r = 20\%$.

c. £251 2 years away, $r = 12\%$.

d. £2,000 9 years away, $r = 8\%$.

Problem 5.3.

At 12 per cent a year, what is the present value of an annuity of £200:

a. for 8 years?

b. for 20 years?

c. for 50 years?

d. for 30 years, between 21 and 50?

e. for ever (a 'perpetuity')

Problem 5.4.

Which would you rather have (starting at the end of year 1):

a. £3,000 a year for the next 20 years, discounted at 20 per cent a year?

b. £2,000 a year for the next 20 years, discounted at 12 per cent a year?

c. £1,000 a year for the next 20 years, discounted at 3 per cent a year?

Problem 5.5.

Which would you prefer:

a. £500 a year for seven years, or

b. £700 a year for five years?

Problem 5.6.

A project is expected to yield £1 million at the end of Year 10. The initial outlay is £410,000. What rate of return does it offer?

Problem 5.7.

A project requiring an initial outlay of £5,400 will yield returns of £1,000 a year for 10 years.

a. What is the rate of return?
b. What annual money returns would be needed to yield a 20 per cent per year internal rate of return?

Problem 5.8.

What is the present value of:

a. £1,200 a year receivable from the end of Year 3 to the end of Year 7 at an interest rate of 20 per cent a year?
b. £4,000 a year payable from the end of Year 5 to the end of Year 10 at an interest rate of 15 per cent a year?
c. £800 a year receivable from the beginning of Year 4 to the end of Year 8 at an interest rate of 12 per cent a year?
d. A pension of £5,000 a year receivable from the end of Year 30 to the end of Year 50 at an interest rate of 15 per cent a year?

Problem 5.9.

Four projects each requiring an initial investment of £4,200 each produce a net present value of zero after discounting at 6 per cent a year:

a. a 5-year annuity of £997.
b. a 10-year annuity of £571.
c. a 20-year annuity of £366.
d. a 50-year annuity of £266.

What happens to the present value of *each* project if the rate of interest falls to 4 per cent a year? What if the interest rate increases to 8 per cent a year?

Problem 5.10.

End of year	0	1	2	3	4
H cash flows (£)	−1,000	+500	+400	+350	+300
J cash flows (£)	−1,000	+400	+400	+400	+400

a. Which of these two projects has the higher net present value at a discount rate of 15 per cent a year? By how much?
b. What is the payback period of each project?
c. What is the discounted payback period of each project?

Problem 5.11.

Project T requires an initial investment of £200,000 (which is non-returnable), and is expected to produce cash inflows of £70,000 a year at the end of each of the next five years. Is it worth investing, if the opportunity cost of capital is 15 per cent a year? Calculate your answer using:

a. Net Terminal Value method
b. Net Present Value method
c. Internal Rate of Return method.
d. Show that the NTV method is precisely equivalent to the NPV method.

Problem 5.12.

A company expects to reduce labour costs by £20,000 a year if it invests £50,000 in new equipment which will last five years. Ignoring tax:

a. What is the annual increase in accounting profit?
b. What is the average accounting rate of return on investment?
c. What is the annual net cash inflow?
d. What is the payback period?
e. What is the NPV at 15 per cent a year?
f. What is the IRR?

CHAPTER 6

More on capital projects

6.1. Working capital

Debtors

Suppose a five-year manufacturing project will generate sales revenue of £220,000 a year; and that debtors of £56,000 will be outstanding at the end of each year. We could show cash receipts as follows: £164,000 in Year 1, £220,000 in each of Years 2 to 5, and £56,000 in Year 6. More usual, however, is to show sales revenues as if they were cash receipts of £220,000 for each of Years 1 to 5; in which case we also need to show an 'investment' in debtors of £56,000 at the end of Year 1, to be recovered at the end of Year 5. (The cash is likely to come in much nearer the end of Year 5 than the end of Year 6.)

Stocks less creditors

If the project incurs cash expenses of £120,000 a year, that may involve stocks of materials, work-in-progress and finished goods. Those will only appear in the profit and loss account as 'cost of sales' when matched later against sales. So we might show an 'investment' in stocks of, say, £40,000 at the end of Year 0, in advance of making any sales. (We would assume that stock is recovered in cash in full at the end of a project, in this case at the end of Year 5.)

Any investment in stocks may be partly offset by the extension of credit from suppliers. Suppose this amounts to £30,000 outstanding at the end of each year. The result would be a net cash investment in advance of only £10,000 (that is, £40,000 in stocks less £30,000 credit from suppliers). We would expect to clear this net amount, as a cash receipt, at the end of Year 5.

Overall position

On the basis of these assumptions, Table 6.1 sets out (in £ thousands) the cash flows in respect of working capital for the project. If the amounts involved were fairly small, it might be simpler to show the net outflow of £66,000 as a single amount arising at one point in time (probably the end of Year 1).

Table 6.1 Investment in working capital (in £ thousands)

End of Year:	0	1	2	3	4	5
Stocks	−40					+40
Creditors	+30					−30
Debtors		−56				+56
	−10	−56				+66

Table 6.2 Present value of investment in working capital

End of Year:	0 £	1 £	2	3	4	5 £
Stocks	−40,000					+40,000
Creditors	+30,000					−30,000
Debtors		−56,000				+56,000
Cash flows	−10,000	−56,000				+66,000
Discount factor:	1.000	0.909				0.621
Present value:	−10,000	−50,904				+40,986
Net present value:	−19,918					

We normally expect to recover the whole of the net amount invested in working capital at the end of a project. But of course in a discounted cash flow analysis we have to allow for the time that it is invested. Thus using a 10 per cent a year discount factor, Table 6.2 shows that the net present value of the amount invested in working capital in this case would be £19,918.

6.2. Taxation

Writing-down allowances

Corporation tax is levied at 30 per cent on taxable profit, rather than on the reported profit in accounts. In computing taxable profit, depreciation of fixed assets charged in arriving at accounting profit is disallowed as an expense. Instead there are tax writing-down allowances ('**capital allowances**') for certain kinds of capital spending.

The writing-down allowance reduces taxable profit and hence reduces tax payments. On plant and equipment, for example, the allowance is normally 25 per cent of cost in the year of purchase and 25 per cent of the **declining balance** in each subsequent year (see Table 6.3).

The cash benefit, of course, is the amount of the WDA multiplied by the relevant tax rate. So in this case, the Year 4 benefit is £26,367 @ 30% = £7,910. This may either go to reduce tax payable, or it may be convenient to show WDA benefits as a separate cash inflow related to the capital investment.

Table 6.3 Writing-down allowances on £250,000 equipment

	Written-down value £	Cash benefit @ 30% £
Cost of equipment	250,000	
Year 1. Writing-down allowance [25% × 250,000]	62,500	18,750
EOY 1 Tax written down value	187,500	
Year 2. WDA [25% × 187,500]	46,875	14,063
EOY 2 Tax written-down value	140,625	
Year 3. WDA	35,156	10,547
EOY 3 Tax written-down value	105,469	
Year 4. WDA	26,367	7,910
EOY 4 Tax written-down value	79,102	
Year 5. WDA	19,775	5,933
EOY 5. Tax written-down value	59,327	
Year 6. WDA	14,831	4,449
EOY 6. Tax written-down value	44,496	
	etc.	

There are special provisions for short-lived assets, such as computer hardware. If such assets are sold within five years, any surplus of the proceeds over the tax written-down value will be subject to a balancing charge. (Any deficit will give rise to a balancing allowance.) After five years, the asset's tax written-down value is transferred into the main pool of plant and equipment for subsequent WDAs; and any ultimate proceeds are then simply deducted from the balance in the pool.

For industrial buildings, the annual writing-down allowance is 4 per cent of the cost of the new building (for 25 years). Offices, shops and wholesale warehouses do not qualify for any tax allowances (except in enterprise zones). Why not? Because there is no tax statute saying they do! (The tax laws, unlike company accounting rules, have nothing to do with 'a true and fair view'.)

Corporation tax

The rate of corporation tax is 30 per cent for taxable profits above £1.5 million. On taxable profits up to £300,000 the tax rate is 20 per cent. (Between £300,000 and £1.5 million the marginal corporation tax rate is 32.5 per cent.)

We need to estimate a capital project's tax effect on the whole company, in order to compute its after-tax incremental cash flows. Table 6.4 shows the extra tax payments resulting from a capital project requiring £250,000 investment in equipment (which we assume to be sold at the end of Year 5 for £59,327 – exactly the amount of the tax written-down value). Extra revenue is £220,000 per year for five years and expenses £120,000 per year (excluding book depreciation). Discounted at 10 per cent per year, the net present value of the tax cash flows comes to −£63,500.

Table 6.4 Amount and net present value of corporation tax (£'000)

End of year	0	1	2	3	4	5	Total
Capital outflow	−250.0					+59.3	−190.7
Sales revenue		+220.0	+220.0	+220.0	+220.0	+220.0	+1100.0
Expenses		−120.0	−120.0	−120.0	−120.0	−120.0	−600.0
Margin		+100.0	+100.0	+100.0	+100.0	+100.0	+500.0
Tax wdas	−62.5	−46.9	−35.1	−26.4	−19.8	0.0	−190.7
Taxable income	−62.5	+53.1	+64.9	+73.6	+80.2	+100.0	+309.3
Tax @ 30%	+18.8	−15.9	−19.5	−22.1	−24.1	−30.0	−92.8
10% factor	1.000	.909	.826	.751	.683	.621	
Present values	+18.8	−14.5	−16.1	−16.6	−16.5	−18.6	−63.5

We assume the investment in equipment occurs in the year before any revenue arises. Where a project reduces taxable profit (as in Year 0 in Table 6.4) the company's overall tax bill will fall, assuming that the rest of the company has taxable profits against which to offset the writing-down allowances. This results in a positive tax cash inflow. Companies not currently paying UK tax can carry forward losses or writing-down allowances for future use. (But, of course, their present value will be somewhat less.)

The UK tax system has recently changed. When the transition is over, corporation tax will be payable by instalments. On average the date of payment will be about the end of the financial year; in other words, for capital project purposes, there will be no time lag between earning profits and paying tax thereon.

6.3. Capital disinvestment

Why projects end

Capital **disinvestment** means disposing of assets a business holds. This may result in receiving sales proceeds for 'second-hand' assets; it may not involve any cash receipts; or it may even require making cash payments to someone for collecting or demolishing the asset or for 'tidying up' after a project has finished (e.g. mining or nuclear energy).

Possible limits to a project's life may stem from the following:

1. Physical exhaustion of equipment. The question may be whether or not to replace the equipment (and if so when).
2. Technical obsolescence of equipment or process. This implies the end of the asset's 'economic' life though not of its physical life. I still possess in good working order a slide-rule which was once quite an 'advanced' piece of equipment!
3. Market factors, such as changing consumer tastes. It may not always be possible to extend a product's life cycle by suitable refinements.

4. Lapse of time, such as a lease for a finite period or expiry of a patent.
5. Political factors, e.g. banning the sale or advertising of a product.

The nature of a capital project may change over time, especially if its expected life extends for several years. Sometimes a firm may need to abandon a project early, if conditions or estimates have changed – perhaps even before it comes on stream. (For example, a new drug where a competitor has got to market first.)

Technically one can compare the NPV of the ongoing project's remaining life with the NPV of stopping it and selling the assets. One question to analyze may be not whether but *when* to stop. Another option for self-contained projects might be to sell them as a going concern to another company. A project which no longer seems attractive enough to Company A might still be of interest to Company B. (This is like any voluntary market exchange, where the different subjective valuations of buyer and seller mean that both parties normally expect to benefit (see Figure 1.1).)

It is sometimes easier to throw good money after bad than to cut one's losses when something has gone wrong with a project. Even though the decision to go ahead may be a '**sunk cost**' – and therefore theoretically irrelevant – in practice, managers can be quite emotional about projects they have championed. (Older readers may recall Mrs. Thatcher and the poll tax.)

Capital recovery

Amounts recoverable at the end of a project's life may represent the proceeds of assets: 1. value of land or buildings; 2. scrap or second-hand value of equipment; 3. working capital, such as stocks and debtors. Or the ongoing value of the project itself to another buyer. These amounts will appear as positive cash inflows at or beyond the terminal date, together with any tax-related cash flows. Of course a firm must discount back to *present value* any amounts (**terminal values** or **residual values**) it expects to recover at the end.

The longer the life of the project, the further away in time the terminal date will be, and for any given discount rate, the lower will be the present value. That is why young people are often rather bored by questions about pensions, while those about to retire find the topic strangely fascinating! (It is an intriguing question how, if at all, one's personal real discount rate varies over the course of one's life!)

In appraising long-life projects it is normal to use an arbitrary horizon period of ten or, perhaps, fifteen years as a rule. Firms do not explicitly consider cash flows beyond the horizon, even if they expect the project to last longer. But of course, including a 'terminal value' at the horizon date in effect does extend the life of the project (though possibly in a different form).

With a fairly high discount rate, this approach seems sensible, since it would make little difference to the amount of the present value. For example, with a 15 per cent a year discount rate, more than trebling a project's horizon period, from 15 to 50 years, would increase the present value of equal annual cash inflows by only

Table 6.5 Extending horizon period from 15 to 50 years at 15 per cent a year

Present value	End of Year 0	End of Year 15	End of Year 50
(a)	5,847a ◄——————— Life		
(b)	6,661a ◄——————————————— Life		
extra 0.814a = 13.3%		◄————————————► extra 35 years	

one-seventh – 13.3 per cent. As Table 6.5 shows (and Appendix B confirms), the discount factor would increase only from 5.847 to 6.661.

6.4. Inflation

What inflation means

So far we have ignored the effect of inflation on the cash flows of capital projects. But it can be significant. Given that many projects last for more than ten years, a 5 per cent annual rate of inflation implies that by the end of a project prices may be at least twice as high as at the start. (For a twenty-year project starting in 1970, the UK multiple would actually have been nearly *seven* times!)

Inflation is not just a technical detail affecting the numbers: it can have a profound impact on business projects. For example, if one country has faster inflation than others, sooner or later its currency will have to devalue against other currencies. Meanwhile there will be much economic and political uncertainty. A devaluation may have a major effect, for example, on export prices, on the cost of imported materials, and so on. Or high domestic inflation may lead in the future, as it often has in the past, to some form of general price control. This too can devastate business profits, since it often amounts to compelling firms to *cut* their prices in real terms.

Inflation and capital projects

In principle there are two different ways to cope with the effect of inflation on capital project appraisal. The key thing is to be consistent: either to discount money cash flows at a money (nominal) discount rate, or to discount 'real' cash flows at a real discount rate.

Forecasting all cash flows in money terms means allowing for any expected specific money price changes. One then needs to discount the future money cash flows at a money discount rate which includes an inflation premium to allow for general inflation. If the rate of inflation varies from year to year, it may be rather messy using a different money discount rate from year to year over a project's life (for the net present value method). (When using the internal rate of return method, of course, one cannot vary the discount rate either between years or between items – say of different riskiness – in the same year.)

An alternative approach is to forecast specific money cash flows as above; then to discount twice – first to allow for general inflation, and then using a real discount rate (adding a suitable risk premium to the real risk-free rate of return).

The real discount rate should be lower than the money discount rate by the expected rate of inflation. For example, if the money discount rate is 15 per cent and we expect 6 per cent inflation (which the money discount rate of 15 per cent includes), then the real discount rate would be only 9 per cent. (Strictly speaking it should be $1.15 \div 1.06 = 1.0849$ (i.e. 8.49 per cent), rather than $1.15 - 1.06 = 1.09$ per cent (i.e. 9.00 per cent). But when inflation rates are fairly low simple subtraction is quite accurate enough.)

It might seem less trouble merely to forecast cash flows in real terms throughout (in effect in terms of 'Year 0 pounds'), and then just discount by the same real discount rate each year. But such an approach has three snags, as follows:

1. General inflation means an increase in the average level of prices (the **retail prices index**). If 'general' inflation is 5 per cent, some items may go up 8 per cent in price, others 3 per cent, and others may go down by 2 per cent. Selling prices, material costs, wage rates, may be critical for a capital project's success or failure. So one does need to forecast *specific* price changes. It will nearly always be too simplistic to assume that inflation will affect all items in the same way over a period of years; though forecasting the precise differences may not be easy.
2. For tax purposes, writing-down allowances relate to the original money cost of certain fixed assets, without adjustment for inflation. Hence in times of inflation tax writing-down allowances will be *falling* in real terms. The effect of inflation on tax may not be simple: even if the money amount of sales revenue and cash expenses were to increase exactly in line with general inflation, the amount of taxable profits (and therefore of tax payable) would increase by somewhat more than that rate.
3. Investment in working capital is also subject to inflation. Stock levels which stay constant in physical terms will require an increasing level of money investment. Likewise, if debtor days outstanding remain constant, the money investment in debtors will grow as selling prices increase in terms of money. (And creditors will tend to grow as suppliers' prices increase.)

Example 6.1

Table 6.1 showed that the five-year project involved a net investment of £10,000 in stocks less creditors at the end of Year 0, and of £56,000 in debtors at the end of Year 1. Table 6.6 shows what happens if there is annual inflation of 6 per cent affecting each item. The sum of all cash flows over the five years is still zero, because we continue to assume that we recover all the net investment in working capital in full at the end of Year 5. The essential point is that working capital 'held constant in real terms' still involves some incremental money cash

Table 6.6 Extra working capital needed with 6 per cent a year inflation (£'000)

End of year	0	1	2	3	4	5
Stocks–creditors	10.00	10.60	11.24	11.91	12.63	
Debtors	0.00	59.36	62.92	66.70	70.70	
Net working capital	10.00	69.96	74.16	78.61	83.33	
Incremental cash	−10.00	−59.96	−4.20	−4.45	−4.72	+83.33
Per Table 6.1	−10.00	−56.00	0.00	0.00	0.00	+66.00
Difference	0.00	−3.96	−4.20	−4.45	−4.72	+17.33
6% discount factor	1.0000	.9434	.8900	.8396	.7921	.7473
'Real' differences		−3.74	−3.74	−3.74	−3.74	+12.95
Net present value	= −2.01					

flows each year. We must allow for these even if we choose to set out the cash flows in 'real' terms not in money terms.

6.5. Capital budgeting

Capital spending

In addition to ways of looking at each project's likely profits or future cash flows, companies need a system of **capital budgeting.** This involves planning aggregate capital spending over the next year or two and splitting it into monthly or quarterly amounts forming part of the cash budget. Among other things, this helps to arrange suitable financing (where necessary) in good time.

Both the amount and the timing of capital projects can change quickly. Business and financial conditions may make it desirable either to speed up or to slow down capital spending. In extreme cases firms may even have to cancel projects after they have begun, though that can be very expensive.

Capital spending takes time. This, more than limited finance, may account for companies sometimes imposing capital rationing. Even if Railtrack, for example, had access to unlimited finance, completing all the projects they would like would still take several years.

Many capital projects are risky, so businesses tend to be cautious about capital spending. Once under way, projects may not be reversible. For specialized plant and equipment there may be almost no second-hand market, and even a potential buyer might only offer a very low price.

That is why companies look carefully before they leap, and insist on thorough procedures for capital project proposals. The larger the amount of money involved, or the greater the strategic importance, the higher up in a company projects must go for approval. Such approval may sometimes seem to be merely 'rubber-stamping', but this is probably because extensive informal discussions have already taken place before the formal submission of the project. In most firms, what goes on informally

Table 6.7 *Ex ante* project appraisal versus *ex post* performance appraisal

In advance	After the event
Main methods: NPV, IRR	Main methods: RI, ROI
1a. Incremental amounts	*1a. Overall totals
1b. relating to discrete 'projects'	*1b. relating to whole business unit
1c. over all (or most) of project's life	*1c. for a single period (often one year)
*2a. Cash flows	2a. Profits (or losses)
*2b. after tax (but before interest)	2b. often before tax (and before interest)
*2c. ignoring depreciation	2c. after charging depreciation
3a. May be constant purchasing power	*3a. Usually monetary units
3b. usually discounted	*3b. not discounted
3c. reinvestment assumption (implicit or explicit)	*3c. No reinvestment assumption
4. Uncertainty clearly relevant	4. Uncertainty often ignored

Note: *Indicates which way cash-flow accounting would probably tend

is at least as important as the formal system, even though it is not so visible. The internal politics of capital budgeting can be crucial.

Evaluation before and after

Table 6.7 compares methods for looking at capital projects in advance and those used for business performance appraisal after the event. Clearly there are several differences.

It has been suggested that using cash flows as the basis for *ex post* performance appraisal (rather than accounting profits) could avoid many of the differences. (The asterisks in Table 6.7 show which way cash flow accounting would probably tend.)

Items 1a and 4 would remain difficult items to overcome. After the event it may often be hard to identify incremental amounts resulting from specific projects which the ongoing business has thoroughly absorbed. (This is a major problem in post-project audits: see below.) Nor will it be easy to make useful guesses after the event about the actual level of risk involved. (This is not easy *before* the event either; but at least *ex ante* one can hardly be unaware of uncertainty.)

Figure 6.1 illustrates the first point: the contrast between looking at incremental amounts relating to discrete projects over a project's whole life, and looking at overall totals relating to the whole business unit for a single accounting period.

Post-project audits

Some larger companies arrange post-project audits for some of their capital projects. As soon as a project is on stream they can check the amount and the timing of the capital spending. But the audit may be more ambitious and try to review operating cash flows too.

Normally such audits take place when a project may still have most of its life to run. It would make little sense to wait until a 10-year project was over before having an

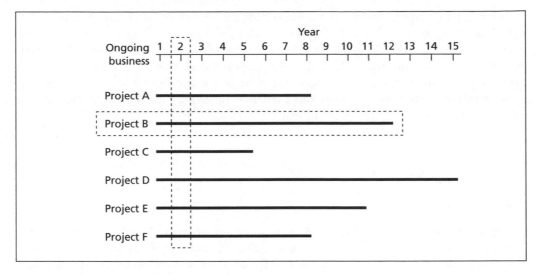

Figure 6.1 Project lives and accounting periods

audit. Conditions would have changed too much, the people involved might have moved on, and any lessons might be out of date. Thus an audit may take place after a project has been running, say, about 1 year. It can compare original estimates with actual outcomes for capital spending and perhaps for the first year's operations. But for later years any comparison may simply be with most recent estimates of future results.

A post-project audit need not be entirely backward-looking. It may sometimes be possible to reassess a project's future as a result. Probably only larger projects, or projects with problems, will be subject to audit. It may not be easy to measure a project's impact after the event.

That implies a need to specify the purpose of post-project audits. It might be dangerous to allocate blame where things have gone wrong. That might induce a risk-averse attitude in managers. It is probably more useful to try to learn what went right, as well as what did not; and how to do better in future. Important aspects to review might include: capital spending, assumptions about market size and market share, operating costs, the timing of events, estimates of project life, and so on.

International aspects

Where a British company proposes to invest in a capital project abroad, it must estimate incremental net-of-local-tax cash flows in the local currency. It probably doesn't matter whether companies assess projects' net present values in terms of local currency or in domestic currency (pounds sterling). But any extra tax payable in the home country must be allowed for, both the amount and the timing. There is, of course, no need to plan for actual conversion into pounds, though we assume there are no exchange restrictions.

If a company expects more inflation in the local currency (than in sterling), the nominal local discount rate should be higher (than a sterling discount rate) to allow for the extra inflation premium. Translation of local currency cash flows into pounds should use the exchange rate expected at the time when the local cash flows arise. The amounts in pounds should thus reflect any expected decline in the local currency's exchange rate against sterling. (But in the short run exchange rates may not fluctuate precisely in line with differences in rates of inflation.)

Problems

Problem 6.1.

Stephen Collier Ltd. is considering an investment project requiring the investment of £50,000 in new fixed assets and £12,000 in additional stocks. The annual sales revenue for the project is forecast to be £80,000, and the annual running costs £60,000 (including S/L depreciation of £10,000). The project's life is expected to be five years. Ignoring tax:

a. show the cash flows year by year
b. should the project be accepted if the firm's cut-off rate is 20 per cent?
c. what is the internal rate of return on the project?

Problem 6.2.

Refer to problem 6.1 above. Additional information is as follows:

1. Existing assets (being replaced) can be sold for £2,000.
2. Tax at 30 per cent is assumed payable on profits on the last day of the year in which they are earned.
3. For tax purposes, S/L depreciation can be ignored; instead tax writing-down allowances of 25 per cent a year on the declining balance are given on the total investment in new fixed assets. Assume that these can be used, if necessary, to reduce tax on Stephen Collier Ltd.'s overall profits.

    a. Show the net cash flows year by year.
    b. Should the project be accepted if the firm's after-tax cut-off rate is 15 per cent?
    c. What is the project's internal rate of return?
    d. What is the profitability index of the project?
    e. How low could the £30,000 annual pre-tax operating cash inflows be and the project still be acceptable?

Problem 6.3.

Colin Park is enthusiastic about a new German machine, which he thinks would enable Park Products Ltd. to reduce operating costs by £20,000 a year (before tax of 30 per cent). The machine costs £60,000. For tax purposes, writing-down allowances of 25 per cent on the declining balance are available. (Ignore any tax time-lags.) At the end of its expected five-year life, the machine could probably be sold for about £5,000. (Ignore any tax consequences at that point.) The company normally requires a return of at least 15 per cent a year (after tax) on this kind of investment.

Should Park Products buy the German machine?

Problem 6.4.

Park Products did go ahead and buy the German machine (G) (see problem 6.3 above). But a month later Colin Park visited Japan in order to keep abreast of the latest technical developments. While he was in Tokyo he learned about an even better machine (J), which would cut Park's operating costs by a further £12,000 a year (before tax) by replacing machine (G). Machine (J) would last five years, with not much salvage value at the end, and would cost £60,000. Unfortunately, machine (G) would have to be sold, and would realize only £25,000.

a. Should Park Products now purchase machine (J)?
b. If machine (J) is purchased, presumably it was a mistake to buy machine (G) in the first place. How much did this mistake cost? How did it come about?

CHAPTER 7

Mergers and acquisitions

7.1. Reasons for acquisitions

Reasons for buying

'**Mergers**' and 'acquisitions' both combine two or more separate businesses into one enterprise, with a single top management and common ownership. The term 'merger' often covers both. Strictly in a merger two companies M and N pool all their assets and liabilities; and shareholders exchange their shares in M or in N for shares in a new **holding company** MN. In an acquisition, A buys all (or most) of the equity shares, or the (net) assets, in B. The purchase price may comprise cash, which buys out the previous ownership interests in B, or shares in A.

Thus an acquisition is simply an example of a capital investment project (from A's point of view). It may involve a larger amount than most normal 'projects'; and the strategic implications may be very important.

The main arguments for mergers are economies of scale, and transferring control of resources to better managers. The main arguments against are the dangers of monopoly, or less competition leading to waste. It is not clear a priori whether higher concentration in an industry will increase or reduce competition. One needs to look at relevant markets, including imports, not merely at 'domestic' production; and one must also consider the impact of potential competition.

Most mergers are **horizontal**, combining firms in the same business: for example, a daily newspaper merging with a Sunday. They are most likely to lead to economies of scale, but they may also tend towards monopoly. Economies of scale vary between industries. They need not apply only to production: there may be savings in marketing, research and even finance. Size can also bring important drawbacks ('diseconomies of scale'): remoteness of management control; extra layers of overhead cost; and rigid bureaucracy.

Vertical mergers combine firms at different stages of production in the same industry. They may aim to control quality, or to ensure sources of supply or retail outlets. Thus a producer of soft drinks might combine 'upstream' with fruit growers or a company making containers, or 'downstream' with a firm running ice cream vans.

Conglomerate mergers combine firms in different industries, perhaps with no obvious connection: for example, a cigarette maker and an insurance company, or a drinks producer and a chain of opticians. Such mergers are fairly rare (they are out of

Table 7.1 Reasons for acquisition

Production
1. Expanding capacity
2. Economies of scale
3. Acquiring technology
4. Vertical integration, for quality control or supply reasons

Marketing
5. Expanding market share
6. Extending product range
7. Gaining entry to new markets
8. Eliminating competition
9. Vertical integration, for distribution reasons

Miscellaneous
10. Target company's shares or assets 'under-priced'
11. Acquirer's shares 'over-valued'
12. Applying superior management skills to the acquiree's business
13. Acquiring management skills to apply to the acquirer's business
14. Preventing a competitor from acquiring the target company
15. Making the acquiring company itself less attractive to a predator
16. Tax benefits
17. Avoiding government interference
18. Diversifying business risk
19. Empire building.

fashion these days). Benefits might stem from tax savings, management skills in the centre, or financial efficiencies. It can be hard to interpret **group accounts (consolidated accounts)** which add together numbers from different industries. Hence group accounts disclose separately their sales, profits and assets in the various different industry segments in which they operate.

The acquiring company may want expansion more quickly than by internal growth. In some industries size may be essential to compete globally. There may be a desire to avoid outside control: it is much harder for governments to interfere with transactions within a group than with 'visible' market deals between separate companies. (This may be an important reason for some global mergers.) Table 7.1 sets out a number of possible reasons for one business to acquire another, some of which may overlap.

Reasons for selling

Many commercial assets are for sale 'if the price is right', even if the owners were not planning to sell. People who have founded a business, or inherited it, may want either to retire or to spread their investment risk. They can defer any **capital gains tax** bill by receiving shares rather than cash; and if they accept shares in a listed company, they can dispose of them whenever they choose.

Another reason for selling a business may be management problems, either succession or lack of ability to manage a larger business following a period of growth. The death or retirement of one or two key people can often reveal a need for new management. Sometimes selling an ailing business may simply be 'a civilized alternative to **bankruptcy**'. Sale as a

---

Table 7.2 Reasons for selling (part of) a business

Ownership
1. Owner wants to diversify risk
2. Owner wants to reduce tax problems on death

Management
3. Manager(s) about to retire, with no obvious successor
4. Poor business prospects under control of present management, possibly following expansion or a change of direction

Part of a group
5. Needs extra source of finance
6. No longer fits with core business or strategy of vendor group
7. Make *vendor* less attractive to a predator

Miscellaneous
8. Needs economies of scale (might justify *acquisition* rather than sale!)
9. Vendor's shares or assets 'over-valued'.

---

going concern will normally produce a better price than winding a firm up; and it will avoid many human and legal problems. Selling a division of a group of companies may make strategic sense if it no longer fits with the 'core' business, or if the group needs extra finance for the rest of its business. It may also make the vendor company less attractive to a predator (by selling the 'crown jewels'). Table 7.2 lists reasons for selling a company.

Management versus shareholders

Managers are likely to have all their eggs in one basket, so they may be keen to merge to reduce their company's total risk. In theory this makes no sense for the company's owners if they hold a portfolio of shares and can thus diversify away most of any company's '**unique risk**' (see Chapter 11). But owners of family companies may not be in this position; hence they too may be quite keen on their company diversifying.

Getting into new areas of business may be exciting for managers, but it may also involve big risks. A famous economist once said: 'People want an *interesting* life.' On average acquiring groups have to pay a **bid premium** of about 25 per cent on the vendor's (pre-bid) share price. This may absorb nearly all of the economic gains from the merger, leaving little if any reward for shareholders in the acquiring group.

Managers may welcome size for its own sake if their pay partly depends on it, whereas shareholders want a good rate of **return on equity**. That is why shareholders would often prefer a higher **dividend payout ratio** than the top managers (see Chapter 12). Merging may also improve a group's credit rating, which may make life more comfortable for managers.

Poor managers, who fail to maximize shareholder wealth, ought in the end to be vulnerable to a takeover bid for control of their company. That could yield large profits for those who organize such a bid. They could either run the business better themselves, or hire other managers to do so, or split it up and sell parts of it off. Private companies, however, may not be easy to take over, hence they are high-risk investments, certainly for minority shareholders. In practice, though, even for listed companies, the short-term pressure on incompetent or unlucky managers may be less than theory suggests.

Joint ventures and minority interests

So far we have been discussing mergers and acquisitions on the basis that they involve 100 per cent of a company's equity shares. But share deals between 'partners' may involve less than 100 per cent of the equity, especially in international transactions. Taking a **minority interest** in a foreign company is often an early stage in learning about operating in a different country.

For example, if a company wishes to expand into a foreign country, it may make sense to proceed by way of a strategic alliance (joint venture or minority interest). In a joint venture, each of two partners owns 50 per cent of the equity. Under the so-called 'equity basis', the accounts normally show the investment at cost plus any share of retained profits, while the profit and loss account reports the share of profits or losses (not just dividends received, if any).

Where the investing company holds only a minority interest in the equity, it will still normally use the equity basis of accounting if the share of equity held is at least 20 per cent (in an **associated company** or 'related company').

Why would a company choose not to own 100 per cent of the equity? It does, of course, reduce the amount it needs to invest in the enterprise. More important, however, is probably the benefit to be gained from the foreign partner's local knowhow and connections, at least for a time.

There may be dangers. Not all cultures may see such relationships in the same light. British Aerospace sold its 80 per cent interest in Rover to the German company BMW, which upset the Japanese company Honda which owned 20 per cent of Rover's equity. British Aerospace seemed to regard its 80/20 'partnership' with Honda as mainly financial, to be ditched if and when a better deal came along; whereas Honda believed its 20 per cent interest in Rover was a long-term arrangement.

In one sense, a minority interest, or investment in a joint venture, may resemble an **option** (see Chapter 8). It may provide an investing company with a springboard for developing 100 per cent interests in the country or industry concerned, when it has learned enough (and also when it has begun to establish a local reputation of its own). On the other hand, the local partner may be gaining access to foreign technology. On this view, such arrangements may often turn out *not* to be long term, but more opportunistic.

7.2. The process of merging

Valuation

An acquiring company may regard an acquisition as a capital investment project. The amount of the investment is the purchase price, plus any extra amount which the acquirer plans to invest in the business (including restructuring costs), less the expected disposal proceeds of any surplus assets. The assets being acquired may be equity shares in the holding company of a group, the assets of the group, or the assets of part of a group. Specified liabilities may also be taken over.

Estimates of the project's future cash flows should allow for **synergy**, or other expected changes, as well as for any further investment. The acquirer may also wish to allow for some terminal value at the horizon date. To find the maximum purchase price payable, the acquirer can discount the estimated future cash flows to present value. The discount rate should represent the rate of return suitable for the riskiness of the business *being acquired* (which may not be the same as the acquirer's cost of capital). (See also Chapter 14.)

As a check it may be useful to employ other valuation methods too, such as price/earnings multiples or even **book values** of assets. For listed companies it has been common for the purchase price to average some 25 per cent more than the acquiree's pre-bid market price per share. This may often leave a demanding task for the acquirer's management to earn a profit on top of that premium. In other words, shareholders in companies being acquired often receive a significant premium; but shareholders in acquirer companies may often not do so well.

Bargaining

In a 'friendly' deal, an acquirer (A) will try to find out why the seller (S) wants to sell. Is S aware of adverse future factors which A does not know about? Or are there personal reasons for selling? And S will try to discover A's motives. Does A value some aspect of the business more highly than S? If so, why? And how much is it worth to A?

Both A and S should take care throughout to keep an eye on other possible choices, as Figure 7.1 shows. A will be comparing S with other possible purchases, or with internal growth. S will be looking around for other possible partners, or thinking of continuing ownership. If there seems to be no feasible alternative for one party to the deal, that party may find it hard to drive much of a bargain.

Both buyer and seller may have in mind a range of suitable prices. If they overlap, a deal should be possible. And the larger the gap between the buyer's maximum price and the seller's minimum price, the more the scope for bargaining. Of course the range may alter during the bargaining. In the excitement of an auction, a 'successful' buyer can easily end up paying far more than he planned; or this may be the price of keeping a deal friendly.

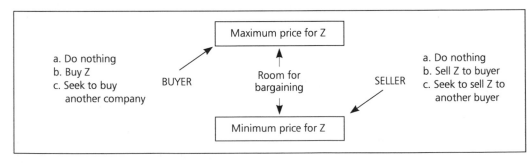

Figure 7.1 Buyer and seller alternatives

The ability to walk away from a deal that is costing too much may not win much glory, but perhaps it serves the interests of shareholders better than expensive 'triumphs'.

Basing the purchase price partly on future profits (**earn-outs**) defers some of the cost and reduces the risk, by protecting the buyer if promised future profits fail to occur. It may also act as an incentive for former owner–managers to continue working well. That is for stand-alone businesses. On the other hand, this kind of arrangement can turn out very messy if the buyer reorganizes the acquired business or combines it with existing business units.

In hostile take-over bids, the interests of the victim's (V) top management may not coincide with those of its shareholders. The management may prefer continuing independence at almost any price. The City Code which governs take-over practice requires V's directors to provide full details of any offer to enable V's shareholders to make an informed decision.

Financing

Combining two formerly separate companies is likely to increase the total equity 'cushion', and thus to reduce the risk for existing creditors. Indeed, by reducing an enterprises's total risk, merging may encourage management to increase **financial gearing (leverage)**.

The method of payment will affect financial structure. For instance, a company with a 35 per cent debt ratio which acquires another company half its size could end up with a debt ratio varying from 23 per cent to 57 per cent, depending on whether it borrowed none or all of the purchase price. (The price might consist of loan stock in the acquiring group; or the acquiring group might borrow itself in order to finance a purchase for cash.)

A well-known advantage of paying in equity shares is to delay any capital gains tax bill for the vendors and to spread any such liability out over time.

Human consequences

Over time most companies develop a style of their own; and it can be difficult to combine two firms with different cultures. Making a merger work takes a great deal of management time and effort. Depending on the nature of the merger (is it horizontal, vertical or conglomerate?), the new group's top management may wish to look in some detail at every significant aspect of the new business: each major product line, every plant, the main markets, all senior personnel.

Human problems often arise among workers as a result of a merger. 'Economies of scale' may be an abstract way of saying that one person can do two people's jobs. So the other person may have to go. Other employees may be demoted, or have to move to a new office or factory, perhaps far away from their present home and friends. Such redeployment may often make good business sense, but to implement it requires great skill and tact on management's part. To avoid uncertainty it is usually a good idea to tell the workers in a newly-acquired business as much as possible about future plans as soon as possible.

Why some mergers fail

Measuring success or failure in the context of mergers and acquisitions is somewhat tricky. Whose point of view is one adopting? Is it the shareholders'? If so, in the acquired company or in the acquiring company or both? Or is it the managers' point of view, the employees', the customers' or the 'national interest'?

There is a fair amount of evidence that shareholders in companies being acquired receive a significant premium over the pre-bid share price – on average around 25 per cent. It seems, though, that shareholders in acquiring companies often get no measurable benefit at all. If this is correct, it suggests a measure of success for mergers overall, with acquiree shareholders getting nearly all the resulting benefit.

From an accounting point of view (as contrasted with share prices), it is not clear that on balance mergers do provide any net benefit. The issue of how goodwill is treated may be important here.

In general terms it seems that – in the opinion of the managers concerned – about half of all large mergers are judged not to have been successful, to have failed. They may not be too worried about the impact on shareholders. What are the main reasons for failure? Significant reasons appear to be:

1. Cultural differences between the two companies.
2. Lack of post-merger integration planning
3. Lack of knowledge of industry or target company.

The implication seems to be that some acquisitions are undertaken with too little thought.

7.3. Accounting

Acquisitions and mergers

When one company buys all or most of the equity shares in another, it normally accounts for the deal as an acquisition. Any difference between the purchase price (whether paid in cash or in shares) and the fair value of the separable net assets represents purchased goodwill. The acquiring concern treats this as an intangible fixed asset and normally writes it off as an expense against (after-tax) profit over not more than twenty years.

But where two groups of shareholders in different companies (A and B) which are combining both get shares in the new group, such business combinations may be treated as mergers if they meet all the following rules:

1. Neither A nor B dominates the new group in size. The larger must not surpass the smaller in size by more than 60:40.
2. Equity shareholders in both A and B receive mainly equity shares in the new group (rather than cash) for their former shareholdings.
3. Managers from both A and B join in managing the new group.
4. Nobody portrays either A or B as 'acquirer' or as 'acquired'.

Merger accounting differs from acquisition accounting in several respects:

1. It combines A's and B's assets and creditors at their former *book* values, so no goodwill arises.
2. It reports as profits of the new group A's and B's combined profits for the entire accounting period in which the merger occurred; and also restates the profits for earlier periods on a combined basis.
3. It leaves the combined retained profits of the merging companies available for payment as dividends by the new group.
4. It includes any new shares issued as part of the deal at their nominal value (with no need for any **share premium** account).
5. It treats as a change in reserves any difference between the new group's called-up share capital and the merging companies' total share capitals.

Because merger accounting does not involve writing off any purchased goodwill as an expense in the profit and loss account, most companies prefer it to acquisition accounting. There is some argument over the difference in accounting treatment: it has no cash effects, so does it really matter? (See Chapter 3.)

Price/earnings multiples and earnings per share

Table 7.3 sets out basic details for Company A and Company B, two firms which are going to combine. A has a **market capitalization** of £1,000 million versus B's £400 million; but B's profits of £50 million (after tax) exceed A's profits of £40 million. Thus A's price/earnings multiple is 25 while B's is only 10. Does it matter which company acquires the other?

Table 7.4 shows what happens if A acquires B (on a 2 shares for 1 basis, implying a 25 per cent premium for B's shareholders) and if B acquires A (on a 3 shares for 4 basis, implying a 20 per cent premium for A's shareholders). In particular it makes a huge difference what one assumes about the price/earnings multiple of the new group.

If one assumes A's price/earnings multiple of 25 is maintained, then the combined market capitalization after the deal *increases* by £694 million! If, however, one assumes B's price/earnings multiple of 10 is maintained, there is a *fall* in market capitalization of £600 million!

Table 7.3 Basic data for A and B

	A	B
Profit after tax (£m)	40	50
Number of shares (m)	400	125
Earnings per share (pence)	10	40
Share price (pence)	250	400
Price/earnings multiple	25	10
Market capitalization (£m)	1000	400

Table 7.4 Alternative acquirers and possible valuations

	If A offers 2 A shares for 1 B	If B offers 3 B shares for 4 A
Purchase consideration (£m)	250m @ 250 = 625 A shares	300m @ 400 = 1200 B shares
Goodwill (£m)	625 − 500 = 125	1200 − 1000 = 200
New group profits (£m)	90 − 6.25 = 83.75	90 − 10 = 80
New number of shares (m)	400 + 250 = 650	125 + 300 = 425
New earnings per share (p)	12.885	18.824
P/E ratio (if unchanged)	25	10
New share price (p)	322	188
Market capitalization (£m)	2094	800
Apparent surplus/deficit (£m)	+694	−600
Market capitalization (£m) − if unchanged	1400	1400
Implied P/E ratio*	16.72	17.50

* Slightly different because of difference in goodwill write-off.

Of course what is far more likely – assuming no synergies – is for market capitalizations in total not to change much, and for the new price/earnings multiple to end up roughly halfway between the two, at around 17. The key lesson is to be careful about what one assumes about price/earnings multiples. They should not be regarded as constants.

Problems

Problem 7.1.

David and Goliath

Goliath plc acquired 100 per cent of David Ltd. for 30 million £1 ordinary shares valued at 400p each on 1 January 2000, when their respective balance sheets were as summarized below.

	Goliath £m	David £m
Fixed assets, net	350	50
Working capital	250	50
	600	100
Long-term debt	100	30
Shareholders' funds:		
Issued ordinary shares	150	20
Retained profits	350	50
	600	100

Required: Show the group balance sheet after the acquisition, assuming that the fair value of David's net assets is the same as the book value, namely £70 million.

Problem 7.2.

Hollyhock plc
Hollyhock plc is proposing to acquire all the equity capital of Snapdragon Ltd. Future cash inflows for Snapdragon as a separate company are estimated at £4 million a year after tax; but Hollyhock's management reckons that economies of scale can add a further £2 million a year after tax, to achieve which an immediate capital investment will be required of £5 million (which is stated net of the effect of tax writing-down allowances).

Regular fixed capital investments needed to maintain Snapdragon's profits are to be taken as equal to the company's current depreciation expense of £2.5 million a year. Surplus Snapdragon assets to be sold immediately after the acquisition (without significantly affecting profits) are expected to realize £1 million net.

If the appropriate after-tax discount rate is 12 per cent a year, what is the maximum purchase price that Hollyhock plc should be prepared to pay for the equity in Snapdragon Ltd:

a. using a horizon period of 10 years?
b. using a horizon period of 15 years?

Problem 7.3.

Beach Products plc
Beach Products plc is planning a major acquisition costing £50 million. The company's present capital consists of 100 million 50p issued ordinary shares, £40 million retained profits and £30 million 10 per cent secured **debentures**. The group's current profit before interest and tax (PBIT) is £25 million a year; which is expected to rise to £35 million a year as a result of the acquisition.

Beach Products can pay for its new acquisition in two ways:

1. issuing 40 million ordinary shares @ 125p each; or
2. issuing £50 million 12 per cent loan stock.

Required: For each of the alternative methods of financing the acquisition, compare:

a. debt ratio
b. interest cover
c. earnings per share

after the acquisition with Beach Products plc's present position. Assume a tax rate of 30 per cent.

Problem 7.4.

Peverill Plastics plc
Peverill Plastics plc is considering making a bid for control of Middlesex Mouldings Ltd. The company's directors have taken a five-year view. Middlesex's predicted cash flow for the first year is a net inflow of £8 million, and it is expected that this will increase by

£1 million a year for each of the next four years. If Peverill's bid is successful, it is believed that the cash inflow can be increased by a further £4 million a year; but only if £10 million is invested at once and a further £3 million invested at the end of each year thereafter to maintain the plant.

a. Set out Middlesex's expected cash flows for each of the next five years.
b. What is the maximum price that Peverill should offer for Middlesex? Assume a discount rate of 10 per cent and a five-year time horizon for the acquisition.
c. How else might Peverill try to value Middlesex Mouldings?

CHAPTER 8

Risk and uncertainty

8.1. Risk

Expected values

We can distinguish between risk and **uncertainty**. Risk is where we know the chance of each possible outcome occurring (as in roulette or with dice). Uncertainty exists where, as is usual in business, one can only estimate the odds (that is, guess).

Suppose that, for a new product, a firm reckons that annual sales levels of 400, 250, or 100 units are possible, and that the chances of each outcome (in order) are 0.1, 0.6, and 0.3. (Of course, in practice we would not expect such discrete outcomes.) By weighting the possible outcomes by their estimated chances of happening, we can calculate an '**expected value**' of sales volume of 220 units (see Table 8.1). We can do the same for the estimated profit at each level of sales, to arrive at an 'expected profit' of £22,000; and in principle we could use the same approach to compute an 'expected Net Present Value' for the project, and make a decision on that basis.

Attaching subjective probabilities to uncertain future events allows manipulation of the numbers. But that hardly makes the process 'scientific'. What confidence can we have in guesses about the chances of various outcomes? Can we even be sure we have considered every possible event? (Why should the probabilities add up to 1.0? "There are more things in heaven and earth, Horatio, than are dreamed of in your philosophy.") Experience suggests that events which in advance seemed quite impossible often

Table 8.1 Subjective probabilities and 'expected values'

Sales volume	Estimated profit (£'000)	Estimated probability (£'000)	'Expected' sales (£'000)	'Expected' profit (£'000)
400	130	0.1	40	13
250	40	0.6	150	24
100	(50)	0.3	30	(15)
		—	—	—
		1.0	220	22

appear afterwards to have been inevitable. (For example, the collapse of the Berlin Wall.)

If we know the true odds, there is no uncertainty, only risk. But we are not safe in extrapolating frequencies for future events from statistics of past occurrences in similar cases. (For example, the millennium bug wasn't much of a problem at the end of the first millennium.) For we are then merely assuming that the past will repeat itself. But trends go on . . . until they stop! And what about unprecedented events? These are more typical of major business opportunities ('the chance of a lifetime'). What are the odds against the United Kingdom (or, perhaps, England) seceding from the European Union in the next fifteen years? Nobody knows (though no doubt it will strike some people as 'politically incorrect' even to raise the question!).

A further problem is that, when dealing with unique events, we can never know if our estimate of the odds was correct – *even after the event*! Thus learning from events is not always easy. It may sometimes be helpful to our thinking about a problem to break it down into a number of simpler sub-problems. That is the idea behind decision trees, to which we now turn.

Decision trees

A **decision tree** is a picture of alternative sequential decisions and the various possible outcomes of those decisions. It is common to incorporate subjective estimates of probabilities of outcomes in order to determine 'expected values' for each decision alternative. By 'rolling back' from the ultimate outcomes, one can (in theory) then simply choose the decision alternative with the highest expected value.

Example 8.1

Zing plc is considering developing and marketing a new gizmo. Development will cost £1.2 million and will take one year. There is reckoned to be a 60 per cent chance that, at the end of that time, the gizmo will work. If it does, marketing the product will then be an option. It is not clear whether or not there will be a competitive product in the market. If there isn't, the net present value of expected after-tax cash flows (at the end of Year 1) is estimated at +£4.0 million. If there is competition, the EOY1 NPV is only +£1.0 million. There is thought to be a 75 per cent chance of competition.

Figure 8.1 portrays the decision tree, distinguishing between decisions [●] and events [■]. By rolling back the expected values of the various outcomes, and giving effect to the estimated probabilities of each outcome, we can 'value' each decision. Obviously, if we believe all the numbers, we would choose the decision with the highest positive value.

Figure 8.1 suggests that the value of developing the gizmo is +£0.57 million, so on the face of it the decision should be to go ahead with development. (Strictly the +£0.57 million is an end of Year 1 amount; which we might want to discount back to present value.)

Of course we can vary some of the estimates and use sensitivity analysis (see below) to test how much difference it makes, for example, if we revise our estimate of the odds (or of anything else). In practice it may be that one of the benefits of decision trees is not so

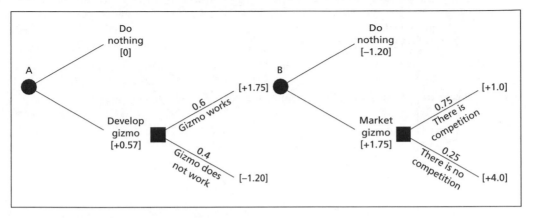

Figure 8.1 Decision tree for Zing's gizmo

much the numerical 'result', but the pictorial representation of the key decisions and events that affect the decisions.

The discount rate

When computing a project's NPV we have to pre-select a discount rate which normally reflects a company's **weighted average cost of capital (WACC)** (see Chapter 11). Some companies use different discount rates for various kinds of project, to allow for differences in risk. For example, they may regard cost reduction projects as low risk, and new product projects as high risk. (Conversely, one large company uses a *lower* discount rate for certain high-risk technical projects, as a deliberate safeguard against falling behind in the technology race.) How much to adjust the 'average' discount rate (the WACC) to allow for high- or low-risk projects is hard to judge.

The same might be done for different periods or for different kinds of cash flow. For example, it may be that the early years of a project are riskier than the later years. Or the expected cash flow resulting from tax writing-down allowances on capital expenditure may be a good deal less uncertain than cash inflows estimated from future sales revenues. One could allow for this by discounting benefits at a lower rate (with a smaller risk premium), and thus, in effect, valuing them more highly.

No method of estimating the cost of equity capital is precisely accurate, to put it mildly. Over the years, the stock market has yielded average returns on equity of about 8 per cent a year (in real terms) more than on risk-free securities. Hence some people regard 8 per cent as the required risk premium to apply to capital investment in the average project. For a lower-risk project, a risk premium of (say) only 4 per cent might be suitable; for an above-average-risk project, a risk premium of perhaps 12 per cent; and for a very high risk project, a risk premium of as much as 20 per cent. These are, of course, crude and arbitrary guesses. If one adopted them, and if the real risk-free rate of return were 2 per cent, then Figure 8.2 shows the real required

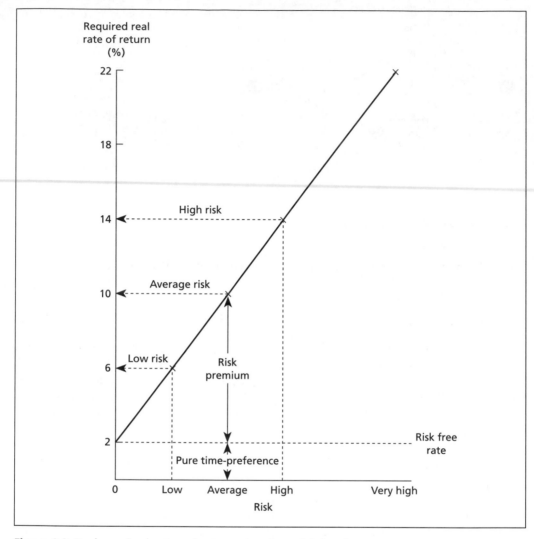

Figure 8.2 Real required rates of return at various risk levels

rates of return for projects of varying risks. (See also Figures 2.3 and 11.3 and the section on 'equity risk premium' in Chapter 11.)

8.2. Uncertainty

Sensitivity analysis

Business managers usually have to plan, control and make decisions on the basis of uncertain estimates about the future. They may know some figures, such as suppliers' prices for the next few months, but about others they may feel very unsure. Where adverse events could badly damage their business, managers need to understand the range and likelihood of possible outcomes. The same is true in respect of favourable outcomes. It would not be very sensible to embark on a project without having any idea that, if everything worked out right, it could be not just modestly successful, but hugely profitable.

One way to try to cope is sensitivity analysis. The first step is often to make a single 'best estimate' ('best' = most likely, not 'optimal') for each item. One might then also make 'optimistic' and 'pessimistic' estimates for each. The spreads may not be symmetrical: for instance, capacity constraints may prevent a firm from exceeding budgeted sales volume by much, whereas in a recession there could be a sharp decline.

Another approach is to vary the most likely estimate for each item in turn, to see how much it would affect the overall result. Some items will not matter much even if they change by a large percentage. So one needs to identify the critical items, where even a fairly small percentage change could make quite a large difference to the overall result.

It is not much use to try changing each item by a fixed percentage (say, 10 per cent); for some items could vary by much more, while others may be unlikely to change by nearly as much. A better method is to define an optimistic estimate of income as one which there was only, say, a 1 in 10 change of exceeding. (There would be only a 1 in 10 chance of falling short of the pessimistic estimate of income.) Of course, guessing the odds is itself not at all easy.

It is also not easy to allow for interdependence among items. Merely to combine the pessimistic estimates of the most sensitive items would be far too gloomy. If pessimistic means a 1 in 10 chance of a worst outcome, for example, with four completely independent variables, there would be only a 1 in 10,000 chance of such a combined outcome. (Admittedly, it is unlikely that the four variables would be completely independent.) Sensitivity analysis may help to answer the question: 'What if . . . ?' – but it does not say how likely 'if' is.

Managing under uncertainty

'**Business risk**' refers to how a business invests its resources, '**financial risk**' to how it finances them. Borrowing to finance assets is risky because the business must legally make regular interest payments and must repay the amount borrowed on the due date. For any change in operating profits (before interest), such financial gearing increases the volatility (= risk) of the profits for equity shareholders. In contrast, equity capital is less risky for the business, since it implies no legal commitments in terms of dividends or capital repayments (see Chapters 9 and 10).

A firm can reduce business risk in a number of ways. Table 8.2, which is certainly not comprehensive, lists three kinds of business actions: contractual, flexible, and uncertainty-reducing. Some actions may either reduce risk or increase it, such as diversifying into different (less familiar) businesses, or building spare capacity.

A survey of 146 large UK companies (Ho *et al*, 1991) found that about 40 per cent often or very often used sensitivity analysis, 39 per cent a subjective-intuitive assessment

Table 8.2 Ways of reducing uncertainty

	Contractual	Flexible	Uncertainty-reducing
Sales	Produce goods only against firm orders not for stock	Avoid over depending on a few customers or products	Research market before launching new products
Purchases	Arrange long-term supply contracts	Arrange more than one source of supply	Stockpile raw materials
Assets	Insure as much as possible	Use general-purpose rather than highly specialized equipment	Retain high liquid resources
Employees	Contract work out rather than use full-time employees	Pay partly by bonus or commission rather than flat rate	Promote from within rather than hire from outside

of risk, and 17 per cent probability analysis. Methods of adjusting for risk (of the 133 companies that did so) most frequently included raising the required rate of return (42 per cent), shortening the payback period (34 per cent), and adjusting estimated future cash flows subjectively/intuitively (63 per cent).

8.3. Options

Derivatives

Derivatives are financial instruments 'derived' from underlying assets. They often amount to bets on changes in prices (such as share prices, commodity prices or interest rates). The performance of the derivative depends on the behaviour of the underlying asset.

There have been a number of spectacular losses connected with derivatives, of which perhaps the best known in this country is Baring's loss of some £900 million on the Japanese Nikkei stock exchange index in 1995 via contracts on the Singapore and Osaka derivative exchanges. That led to the bank's collapse. The problem in Baring's seemed to be that top management was not aware of what was going on and had inadequate internal control mechanisms.

There is nothing necessarily wrong in speculating in business, if it is a calculated risk. Indeed one could argue that most business activity contains an element of speculation. The main reason for the enormous growth of activity in derivatives over the last several years, however, is to do with the power of derivatives to *reduce* business risk rather than increase it.

For example, suppose a British company exports to Germany and is owed 5 million euros due in three months' time. There is no absolute need to do anything. The company could simply wait for three months and then receive 5 million euros. But if the company wishes to protect itself against a fall in the euro between now and then it might enter into a three month forward contract with a bank. The deal would be that the company would agree to pay the bank 5 million euros in three months time in return for receiving in three months' time a sum in pounds sterling agreed now. Thus the company protects itself ('hedges') against an unwelcome fall in the euro. In a sense, one might argue the company is needlessly speculating on the strength of the euro if it does nothing.

Another example might be a firm which manufactures chocolate bars, for which it needs large quantities of cocoa. It could simply buy the cocoa on the commodities exchange when it needs it for manufacturing purposes. In that case the firm is vulnerable to an increase in the price of cocoa. An alternative would be to buy forward, at a price agreed now. This reduces the risk of suffering from a price increase, though of course it also means the firm will not gain so much if cocoa prices fall. Such a company might take the view that its core business is making and selling chocolate bars, rather than speculating on the price of cocoa. It may thus choose to eliminate some of the risk of changes in the cocoa price.

Share options

An option is a contract giving the holder the right (but not the obligation) to buy ('call') or sell ('**put**') a financial instrument or other asset at a given ('exercise') price on or before a given date. In respect of shares, there are two different types of options: **American**, which can be exercised *at any time* up to the expiry date, or **European**, which can be exercised *only* on a given future date.

Private investors may choose to speculate with **call options**, risking a relatively small amount of money in the hope of a large gain. For instance, suppose you thought it likely that convincing scientific evidence would shortly be published showing that smoking cigarettes did *not* cause lung cancer. One way to 'cash in' on this expectation might be simply to purchase shares in tobacco companies. So, for example, you might invest £120,000 in buying, say, 20,000 shares in British American Tobacco plc. Let us suppose you expect the share price to double when the news is announced. In that case, if all goes to plan, your 20,000 shares would become worth £240,000, and you would have made a profit of £120,000 (= 100 per cent) on your investment.

An alternative would be to buy call options in BAT. Let us suppose that a 3-month call option would cost 60p per share, while a 6-month call option would cost 80p. If you go for the 3-month option, for £120,000 you could purchase options to buy ('call') 200,000 shares in BAT at a price of 600p each. If the news you expect is duly announced *within three months*, then you could buy 200,000 BAT shares for 600p, costing a total of £1.2 million. But you would be able to sell those 200,000 shares at once for 1200p each (assuming you were correct in expecting the share price to double), thus yielding £2.4 million. Your profit would be £1,080,000 (£1.2 million less the £120,000 cost of the options) on your investment of £120,000. That amounts to a profit of no less than 900 per cent!

Of course, if your expectation is wrong – either the news is not announced within the period of the option, or, if it is, the share price doesn't increase as much as you expected – then you may not do so well. In particular, if you get the timing wrong, the option may simply lapse and you will have lost your entire 'investment' of £120,000 in call options. If you had instead chosen to buy 20,000 BAT shares outright, at least you would still own the shares. They might not (yet) be worth 1200p per share, but they might still be worth about 600p per share.

We have been looking at the position of an investor; but many companies use call options as one way to pay their senior managers. 'Executive share options' are provided, on certain terms, to directors and other senior managers. If their company's share price goes up enough – over a period of years – they may stand to gain very large sums of money. There are several possible shortcomings to such schemes, mostly enabling the managers to gain at the shareholders' expense.

For instance, if a company chooses not to pay out all its earnings in dividends, one would expect the share price to go up to reflect the 'retained' earnings. There's not much reason to pay managers for that. Similarly, if there is inflation, one might expect the share price at least to maintain its 'real' value over time, so again why should one reward managers for that? Given that share prices, and the stock market in general, will probably be sensitive to interest rates, if share prices in general rise as a result of falling interest rates, again it seems wrong to reward senior managers for that.

Apart from the unnecessary cost to companies of poorly-designed executive share options schemes (sometimes called Long-Term Incentive Plans, or L-TIPs), there is a further difficulty. The profit and loss accounts of companies with such schemes never fully reflect their true cost. Admittedly once the options have been exercised, the earnings per share calculation will allow for the extra number of shares in issue. But profit will be overstated, in that no expense will have been charged in respect of the value of the options granted.

The managers who participate in company schemes stand to gain large amounts if the share price goes up, but don't lose anything if the share price goes down. That potential benefit is worth something. It is often not at all easy to value the options in executive incentive schemes, because the terms are usually much more restricted than the kinds of options traded on the derivatives exchange. Even so, it should be possible to estimate the real cost to the company. But at present the accounting standard-setters have not managed to produce an acceptable way of doing so.

In general a call option will increase in value the greater the volatility of the underlying asset and the longer the time period involved. Why is this valuable, if investors are risk-averse? Because since the holder can always choose *not* to exercise the option, he ignores downside risk. Thus the only relevant volatility is 'upside risk' – and the more of this the better! Again there must be a question whether encouraging managers to increase the volatility of their company's shares is likely to be in the interests of most shareholders.

Real options

Some kinds of 'real options' may be relevant for managers making capital investment decisions, including the chance to invest more in future, after the outcome of particular events has become less uncertain. For instance, several large companies have chosen to invest in China, even though the immediate prospects for profit may not be good. They are probably positioning themselves to prosper in a very large market many years down the line, and assuming that if they don't start now they may seriously damage their prospects for the future. In effect they are buying a call option, which in some circumstances they may choose to exercise in future.

Real options like this can be difficult to value with basic DCF techniques, because the various possible outcomes may affect the proper discount rate to use. Some kind of decision-tree approach (which we briefly examined earlier) may be most suitable.

8.4. Foreign exchange risk

Transaction risk

Transaction risk (or exposure) arises because money amounts are payable in terms of a foreign currency. If the exchange rate changes, so does the equivalent in domestic currency. Suppose a company invoices a credit sale abroad in US dollars for $120,000. If the exchange rate at the date of sale is £1 = $1.50, the sterling amount due is £80,000. But if the exchange rate at the date of *payment* is £1 = $1.60, then the sterling amount is only £75,000. There has been a loss of £5,000. Whenever a company invoices sales in other than its own domestic currency, there is a risk of this kind of loss if the exchange rate moves in the wrong direction. (Of course, companies can equally well 'gain' when the exchange rate moves the other way.)

It is hard to predict how future (forward) exchange rates will differ from current (spot) rates. So in the long run it may be best simply to convert foreign currencies into sterling when received, without attempting to buy or sell forward in order to avoid the transaction risk. The trouble is, in the short run there may be significant exposure; and risk-averse finance managers might prefer to hedge, even at some cost.

An additional point arises on borrowing in foreign currencies, where the tax treatment of interest payable and of gains and losses on foreign exchange may not be the same. The rate of interest should include an inflation premium to allow for any expected difference in the future rate of inflation compared with the domestic currency. That is what purchasing power parity theory suggests (see Chapter 2).

Suppose that interest expense is fully tax-deductible (as would be normal), but that gains on foreign exchange are not taxable. The interest expense will be deductible for tax purposes, but any gain on the transaction exposure, if the foreign currency does fall against the domestic currency, may not be taxable (under some tax regimes). Thus it might pay – on an after-tax basis – to borrow in weak currencies with high rates of inflation. For a similar reason, one might prefer to lend in strong currencies.

This effect is similar to that which constant purchasing power (CPP) accounting can reveal in times of inflation. A company with a 'cash mountain' in a high-inflation currency will be taxed on its apparently high money interest income. It will not, however, get any tax relief in respect of the real loss of purchasing power. This effect exists even if the high inflation is fully anticipated.

Accounting translation exposure

When a group consolidates the accounts of its foreign **subsidiaries**, there is the question of what exchange rate to use for translation. ('Translate' means 'restate for accounting purposes', whereas 'convert' means 'exchange one currency for another'.) The choice affects the domestic currency amounts in the group accounts.

Should one use the exchange rate at the balance sheet date (the 'closing rate' method)? This would normally be the exchange rate for monetary items. But what about the profit and loss account? Should one translate at the closing rate or at an average rate for the period? (The latter is becoming the most usual method.) For fixed assets the closing rate method is normal. An alternative method – which accounting standards no longer permit – is the 'temporal' method, which uses the exchange rate on a fixed asset's date of purchase.

There is reason to think that purely accounting differences, such as would arise from using one method rather than another, have no real effect (for example, on share prices). Hence accounting translation exposure should not really matter. But many finance managers seem reluctant to accept this conclusion.

Economic exposure

Economic exposure means that the present value (in terms of domestic currency) of future operating cash flows may vary due to exchange rate changes. The future cash flows may relate either to domestic or to foreign operations.

The direct impact works as follows. In foreign markets, if the pound is strong against foreign currencies, compared with foreign companies a British firm's prices may be higher (if it maintains the sterling equivalent price) or its profit margins may be lower (if it maintains the foreign currency price and thus reduces the sterling equivalent price). Table 8.3 shows an example.

In the home market, if the pound is strong, then compared with British firms foreign companies will be able either to reduce their sterling price (if they maintain the foreign

Table 8.3 Effect of strong pound on British exporter

Export to EMU-land, originally		£160,000 @ 1.50 = 240,000 euros
If £1 strengthens to £1 = 1.60 euros:		
a.	High euro price (same sterling equivalent)	£160,000 @ 1.60 = 256,000 euros
b.	Same euro price (reduces sterling margin)	£150,000 @ 1.60 = 240,000 euros
c.	Some combination of the two	£155,000 @ 1.60 = 248,000 euros

currency equivalent) or increase their profit margins (if they maintain the sterling price, and thus increase the foreign currency equivalent).

In addition, there may be an effect on the sterling cost of imported goods (in the opposite direction). Questions also arise about the price-elasticity of demand and about the permanence of any change in exchange rates. There may also be other less direct effects.

It is obvious that trying to calculate all the likely effects is very complex. One possible way to get some protection might be by means of suitable foreign currency financing. This would aim to roughly match the finance with the foreign currency exposure.

CHAPTER 9

Borrowing

9.1. General features

Background

A company must repay amounts borrowed ('debt') as they become due ('mature'), and pay the regular agreed amount of interest on the debt outstanding. Failure to do so entitles the lender to take legal action at once to recover the principal and any unpaid interest. Both lender and borrower will want to see a good margin of safety. Then they can both be confident that a company can meet its legal commitments even if things don't go quite as planned.

A lender will be concerned with the borrower's honesty and with his competence. The borrower will have to say *why* he needs the money, *how much* he requires, and for *how long*. He must also explain how he expects to be able to repay the loan in due course. Detailed cash forecasts covering (at least) the whole period of the proposed loan may help to answer many of these important questions. It may be useful to prepare more than one set of forecasts, based on different assumptions, to give an idea of the margin for error.

A firm's financial director or managing director should be sure to talk to the bank manager regularly. If everything is going well, this may simply amount to a friendly chat. It will keep the bank abreast of general trends, opportunities and challenges facing the business. If there are financial problems, there may be a need for longer and more detailed meetings.

In addition, the business should keep the bank manager informed of its financial progress, at a minimum sending the bank the firm's annual accounts (and, of course, any interim accounts, too). It might also be sensible to send a copy of the cash forecasts for the ensuing year. Some businesses do not even prepare such forecasts on any formal basis for their own internal use. Needless to say, they are the ones most likely to find themselves suddenly in need of 'unexpected' bank borrowing. (What bad luck! It was Gary Player who remarked that he found the more he practised, the 'luckier' he became!)

Short-term borrowing

A bank overdraft is a popular form of short-term borrowing which is convenient and flexible for borrowers. Its main drawback is that it is legally repayable 'on demand', hence balance sheets show overdrafts as current liabilities (creditors due within one year). Only the amount actually overdrawn bears interest, though there may be a small 'commitment fee' on the agreed maximum limit. Interest accrues from day to day, at a rate which varies with market conditions. It is often expressed as 'x per cent over base rate'.

Term loans range from periods of less than a year to more than five years. They may provide for borrowing in tranches, and for repayment by instalments (rather than a single **'bullet' repayment** on maturity). In **project finance** the timing of repayment may depend on how well a project performs. Term loans may be more expensive than overdrafts, often with a penalty on early repayment. Interest rates on term loans often vary, because volatile rates of inflation can make fixed rate loans risky both for lenders and for borrowers. Longer-term loans often carry higher interest rates than short-term borrowings (see Chapter 2). And smaller or riskier firms will have to pay higher rates of interest than larger or more secure borrowers.

Also included among current liabilities may be parts of loans originally arranged for more than one year. This may be the entire principal of a loan now nearly due for repayment; or it may comprise a part of the total amount, for example, of finance leases (see below). For purposes of measuring gearing (see Chapter 12), it is probably best to include in total 'debt' *all* negotiated interest-bearing finance, both short term and long term, leases as well as loans.

Long-term borrowing

Long-term loans to companies (often called debentures, from the Latin 'they are owed') may be with or without **security** (see below). The borrower of a long-term loan must repay the whole amount on the due **redemption** date A company whose financial position has worsened may find it hard to repay a loan or to arrange new borrowing (refinance). Inability to repay debt is one of the main causes of corporate failure. In order to reduce the risk, some kinds of finance may provide for partial repayment at regular intervals.

Divisions of a large group often plan investment in fixed assets themselves, but borrowing is usually arranged centrally by the whole group. This is partly to reduce the lender's risk (and therefore the interest rate), since the whole group's assets, not just a single division's, will then be available to cover the loan. Also it may make sense to concentrate borrowing expertise in a single group treasury department.

The 1980 Wilson Committee, in respect of large and medium-sized companies, 'could not find a single example of an investment project which had not gone ahead because of the inability to raise external finance...' It expressed no view about whether banks tended to be too cautious with respect to gearing and security conditions for small firms. The conclusion is that for larger firms the capital market is probably very effective; but this may be less true for small firms.

The stock exchange may 'list' loans to larger companies just like government borrowings. The original lender can then recover the investment, not by the corporate borrower repaying, but by selling the **loan stock** to another investor. At the maturity date the borrowing company will repay the principal amount to the current holders of the loan stock. (Some companies start to buy in their own loan stock towards the redemption date to reduce the total amount of cash needed on final maturity.) Smaller firms may arrange loans from banks, insurance companies, pension funds, or private investors. With only a single lender it may be possible to renegotiate certain loan conditions if circumstances change. That is not feasible with listed loan stocks where the lenders are widely dispersed members of the public.

Key aspects of debt

Three key aspects of debt are: the term, the interest rate and the currency.

The *term*, or maturity, may vary from overnight to infinity. 'Short-term' borrowing is any debt repayable within twelve months. (Bank overdrafts, although legally repayable on demand, may in fact continue beyond one year.) Some people would define 'long-term' as meaning any borrowing longer than 'short-term'. Thus balance sheets use 'long-term' to refer to any debt repayable more than one year ahead.

It would be normal to define 'medium-term' borrowing as debt repayable between one year and about five years ahead. On that basis, long-term debt would have a maturity more than five years ahead. Some borrowing may be perpetual (**irredeemable**); but most long-term debt has to be repaid one day. So what starts as long-term debt ends up as very short term.

The *interest rate* may be fixed or floating. (Bank overdrafts nearly always have a floating rate.) Fixed interest rates (or **coupon rates**) do not change during the life of the debt. Floating rates, in contrast, may change since they are linked to a benchmark rate. For example, a debt instrument might define the interest rate as '1 per cent over LIBOR'. Then when the **London Interbank Offered Rate** changes, the interest rate on that debt will change too.

Fixed rate debt became unpopular in the 1970s, when in many countries inflation rates were high and volatile. Often neither borrower nor lender was keen to speculate on future changes in the rate of inflation. Allowing the rate to float meant that changes in inflation rates would penalize neither party.

The third key aspect of debt is *currency*. Companies with overseas assets may choose to borrow in foreign currencies rather than in sterling. That provides some protection against changes in the exchange rate (see Chapter 8). The interest rate may differ from sterling interest rates, depending mainly on the expected relative rates of inflation. But different term structures may also be relevant: at the time of writing, sterling interest rates are much higher than euro rates for short-term borrowing, but slightly lower than euro rates for very long-term borrowing.

If the exchange rate changes during the term of the loan, then the true cost of the borrowing comprises the interest payable plus or minus any loss or gain on exchange. (The tax effects may be relevant here, as noted in Chapter 8). Borrowing in foreign currencies can be risky if overseas earnings/assets do not fully cover the interest and principal.

9.2. Reducing the lender's risk

General considerations

In general the return to lenders is fairly low (unlike possible gains on equity invest-ments); so most lenders only want to take small risks. Hence they will be concerned with the margin of safety on business lending. For example:

- How far might profits and cash inflows fall in a downturn?
- To what extent could the company reduce planned spending at lower levels of output?
- How quickly could the borrower liquidate current assets if need be to pay loan interest or to repay principal?
- In a crisis, how quickly could the borrower sell off fixed assets? How low, at worst, could their second-hand value be, if the whole industry is in a downturn?
- Is the borrower both honest and competent? What is his track record? What about his character: would a possible default really concern him? If his financial position were to get much worse, would he continue to provide regular accurate up-to-date reports?
- What sort of business is it? Profitable? Risky? Stable? How good is the management, especially financial management and management **control**? Is there adequate *depth* of management?

Personal guarantees

In a limited company the liability of the shareholders is limited (hence the name) to the nominal amount of the issued ordinary share capital. So when the shares are 'fully-paid-up', shareholders have no further potential liability to the company. In contrast, the creditors of **partnerships** or sole traders ('unincorporated' businesses) can, if need be, look for repayment to the private assets of the individual proprietors (owners), *in addition* to any assets of the firm itself. Thus the potential liability of sole owners or partners in a firm is normally unlimited.

A small business is likely to be risky, especially if it is new. So anyone lending money to a small limited company may want to get a personal **guarantee** of repayment from the main shareholder(s). This will put the lender in the same position as if he were lending to a sole trader or partnership.

The reverse side of this coin is that giving a personal guarantee is a major step. At the time, it may seem almost like a 'free' way of improving a small company's credit rating. But giving a personal guarantee *fundamentally* changes the legal position of whoever gives it (whether the controlling owner, a director or a friend or relative). If things go wrong, the consequences may be extremely serious. And once given, it is not always easy to 'withdraw' a personal guarantee. *Caveat emptor* ('let the buyer beware') may nowadays not have quite the weight it once carried; but *caveat guarantor* is still essential advice.

Security

Another way for a lender to reduce his risk of loss is to arrange for certain assets to serve as formal **collateral** for the loan. On liquidation of the business this gives him priority: the proceeds from selling those assets will go first to repay his **secured loan**. Anything left over will go into the company's general pool of funds to pay other, unsecured, creditors. What if the proceeds from selling assets serving as collateral do not cover the full amount of a 'secured' loan? To the extent of any shortfall, the creditor will rank as unsecured.

Debtors, some kinds of stocks, and general equipment can serve as collateral for loans, as well as land, buildings, and marketable investments. For highly specialized assets there may be no resale market. Legal title to the asset needs to be easily transferable; and the asset's value should be fairly stable and easy to determine. It should also cover the amount of any loan by a fair margin.

Instead of securing a loan on specific assets, a lender may obtain a **floating charge** on all a borrower's assets. This comes into effect ('crystallizes') only if a company goes into liquidation – and thus permits the sale of assets in the normal course of business. (An asset which is serving as security for a loan can be sold only if the lender agrees.) On a **winding-up**, certain debts (for example, certain wages and taxes) come before the claims of unsecured creditors (see Chapter 13). They also have priority over any floating charges – though *not* over a fixed charge on a specific asset.

Covenants

Corporate lenders usually insist on certain conditions (**covenants**). Their main functions are as follows:

1. To prevent the sale of substantial parts of the business, or the granting of prior claims on assets to other subsequent lenders.
2. To require the maintenance of certain financial ratios at stated levels, or the maintenance of physical assets in good condition.
3. To assure the provision of regular up-to-date financial information.
4. (For smaller companies) To restrict the amount of directors' salaries or dividend payments.

Breaches of covenant (like failure to pay interest when due) can entitle the lender to require immediate repayment of the loan. But a breach may simply act as a 'trigger': it alerts the lender to an unexpected event, and suggests a need to discuss the current state of the business with the borrower.

9.3. Other types of debt

Leases

Leases allow the lessee use of an asset in return for regular payments of lease rentals to the lessor, who remains the legal owner. **Operating leases** are short-term, and often for small amounts, and firms simply treat the lease rentals as expenses. In contrast, non-cancellable **finance leases** normally cover almost the whole of an asset's useful life. In effect, finance leases put the lessee in almost the same position as if he had borrowed and purchased the asset outright. So the lessee's balance sheet **capitalizes** finance leases and shows fixed assets at 'equivalent cost' matched by long-term 'liabilities'. The annual accounts treat part of each year's lease rental as interest expense and part as repayment. (In addition, depreciation is charged on the fixed asset.) A similar approach applies to **hire-purchase** deals where, following a 20 per cent down payment, firms acquire assets by instalments over up to five years.

In capital project appraisals, one may discount future finance lease payments ('deferred investments') at a very low discount rate (suitable for debt), or else replace them with a 'payment' at the start of the project equivalent to the capital cost of the asset. In either case, tax reliefs on the lease payments need to be taken into account.

Income bonds

Income bonds are debt instruments on which interest is payable only if earned in the period, though borrowers have to accumulate any missed interest payments and make them up later. Some people argue that income bonds offer all the advantages of **preference share capital** (see below), together with the tax advantages of debt. The issuer must redeem income bonds at a fixed amount on a specific date.

Convertible loans

Some long-term loans may be **convertible** into ordinary shares at the holder's option on pre-arranged terms. As long as a loan is not converted, it counts as debt on the balance sheet. It continues to incur regular interest payments, and ranks as a creditor in the event of winding-up. But upon conversion it ceases to bear interest, and becomes ordinary share capital ranking for dividends. The option to take up equity if the company prospers may reduce the nominal interest rate payable on convertible loan stocks. Where it makes much difference, **earnings per share** and book amount of equity per share may be computed both as they are now and as they would be on a **fully diluted** basis.

Preference share capital

As a form of corporate finance, preference share capital lies in between long-term borrowing (debt) and ordinary share capital (equity). From a financial point of view many of its features are similar to debt, but legally it forms part of shareholders' funds. (These are now split between 'equity' – normally ordinary share capital – and 'non-equity' – which would certainly include preference share capital.)

Debt interest must be paid before there can be any question of declaring preference dividends; and until a company has repaid lenders in full on winding-up, the preference shareholders will get nothing back at all. But preference capital has priority over

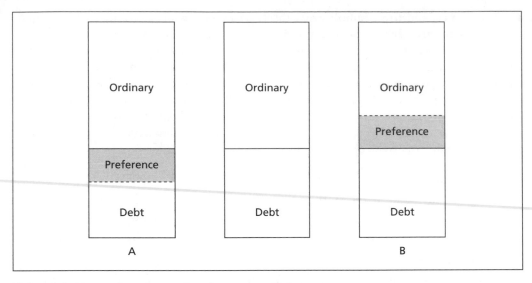

Figure 9.1 Alternative views of preference capital

ordinary capital, both with respect to dividends and with respect to ultimate capital repayment. Both the amount of any preference dividend and the amount of preference capital repayable on redemption are normally fixed money amounts.

Mainly because they are not deductible for tax purposes, preference dividends are usually more expensive for a company to pay than debt interest. Where preference shares exist, failure to pay preference dividends will prevent payment of any ordinary dividends. No company contemplates that except in dire crisis, so in practice preference dividends may seem nearly as much a commitment as debt interest. Yet if the worst comes to the worst, there is a big difference between a company being highly embarrassed if it has to omit preference dividends for a period or two or being *liquidated* if it fails to pay interest due on its debt.

As Figure 9.1 suggests, it may be better to view preference share capital as an alternative to ordinary share capital (B), not to borrowing (A): as a useful way to increase financial gearing without too much risk. Indeed, preference shares will be much cheaper than ordinary shares (being so much less risky to the holders), yet (from the company's viewpoint) much less risky than debt.

Provisions for liabilities and charges

UK accounts charge deferred taxation as an expense 'to the extent that it is probable that a liability will crystallize' in the foreseeable future. This is not a straightforward definition (and the treatment of deferred tax is currently being reconsidered). Deferred taxation:

- does not bear interest
- is not a legal liability on the balance sheet (merely the 'other side' of the extra amount charged as tax expense in the profit and loss account)

- (like provisions for pensions) is not normally regarded as part of a company's negotiated interest-bearing debt.

9.4. Valuing debt

Risk-free securities

About 75 per cent in value of all stock exchange transactions in the United Kingdom is in government (gilt-edged) securities. These are regarded as 'risk-free' (see Chapter 2). This market is important because it reflects expected future interest rates. We have seen how critical these are in many financial decisions.

The government issues new gilts for periods varying from three months to more than twenty-five years. Certain outstanding gilts have no redemption date – they are irredeemable, and simply promise to pay a stated coupon rate each year for ever. Some of these perpetuities have been in issue for more than one hundred years, so they provide long-term trends for gilt-edged prices and risk-free interest rates. The coupon rates on outstanding gilts vary widely, mainly as a result of different interest rates on the various dates of issue (due to varying levels of inflation at the time). Some of the difference in coupon rates is also due to UK tax reasons.

In Chapter 5 we saw how to 'value' future cash flows from a capital investment project, by discounting them back to 'present value'. We can use exactly the same approach to value shares or other assets.

Imagine a risk-free government security, paying interest of £4 per £100 nominal of stock, once a year for ever (a **perpetuity**). Ignoring tax, what would we expect its market price (= present value) to be? We assume we know the amount and the timing of all future cash receipts. The only other thing we need to find out is what interest rate to use to discount them back to present value. The proper discount rate to use is the opportunity cost – the rate of return which could be earned on similar-risk (in this case, risk-free) investments.

Example 9.1

If the current interest yield on perpetual risk-free securities is 5.0 per cent a year, then the present value of '£4 a year for ever' should be £80 – since this gives the required interest yield of 5.0 per cent (= £4/£80). To find the capital value of a perpetuity we simply divide the amount of the annual interest payment (a) by the relevant interest rate (r). In general: a/r. In this case £4/.05 = £80.

If the interest rate were now to rise to 8 per cent a year, investors would sell the £4-a-year perpetuity until its market price reached £50 (= £4/.08). At that point it would just yield the current rate of interest of 8 per cent (= £4/£50). Why would people sell the £4-a-year perpetuity if its market price were above £50? Because they would then be able to acquire – risk-free – a larger annual income for ever. Suppose the market price remained at £80. By selling the perpetuity, and reinvesting the £80 proceeds in a risk-free security yielding the

Table 9.1 Current market values (£) for a £7-a-year security with varying maturities and current interest rates

Current interest rate:	3.5%	7%	10.5%	14%
Redemption:				
• Tomorrow	100	100	100	100
• Year 10	154	100	79	64
• Never (perpetuity)	200	100	67	50

'going' rate of interest of 8 per cent a year, someone could achieve an income of £6.40 a year for ever (= 8 per cent × £80).

Suppose the term structure of interest rates were absolutely flat, at 7 per cent a year whatever the maturity of the (risk-free) stock. We know that a *perpetuity* carrying a coupon rate of 14 per cent would carry a market price of £200; while one with a coupon of £3.50 per cent would have a market price of £50.

Similarly, we can consider a security with a coupon rate of, say, £7 a year and current rates of interest (for equivalent-risk securities) which vary from time to time. The value of such a security will vary both with the current rate of interest and with the redemption (maturity) date, as set out in Table 9.1.

If the redemption date were *tomorrow* then the market price would clearly be very close to £100 (the **nominal amount** repayable) whatever the current rate of interest. (That rate of interest, or 'discount', would apply for only a single day.) We already know that for a perpetuity (never redeemable) the market value will be simply the coupon rate divided by the current rate of interest.

The calculation is somewhat more complex where there is a redemption date some years in the future (say, after ten years). In that case we have to calculate the value of a ten-year annuity at various interest rates, together with the present value of £100 ten years in the future also at various interest rates. In the case shown, the value would be £154 if current interest rates are 3.5 per cent and £64 if current interest rates are 14 per cent.

In each case the **redemption yield** would be the current rate of interest, since we are taking into account both the annual interest amounts and the ultimate £100 receivable in ten years' time. (The contrast is with the **flat yield**, which simply represents the annual interest divided by the current market price. Thus for the ten-year redemption securities, the flat yield is respectively: 4.5%, 7.0%, 8.9% and 10.9%.)

Corporate debt

Valuing corporate debt is very like valuing risk-free securities, except that companies (even large ones) are normally riskier to lend to than governments with control of the printing presses. (That may not be true of certain governments in Euro-land, since the Treaty of Maastricht says the European Central Bank will not be responsible for the debts of national governments.) Hence the required rate of interest will include a risk premium, though it may be fairly small.

Again ignoring tax, suppose with the current risk-free rate of interest being 7.0 per cent a year, BIG plc can borrow at 9.0 per cent a year – that is with a 2.0 per cent risk premium. Let us suppose the coupon rate on this debt is 14.0 per cent, as BIG plc borrowed the money when interest rates were much higher than they are now.

If the loan were repayable tomorrow, it would, of course, stand at almost **par** – say £100 value per £100 nominal of loan stock. If the loan were a perpetuity, it would stand at £156, giving a yield of 9.0 per cent a year (= £14/£156). Finally, if the loan were repayable in ten years' time, its current value would be about £132 – well above par because interest rates are lower than when the loan was borrowed.

If the riskiness of the loan were to increase, then so would the required risk premium, say to 3 per cent (rather than 2 per cent, as before). Then the current required rate of return would increase from 9 per cent to 10 per cent. (In other words, the current market value of the loan would fall – in this case, for the ten-year maturity, from £132 to £125.)

It should be obvious that the market price of long-term loans will be more sensitive to a change in interest rates than will the market price of short-term loans. (If it isn't, look again at Table 9.1.)

Deep discount bonds

Debt normally carries a coupon rate close to the current rate of interest (for the maturity) at the date of issue. But sometimes securities are issued which pay no interest at all during their life (**zero coupon**), or perhaps only a very low rate. The amount due on redemption then has to cover not merely the 'principal', but also the interest which has accrued during the life of the **deep discount bond**.

For instance, suppose the current interest rate (ignoring tax) is 10 per cent a year; and a company borrows £5 million cash for five years, with no interest payable until redemption. The cash due at the end of Year 5 will be £8,052,550. The interest mounting up each year (on the start-of-year amount outstanding), and the liability shown on the balance sheet at the end of each year, will be as shown in Table 9.2. The 'deep discount', in this case, merely represents the interest which is being deferred (or 'rolled up') until the final redemption date at the end of five years.

Table 9.2 Build-up of cumulative interest on a deep discount bond

End of year	Interest charged in year £'000	Liability at end of year £'000
0	—	5,000
1	500	5,500
2	550	6,050
3	605	6,655
4	665.50	7,320.50
5	732.05	(8,052.55)

Problems

Problem 9.1.

What is the value of a perpetuity of £6 a year if the interest rate is 12 per cent?

a. What happens to the value if the interest rate falls to 10 per cent a year?
b. What happens if the interest rate rises to 15 per cent?

Problem 9.2.

The Arcadian government's irredeemable 4 per cent stock stands at 60.

a. What is the risk-free rate of interest?
b. What will the price of the stock be if the interest rate is:

  (i) 5 per cent
  (ii) 3 per cent?

Problem 9.3.

If the rate of inflation falls from above 6 per cent a year to about 2 per cent a year, what would you expect to happen to the yield on an index-linked government bond which now stands at 3 per cent a year? Why? What would happen if there were deflation (negative inflation) of about 2 per cent a year?

Problem 9.4.

Dodgy plc borrowed £36 million last year at an interest rate of 9 per cent. Of this, 2 per cent represented pure time-preference, 3 per cent inflation premium and 4 per cent risk premium.

A year later the risk-free money rate had fallen from 5 per cent to 4 per cent as inflation expectations fell. At the same time, the risk premium applicable to Dodgy's debt rose to 6 per cent. What would happen to the value of Dodgy's debt:

a. if it were a perpetuity?
b. if it were redeemable 16 years after it had been borrowed?

CHAPTER 10

Ordinary share capital

10.1. Shareholders' funds

The nature of ordinary shares

From the company's viewpoint, **ordinary share capital** (equity) is less risky than borrowing (debt) as a source of funds, for three main reasons:

1. There is no legal commitment to pay any dividend (unlike interest on debt).
2. As long as the company exists it need never repay equity capital to shareholders, whereas it must legally repay debt on the due maturity date.
3. Equity capital is free from the restrictions which lenders often attach to debt by way of covenants (see Chapter 9).

For shareholders it is the other way round: owning equity shares is more risky than lending a company money. On a winding-up, only after the company has repaid all other suppliers of finance in full will ordinary shareholders then get anything that remains. So in a successful company their potential reward is limitless. But if the company is unable to pay all its creditors in full, the ordinary shareholders get nothing at all. In a limited company, however, the company cannot call on ordinary shareholders to subscribe any more money. Once the shares are fully paid-up, the most they can lose is what they have already invested. (Historically this limitation proved vital in encouraging rich investors to finance companies, knowing that only a small part of their wealth was at risk.)

In theory dissatisfied shareholders may vote to replace a company's directors at the annual general meeting. But in practice they will usually simply sell their shares. The trouble is that by then the market price of the shares may already have fallen, to reflect past performance and poor future prospects. Large shareholders, in contrast, may prefer to remain as investors and try to find ways to get the managers to improve the company's performance (or to replace the chief executive).

In **unlisted companies** it may be very difficult to influence a company's policy, since the directors are often also major shareholders (with their families). It may also be difficult for an 'outside' shareholder to sell his shares, at least not at anything like the expected price. In fact, outside equity capital is likely to be difficult and expensive for small companies to raise, and probably it will be available – if at all – only to the most successful and promising ventures.

Ordinary shareholders' funds in accounts

The Companies Act 1985 sets out five headings under 'Capital and Reserves' (shareholders' funds):

1. Called up share capital
2. Share premium account
3. Revaluation reserve
4. Other reserves
5. Profit and loss account

For most companies this boils down to three kinds of item:

1. Amounts received for new shares issued
2. Revaluations of fixed assets
3. Retained profits

For practical purposes there is little point in splitting amounts received for new shares issued between the nominal amount per share and any share premium. In both cases it normally amounts to permanent capital. But one does need to distinguish between ordinary (equity) shares and preference (non-equity) shares, even though both of them legally count as shareholders' funds.

Revaluations of fixed assets mainly comprise the following:

1. Increases above cost in the book value of land and buildings (which some countries do not permit).
2. Adjustments resulting from changes in foreign exchange rates.

Revaluations of fixed assets (whether up or down) do not directly affect a company's finances – the **revaluation reserves** are 'merely' book-keeping entries. They may affect depreciation charges, but in the United Kingdom there are unlikely to be any tax consequences. But they will affect certain ratios, such as **debt ratio** and return on net assets or return on equity. Any downward revaluation to fixed or current assets would normally be charged as an expense in the profit and loss account.

Retained profits comprise the cumulative total to date of profit for ordinary shareholders (profit after tax less minority interests and preference dividends) less **net dividends** paid and payable. For most companies this is a more important permanent source of finance than either new issues of shares or borrowing.

10.2. The stock exchange

Economic functions

The stock exchange is a market on which investors can buy and sell securities of leading British and international companies, and of governments. In June 1999 there were about 100 different British government stocks outstanding with a total market value of some

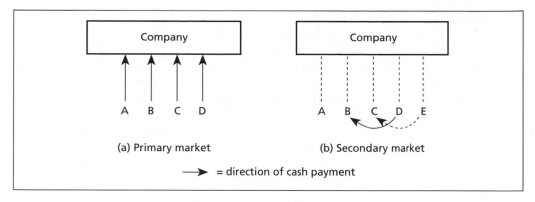

Figure 10.1 The stock exchange: primary and secondary markets

£336 billion (with a *daily* turnover of £4 billion). UK-listed shares of about 1,850 companies had a total market value of about £1,650 billion.

The trend of the past forty years shows a decline in the proportion of listed equities held by individuals, and an increase in that held by insurance companies, pension funds and unit trusts (see Table 1.1).

The main function of unit trusts and investments trusts is to invest in ordinary shares on behalf of individuals, who thus get the benefit of expert management and lower dealing costs, and perhaps a **diversified** portfolio (see Chapter 11). A unit trust is open-ended – it can expand if people want to buy more units, or shrink if people want to sell back units. An investment trust is simply a limited company whose purpose is to invest in securities.

Most stock exchange transactions involve the exchange of existing securities between investors. Only a small proportion of transactions comprises new issues, by companies or by governments. New issues of ordinary shares are a far less important source of equity funds for most companies than retained profits.

Since investors value **liquidity** – the ability to sell quickly at close to current prices if they need the money – the existence of **secondary markets** makes it much easier to raise money on the **primary market** than it would otherwise be. Figure 10.1 illustrates the difference between (a) the primary and (b) the secondary functions of the stock exchange.

In (a) the company is issuing new shares to A, B, C and D and receives the cash. In (b) the company is not directly involved in the transactions and does not receive any cash. Shareholder A is not dealing; B is selling shares to D; and C is selling shares to E, at the market price at the time of each deal. The **privatizations** of nationalized industries were mostly type (b): one shareholder (the government) was selling its shares to the public.

The capital invested by companies and by governments is often reflected in fixed physical assets, such as equipment, buildings, roads and so on. Thus businesses may tend to be anchored to a specific location or type of business. This may also be true to some extent of employees and suppliers. But if a market exists where shareholders can buy and sell shares in the ownership of these assets, a shareholder possesses wealth which is mobile. He can sell his shares to someone else if he needs the cash for consumption; or if he wants to invest in another kind of business or in another country; or if he just loses confidence in a particular company or country. Any restrictions on investors' freedom to escape from a particular investment would almost certainly make them much less willing to invest in the first place.

The presence of short-term **speculators** helps the market. **Bulls** buy shares expecting them to rise (probably in the fairly short term), while **bears** look for prices to fall. They either sell shares they do not even own ('**selling short**'), hoping to buy them back later at lower prices; or at least refrain from buying yet, planning to do so more cheaply later. They may also deal in options (see Chapter 8) – though these can be used to *reduce* risk as well as to speculate.

If on balance speculators make profits, that implies that their views are somehow 'more correct' than other people's. Their actions drive market prices sooner to levels they would otherwise take longer to reach. (This may also be true of **insiders**.) In this way – and without intending it (Adam Smith's 'invisible hand'!) – they help improve the trustworthiness of market prices as signals to investors and others.

Global markets

Most developed countries have stock exchanges. Table 10.1 lists the largest as at 31 December 1998, by market capitalization The US market is easily the largest, with

Table 10.1 National stock markets by size at 31 December 1998

	Market capitalization $ billion	% of total
United States	10,362	53.2
Japan	1,974	10.1
United Kingdom	1,947	10.0
Germany	829	4.3
France	727	3.7
Switzerland	605	3.1
Netherlands	517	2.6
Italy	449	2.3
Canada	365	1.9
Spain	261	1.3
Australia	226	1.2
Sweden	215	1.1
Hong Kong	208	1.1
Belgium	178	0.9
Finland	111	0.6
Remainder	508	2.6
TOTAL	19,482	100.0

Japan and the UK next. Between them these three countries have nearly 75 per cent of total world stock market capitalization.

A number of aspects of European countries merit noticing. The UK's stock market capitalization is practically as large as the stock markets of France, Germany, and Italy combined. Switzerland and the Netherlands have larger stock markets than their economic size as countries might lead one to expect. And the market capitalization of Euro-land countries (at $3,186 billion) is only slightly larger than that of non-euro European countries ($2,909 billion). It is also obvious that these valuations in US dollars are affected by changes in exchange rates. Thus the 15 per cent fall in the euro between January and December 1999 may have affected some of the above comparisons considerably.

Efficient markets

Are stock markets reasonably efficient in pricing the equity shares they list? If so, investors can be confident of fair prices when they buy and sell shares. And corporate managers too can rely on stock market prices, so they can aim to maximize share price as a proxy for maximizing shareholders' wealth. Managers can also choose which projects are worth investing in by using stock market prices to estimate the rates of return which investors require.

We can distinguish three levels of market efficiency:

1. *Weak form*: share prices reflect all information conveyed by past prices. This implies that **technical analysis** of the past trend of share prices (chartism) cannot help anyone to make consistent profits from stock market dealings.
2. ***Semi-strong form***: share prices reflect all publicly available information. This implies that fundamental economic analysis of company performance cannot help anyone to make consistent profits, because markets respond rapidly to new data. There is a paradox here: the so-called '**efficient markets hypothesis**' may only continue to be true if some people don't believe it!
3. *Strong form*: share prices reflect all knowable information, whether public or private. This implies that even people with relevant inside information cannot make consistent profits from stock market dealings.

In general the evidence suggests that, after allowing for transactions costs, the stock market *is* efficient in both the weak form and the semi-strong form. But there is reason to believe that insiders can profit from their private knowledge. (It is arguable that public policy should allow insiders to deal and make profits in order to let share prices more quickly reflect *all* relevant information.)

If share prices at any moment reflect all available information, they will only change if new information appears. But the next bit of 'news' (by definition) is independent of the last bit. Hence share price movements will tend to follow a 'random walk'.

Widespread acceptance of the efficient markets hypothesis has led to a large number of passive **index funds** being content simply to track some stock market index, rather than seeking vainly (and at some extra expense) to out-perform it.

10.3. Stock market indices

UK indices

There is interest in the equity market as a whole, as well as in specific industries and companies. Three main indices show how the equity market is performing.

1. The FTSE 100 share index

The FTSE 100 share index ('Footsie') began in 1984. The Footsie index is calculated minute by minute on the basis of the 100 largest listed companies (in terms of market capitalization). The constituents have changed frequently at the margin, in particular as large utilities were privatized. Together the 100 constituent companies comprise about two-thirds of the total value of the UK-listed equity market. Figure 10.2 shows the level of the FTSE 100 share index as at 1 January each year (in constant January 1999 terms).

Clearly the market has been on an upward trend over the past fifteen years. It has nearly tripled in real terms, increasing on average by more than 7 per cent a year. It is striking that the 'crash' of October 1987 (when the index fell by about 25 per cent overnight) is not visible on the chart.

Table 10.2 shows the market value of the largest ten UK companies in June 1999. Three of them are pharmaceutical companies, and there are two banks, two oil

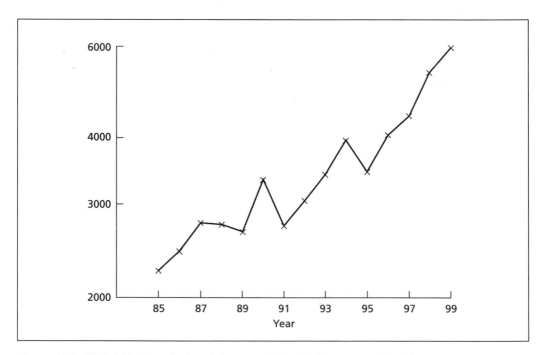

Figure 10.2 FTSE 100 share index, 1 January 1985–99 (January 1999 £s)

Table 10.2 Ten largest UK companies, 10 July 1999

	£ billion
BP Amoco	118
Vodafone Airtouch	82
BT	72
Glaxo Wellcome	64
Shell Transport	53
SmithKline Beecham	47
Lloyds TSB	46
AstraZeneca	43
Barclays Bank	27
Diageo	24

companies and two telecommunications companies. Several of the largest have been involved in mergers in the last few years, as the names reveal.

2. The FT-Actuaries Non-Financials

The Non-Financials Index evolved out of the 500-share index (started in 1962), which is computed as an **arithmetical average**, hence is suitable for looking at long-term trends. There are currently 570 shares in the index; and adding the 233 Financial shares gives the 803 shares currently in the All-Share index.

The All-Share index comprises ten industry sectors, sub-divided into 39 sub-sectors. Table 10.3 sets out the ten industry sectors currently in use (they change from time to time).

The four largest sub-sectors should be no surprise, in the light of Table 10.2. showing the ten companies with the largest stock market capitalizations. They are: Banks (15%); Telecommunications (12%); Oil & Gas (10%); and Pharmaceuticals (10%). It will be seen that these four (out of 39) sub-sectors make up 47% of the All-Share Index's capitalization.

Table 10.3 Industry sectors in the FTSE All-Share index

Industry sector	% of All-Share index
Resources (16)	12
Basic industries (80)	4
General industrials (77)	4
Cyclical consumer goods (16)	1
Non-cyclical consumer goods (81)	17
Cyclical services (219)	16
Non-cyclical services (22)	15
Utilities (20)	4
Information technology (39)	1
Non-financials (570)	**74**
Financials (233)	**26**

Table 10.4 FTSE Industry sub-sectors, 9 July 1999

Industry sectors	Industry sub-sectors
Resources (16)	Mining (5); Oil/Gas (11).
Basic Industries (80)	Chemicals (18); Construction/Building Materials (59); Forestry/Paper (2); Steel/Other Metals (1).
General Industrials (77)	Aerospace/Defence (9); Diversified Industrials (4); Electronic/Electrical Equipment (20); Engineering/Machinery (44)
Cyclical Consumer Goods (16)	Automobiles (7); Household Goods/Textiles (9).
Non-Cyclical Consumer Goods (81)	Beverages (9); Food Producers/Processors (22); Health (12); Packaging (10); Personal Care/Household Products (4); Pharmaceuticals (21); Tobacco (3).
Cyclical Services (219)	Distributors (22); General Retailers (40); Leisure, Entertainment/Hotels (29); Media/Photography (43); Restaurants, Pubs/Breweries (21); Support Services (35); Transport (29)
Non-Cyclical Services (22)	Food & Drug Retailers (13); Telecommunications (9).
Utilities (20)	Electricity (7); Gas Distribution (2); Water (11).
InformationTechnology (39)	I.T. Hardware (4); Software/Computer Services (35).
Non Financials (570)	
Financials (233)	Banks (11); Insurance (19); Life Assurance (8); Investment Companies (117); Real Estate (48); Speciality/Other (30).
All Share (803)	

Table 10.4 shows the list of industry sub-sectors on 10 July 1999. (A similar classification is used for European stocks.)

3. The Financial Times 30-share index

The 30-share FT industrial ordinary share index contains leading shares from most business sectors. It began as long ago as 1935, though nearly all the shares comprising the index have changed since then. The index shows how leading shares have moved in the short term, from hour to hour. It is a **geometric average** (taking the 30th root of the product of all the share prices multiplied together), and is not suitable for long-term trends. It is not often quoted these days as a measure of market behaviour, having been dislodged by the FTSE 100 share index.

US indices

The two best-known US indices are the 30-share Dow-Jones Industrial average and the Standard & Poor's 500-share index. There has been some concern that the Dow-Jones index, which is probably still the most widely quoted, may not be very representative of the whole equity stock market in New York. (This may be worrying if it is the basis for index funds.)

Figure 10.3 shows the Standard & Poor's Industrial share index since 1979. Like the UK market, Wall Street has evidently been on an upwards trend for several years. That does not, of course, mean it must now be 'too high'. It could have been 'too low' before;

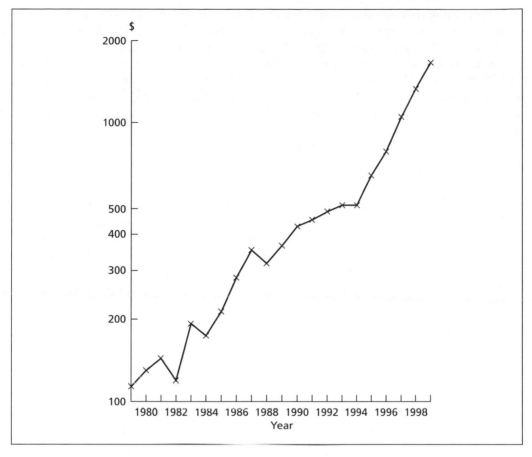

Figure 10.3 Standard & Poor's Industrial share index, mid-year 1979–99

or there may have been events (such as increasing profits or reduced interest rates) that have 'justified' the rise in share prices.

10.4. Issuing equity shares

Going public

A company may wish to list its ordinary shares on the stock exchange for two main reasons: to raise more share capital from the public; or to enable existing shareholders to sell some of their shares. When a company 'goes public' it must issue a **prospectus** naming the directors and giving the company's history, its recent financial results and certain other details.

Normally a company must offer at least 25 per cent of the ordinary shares to the public in order to ensure a reasonably liquid market in the shares. For small companies, the **alternative investment market (AIM)** has less stringent requirements. For example, an AIM company need offer only 10 per cent of its shares to the public.

The costs of issuing shares to the public can be high. There would need to be a price discount (of between 10 and 20 per cent) to attract buyers of risky shares in a little-known company. Moreover underwriting costs, fees to advisers, printing and promotion costs, would total at least 5 per cent of the proceeds, possibly much more for small issues. And for small companies the cost in terms of management time can be significant.

There are three main methods of going public, as follows:

1. An **offer for sale** offers shares to the public at large, at a fixed price. This is a common method for larger issues. The issuing house may itself take up all the shares before selling them on to the public. Pricing new shares may be difficult if there are few companies to compare with. If the price of a new issue (fixed some days in advance) is too high, nobody will buy, and the **underwriters** will have to take up the shares; but if the price is too low, the issuing company's existing shareholders will find their equity interest **diluted**.
2. The issuing house may '**place**' a new issue (below a certain size) privately with its clients, including financial institutions, at a price fixed in advance. A proportion must be made available to market-makers to ensure a market in the shares. There may be lower expenses than for other methods of issue, but a larger market discount.
3. The **tender method** sets no fixed price in advance. Instead it solicits offers from the public; and the highest price which will raise all the required money becomes the asking price for all successful purchases. The market discount is likely to be small, which discourages **stags** (bulls of new issues).

A fourth method, which is fairly rare, is an 'introduction'. This is used when an established company is being listed, but not seeking to raise any new money. A recent example was Anglo-American Corporation of South Africa, which was transferring its listing from Johannesburg to London.

Several of the privatized enterprises used the offer-for-sale method, and in many cases the fixed price at which the shares were offered was much lower than the level to which the shares later rose on the market. The general view is that the government sacrificed large sums in order to ensure the political success of these issues. (See Chapter 13)

When a company offers some of its equity shares to the public for the first time, it is often an opportunity both for the company itself to raise some new money and for existing shareholders to sell some of their holdings (possibly in order to diversify). Thus the total proceeds of the issue may need to be split between the company and its existing shareholders.

Rights issues

The methods of issue just described apply to unlisted companies going public for the first time. Companies whose shares are already listed normally use a **rights issue** to raise more equity money (over and above equity funds raised by retaining profits rather than distributing them in dividends). This is because the stock exchange regards rights issues as normally being fairest to existing shareholders.

A rights issue offers extra shares to existing shareholders, in proportion to their holdings, priced at some discount to the current market price per share. (Of course, the offer price of a rights issue must be below the current market price, otherwise anyone who wants to buy more shares would simply do so in the market, not by way of the rights!)

In theory the *price* of a rights issue does not matter! An existing shareholder who is unwilling to take up the new shares can (in the UK) always sell his rights in the market and thus avoid any loss from dilution. (The bigger the rights issue discount from the current market price, the more the rights will be worth.) Indeed, the company itself will automatically sell the rights on behalf of any shareholders who do not take up their rights.

Example 10.1

Thomas Lodge plc has 50 million ordinary shares already in issue, with a current market price of 150p each. The company plans to raise an extra £20 million of equity capital by means of a rights issue. Table 10.5 shows two different ways of achieving this (ignoring transaction costs): either issuing 1 for 1 @ 40p, or else issuing 2 for 5 @ 100p.

Alan Yarrow (AY) owns 1,000 shares and decides to take up his rights in full; while Norman Oliver (NO), who also owns 1,000 shares, decides to sell all his rights. Table 10.6 shows that in each case the market value of AY's holding goes up to reflect the amount of extra cash (£400) he has invested; and the market value of NO's holding goes down by exactly the amount of cash he receives in each case for selling his rights.

Bonus issues and share splits

So far we have been discussing two kinds of share issues on the stock exchange: new listings, which usually raise new money for a company, but which may merely transfer shares from existing shareholders to new ones; and rights issues, by which listed companies raise new capital from their existing shareholders (or from those who buy the rights to subscribe for new shares).

Table 10.5 Rights issue: alternative issue prices

	1 for 1 @ 40p	2 for 5 @ 100p
Number of new shares to be issued	50 million	20 million
New total number of shares (n)	100 million	70 million
New share price ($£95m/n$)	95p	135.71p
Value of the rights per share	55p	35.71p

Table 10.6 Taking up or selling rights

£	1 for 1 @ 40p		2 for 5 @ 100p	
	AY	NO	AY	NO
Opening holding @ 150p: 1,000 shares	1,500	1,500	1,500	1,500
Buy 1,000 shares @ 40p	400			
Buy 400 shares @ 100p			400	
Sell 1,000 rights @ 55p		(550)		
Sell 400 rights @ 35.71p				(143)
Closing holding @ 95p [135.71p]				
AY: 2,000 [1,400] shares	1,900		1,900	
NO: 1,000 [1,000] shares		950		1,357

Two kinds of share issues raise no new money for companies, but can affect the meaning of certain stock exchange ratios. They are respectively **bonus issues** and **share splits**.

1. Bonus issues (scrip issues) capitalize some of a company's reserves, by transferring them on the balance sheet to called-up share capital. This is purely a book-keeping entry. The *total* amount of shareholders' funds remains the same as before, since the company has raised no new money: it has merely turned some of its retained profits or other reserves into called-up ordinary share capital (so they are no longer available to pay out in dividends).
2. Share splits simply split shares into smaller units without even affecting balance sheet amounts.

Example 10.2

Giant plc has 600,000 ordinary £1 shares in issue, with a market price of £12 each (1200p). After the company makes a '4 for 1' share split, it will have 2.4 million ordinary shares of 25p each in issue, each with a market price of 300p. Notice that a '4 for 1' share split means 4 new shares *instead of* each existing share in issue; whereas a '4 for 1' bonus issue means 4 new shares *in addition to* each existing share held, making 5 in all.

In comparing earnings per share (or other 'per share' amounts) over time, one may need to adjust earlier years' figures to allow for subsequent share splits or bonus issues.

What is the purpose of making bonus issues or splitting shares? They 'give' shareholders nothing they did not already own: they do not increase the total market value of the equity capital. One obvious effect is to reduce the per-share market price of the stock exchange; but there is no reason – either in theory or in practice – to think this matters.

Problem 10.1.

A company has issued 250,000 8 per cent preference shares of £1 nominal value and 400,000 ordinary shares of 25p nominal value. The directors retain for expansion half of anything that remains once the preference dividend has been paid. Calculate the rate of preference dividend and the amount of ordinary dividend per share if profits are:

a. £20,000
b. £60,000
c. £100,000

Problem 10.2.

Nancy King plc has 240 million ordinary shares already in issue, with a current market price of 330p per share. The company plans to raise an extra £180 million of equity capital by means of a rights issue. Two possible ways of achieving this (ignoring transaction costs) are being considered: either (a) issuing 3 for 2 @ 50p or else (b) issuing 1 for 4 @ 300p.

For each alternative, calculate:

- what the new total number of shares would be
- what you would expect the new market price per share to be
- the estimated value of the rights.

Also calculate the position of two holders of 2000 ordinary shares. The first, Olivia Knox, plans to take up the rights to which she is entitled; while the second, Colin Berry, proposes to sell his rights for cash. Show in each case, and for each of the alternative methods of making the rights issue: how much cash will be paid (by OK) or received (by CB), and how many shares each will own after the rights issue, and what those shares will be worth.

Problem 10.3.

Knight plc, Terry plc and Lincoln plc each have an issued ordinary share capital of £120 million in £1 shares, an accumulated balance on profit and loss account of £70 million, and no other reserves. The authorized ordinary share capital in each case is £200 million. The current market price per share in each case is 240p.

The companies make the following ordinary share issues, and you are asked to show for each company the details of share capital and reserves after the issue:

a. Knight plc issues 20 million new shares to employees @ 150p each.
b. Terry plc makes a 1 for 3 bonus issue.
c. Lincoln plc makes a 1 for 4 rights issue @ 200p.

What would you expect the market price per ordinary share to be after the share issue in each case?

Problem 10.4.

George Shackle Ltd., an unquoted company planning to go public, wants to raise £20 million additional capital net of all expenses. The two controlling families own 40 per cent of the 6 million ordinary 50p shares currently in issue; and they plan to sell one third of their combined holdings. After a proposed 10 for 1 share split, the directors expect that the ordinary shares can be sold on the market for 160p each; and it is thought that 150p per share will be left after underwriting commissions and certain other costs. In addition, printing and advertising costs, together with professional fees, are expected to total £1 million.

a. How many shares will be offered to the public?
b. If the shares go to a 10 per cent premium over the issue price, what will the market value of the enlarged equity amount to?
c. If a net dividend of 4.0p per share is expected to be paid on the enlarged capital, with a dividend cover of 2.5 times, what is the envisaged price/earnings ratio based on the issue price?

CHAPTER 11

Cost of capital

In this chapter we first discuss the cost of debt. We then tackle the very tricky topic of the (opportunity) cost of equity capital. We look at two methods of approaching this: first, modern portfolio theory and the Capital Asset Pricing Model (CAPM) and, second, the **Dividend Growth Model**. Then we discuss how to *combine* the cost of debt and the cost of equity to estimate the Weighted Average Cost of Capital (WACC).

11.1. Cost of debt

Direct cost

The direct cost of borrowing is the payment of interest to the lender. Debt interest is a business expense for tax purposes, so the after-tax cost of debt is usually less than the nominal (coupon) rate of interest. For example, suppose a company pays loan interest of 8.0 per cent a year and tax on profits is 30 per cent. Then the after-tax cost of debt interest is 5.6 per cent a year:

$$8\% \times (100\% - 30\%) = 8\% \times 70\% = 5.6\%$$

A loan to a higher-risk small company might cost 10 per cent a year, to include a larger risk premium. But that company might be subject only to the 20 per cent 'small company' tax rate on profits. So the debt's after-tax cost would be 8 per cent a year – nearly half as much again:

$$10\% \times (100\% - 20\%) = 10\% \times 80\% = 8.0\%$$

A company may be paying no tax on profits, either because it is making losses or because of high tax allowances against profit. In that case there will be no reduction due to tax in the direct cost of borrowing.

The tax laws mostly refer to money, so any 'real' gain to the borrower in respect of inflation is not taxable. This can have a big effect in reducing the real after-tax cost. The overall nominal *ex ante* rate of interest includes an inflation premium. To keep it simple, the following example assumes that this turns out to be precisely correct vis-à-vis the actual rate of inflation *ex post*. (The actual rate of inflation may in fact be very different from what was expected.)

Table 11.1 Real rates of after-tax interest on debt

Inflation	0%	3%	6%	12%
Before-tax interest	5.00	8.15	11.30	17.60
Tax @ 30%	1.50	2.45	3.39	5.28
After-tax interest	3.50	5.70	7.91	12.32
less: purchasing power gain	*0.00*	*2.91*	*5.66*	*10.71*
Real after-tax interest	**3.50**	**2.79**	**2.25**	**1.61**

Example 11.1

Suppose an 8 per cent annual interest rate comprises the following:

- 3 per cent pure time preference
- 3 per cent inflation premium (assumed correct)
- 2 per cent risk premium

Then the amount of purchasing power needed to repay a loan will be 3/103 (= 2.9 per cent) a year less than the amount that was borrowed.

Table 11.1 includes four columns to show the real after-tax cost of four different loans. 3 per cent pure time preference and 2 per cent risk premium is the same in each case. But the four loans have different inflation premiums (in each case assumed correct), of zero, 3 per cent, 6 per cent and 12 per cent. Notice how the real after-tax cost of interest declines as the nominal interest rate increases!

Indirect costs

The direct cost of debt is interest payments, taking into account both tax and inflation. But there may also be an indirect cost to a company as the level of gearing rises, in that then the riskiness (volatility) of the residual equity increases too. So the cost of equity may rise as a result.

Whatever the financial cost of debt and equity to the company, as the level of debt rises it is likely to restrict managers' freedom of action. External lenders will tend to demand more stringent covenants. And managers themselves prefer not to borrow too close to the perceived limit in order to maintain some spare borrowing capacity in case of urgent need. (Companies in serious trouble may have to borrow as much as they can get their hands on; but it is internal, not external, decision-makers who normally choose how much companies borrow.)

11.2. Cost of equity (CAPM)

Modern portfolio theory

Modern portfolio theory (MPT) holds that investment involves two different kinds of risk: **market risk** and unique risk. Equity investors cannot avoid market risk, which

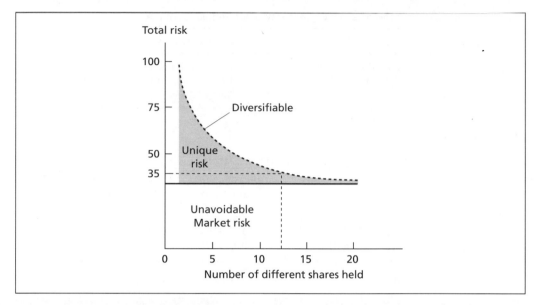

Figure 11.1 Unique risk and market risk

stems from the uncertainties of the whole economy. In contrast, unique risk relates to a particular company or a specific project. Shareholders can, in effect, dilute such risk by investing in several different kinds of projects (or shares).

An investor who splits his equity equally among a dozen different shares (of companies in different industries) can diversify away *more than half* the total risk he would bear by investing everything in shares of a single company. In effect, a portfolio averages out the unique risks of the different shares. But investors *cannot* diversify away about one-third of the total risk of a single share however many different shares they hold. That represents the residual risk to which all shares (and projects) are subject. As Figure 11.1 shows, increasing the number of equal holdings beyond about a dozen equity investments makes little further difference in reducing unique risk.

This points to an important difference of outlook between managers of a company and its shareholders. Managers (like workers) are normally committed largely to a specific company, and may therefore be concerned with its total risk (that is, both market risk and unique risk). Shareholders, on the other hand, are mobile and can normally hold diversified portfolios. So the theory says, if they do, they need care only about market risk. One important question is the extent to which market pressures force managers to act in the interests of shareholders (by worrying only about market risk, as opposed to total risk).

This theory concerning risk, and how the market values assets (it is often referred to as the **capital asset pricing model** – or simply CAPM), also has implications with respect to profit-seeking. Is it really, as the theory implies, more rational for shareholders to hold diversified portfolios, in order to avoid risks for which they cannot expect to get any reward? Or is it, as some successful investors believe, better to 'put all one's eggs in one basket'– *and then watch the basket*?

Table 11.2 Synonyms for two different kinds of risk

Market Risk	Unique Risk
Non-diversifiable risk	Diversifiable risk
Systematic risk	Unsystematic risk
	Specific risk

Market risk

Modern portfolio theory says that no investor *needs* to take on most unique risks: he can get rid of them by holding shares in several different companies. Hence market returns will compensate only for market risk. These two kinds of risk have several different names each, as listed in Table 11.2.

The theory says that the required return on any particular equity share bears a definite relationship (known as **beta**) to the return on an investment in the market as a whole. 'Return' here means dividend plus capital gain. An investment with a beta of less than 1.0 is less risky than the whole market; with a beta of more than 1.0, more risky. (In this context, 'risk' means the *volatility* of a share's returns.) Figure 11.2 shows the spread of

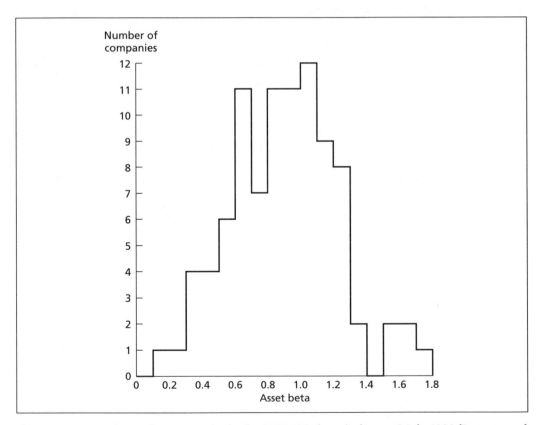

Figure 11.2 Asset betas for companies in the FTSE 100 share index on 6 July 1999 (Datastream)

Table 11.3 Required rates of return for Project E and Project F

Project	Required after-tax risk-free return	Estimated beta	Required market risk premium	Required project risk premium	Required project rate of return
E	4%	+ (0.75	×8%	=) 6%	=10%
F	4%	+ (1.5	×8%	=) 12%	=16%

asset betas for companies in the FTSE 100 share index on 6 July 1999, according to Datastream. It is not easy, even for listed companies, to translate the company's beta into a beta for a specific project.

To find the required (minimum) after-tax rate of return for a particular investment one must add a risk premium to the after-tax risk-free rate of return. In MPT this risk premium is the whole market's after-tax risk premium multiplied by the investment's beta. Based on actual past results over many decades (similar in the United Kingdom and the United States), an investment in the equity stock market as a whole requires a real after-tax risk premium of about 8 per cent a year on top of the risk-free rate of return on government stocks. (But see also the next section for further discussion.)

Example 11.2

Project E (which might be an ordinary share in Company E), with an estimated beta of 0.75, will have a risk premium of 6.0 per cent; while Project F, with an estimated beta of 1.5, will have a risk premium of 12.0 per cent. Assuming the required risk-free after-tax money rate of return is 4.0 per cent, the required project rates of return (or 'cost of equity capital') will be 10 per cent and 16 per cent respectively, as set out in Table 11.3. These are money (nominal) costs of capital: if we wanted to determine *real* **costs of capital**, we would need to use the *real* after-tax risk free rate of, say, 2.0 per cent. That would then give real costs of capital of 8 per cent for Project E and 14 per cent for Project F.

Figure 11.3 shows the capital market line with a straight-line relationship between market risk (beta) and required rate of return. It starts from the after-tax risk-free rate of return (assumed to be 4 per cent in money terms) and adds a risk premium – the market risk premium of 8 per cent multiplied by the project's own beta. (Both these numbers are only estimates.) The beta refers *only* to market risk. It ignores a project's unique risk (also called **specific risk**) on the grounds that any investor can choose to avoid it by holding a diversified portfolio.

If Project E has an expected return of 12 per cent in money terms, and if Project F has an expected return of 14 per cent, then Project E is acceptable but Project F (which has a higher expected return but is also higher-risk) is not.

The equity risk premium

The last section stated that, based on actual past results over many decades, an investment in the equity stock market as a whole requires a real after-tax risk premium of

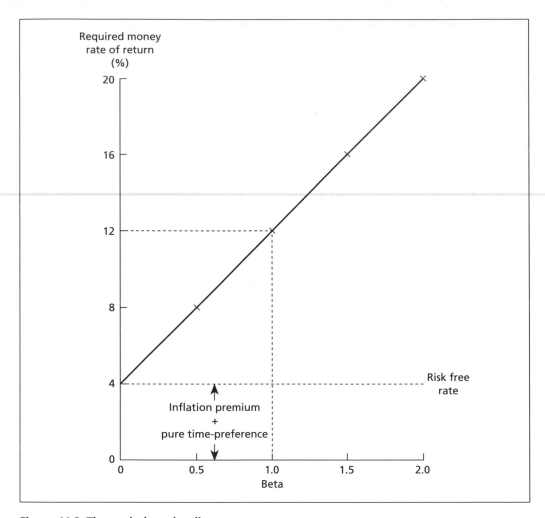

Figure 11.3 The capital market line

about 8 per cent a year on top of the risk-free rate of return. But that statement is controversial. There is a wide range of rates which is now advocated for the equity risk premium (also called the market risk premium).

Brealey and Myers (1996) say: 'Over a period of 69 years the market risk premium has averaged 8.4 per cent a year.' According to Buckley (1996), since 1926 (based on long-term government bonds), the excess real return in the US has been 7.2 per cent and since 1919 in the UK it has been 8.4 per cent. These numbers use an arithmetic index: they would be lower (US 5.6 per cent, UK 6.2 per cent) using a geometric index.

Van Horne (1998) says: 'The *expected* return on the **market portfolio** has exceeded the risk-free rate by anywhere from 3 to 7 per cent in recent years.' He stresses, however, that this is *ex ante* expectations, not the range of risk premiums actually realized.

Siegel (1998) suggests that the standard deviation of average annual real returns has actually been lower for equity stocks than for risk-free bonds for investors with a holding period of twenty years or more. It has been much higher for equity stocks (than for bonds) for holding periods of one or two years, and slightly higher for holding periods of five or ten years.

Thus there are at least four points at issue:

1. whether to use past results as proxy for future *ex ante* estimates (as is normally done for betas);
2. whether to use an arithmetic index or a geometric index (the former produces results about 1.5 to 2.0 per cent year higher);
3. whether to use very short-term or long-term risk-free bonds (the former produces results about 0.5 to 1.0 per cent a year higher);
4. whether to use a one-year holding period or a longer period, possibly much longer.

The trouble is, as Figure 11.4 shows, that if the 'correct' equity risk premium may vary from (say) 3 per cent to 9 per cent, the range of answers given by the CAPM approach is so wide as to be almost meaningless.

One's view on this may also influence one's view on the level of the stock market. If Wall Street's Dow-Jones Index, standing at 11,200, is using a market risk premium of 5 per cent, a real risk-free rate of 2 per cent and an assumed real growth rate of 2 per cent, then a shift to using a market risk premium of 8 per cent (other things unchanged) would reduce the Index by 37½ per cent – to 7,000!

Problems with CAPM

The CAPM formula for the cost of equity capital is: $R_f + \beta(R_m - R_f)$. In interpreting the meaning of this formula, a number of problems arise. We can take the three main components in order:

R_f, the risk-free rate of return

1. What time period should we use? Is it very short-term government securities, such as 90-day Treasury Bills? Or should we be matching the term with the 'typical' life of a project, say ten to fifteen years? (The answer needs to be consistent with the way we define 'R_f' in the expression $(R_m - R_f)$.)
2. The market risk premium term $(R_m - R_f)$ is in 'real' terms. So if we need to allow for inflation, we modify the 'R_f' term. To get a *money* (nominal) cost of equity capital, we use a money risk-free rate, based on the current yield on government securities. But what if we require a 'real' cost of equity capital? To get a real risk-free rate, can we simply take the yield on index-linked government securities? Or is it really somewhat less than that?
3. What about tax? Should we assume the typical equity investor is a financial institution? Or a higher-rate personal taxpayer? Their tax positions are different.

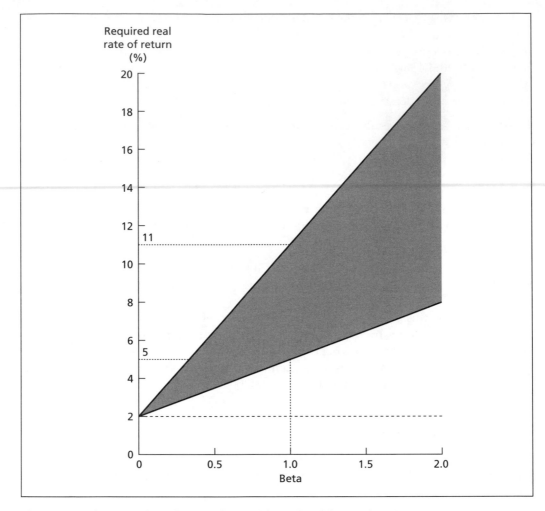

Figure 11.4 The capital market 'wedge', with equity risk premium 3–9 per cent

β, *the relationship to market risk*

4. Is it true (as Van Horne suggests) that company betas vary 'considerably' depending which version of the stock market you use? And how unstable are company betas over time? Why is a sixty-month past period right to calculate a company's beta, rather than six months or fifty years (= 600 months)?

5. How can we modify the estimated beta of a listed company into a suitable beta for a specific project? And what about unlisted companies?

6. Should we use a geared equity beta (what the published numbers usually are), which relates to the cost of equity capital in a geared company? Or should we use an ungeared asset beta, which is the weighted average cost of capital in a geared company? (That means, what the cost of equity capital would be if the company

were ungeared, i.e. had only equity capital.) In 'ungearing' a geared beta, should we somehow allow for the tax-deductibility of debt interest?

$(R_m - R_f)$, *the market risk premium* (see also previous section)

7. Is it correct to use simply the domestic stock market in order to calculate the required market risk premium (sometimes called the equity risk premium)? Or should we aim to cover global markets or use a much wider set of assets than just listed securities?
8. Over what past time period should we calculate the actual 'achieved' risk premium? The last five years, the last twenty-five, or the last seventy-five years? In any case, are we right to assume that the future will be like the past? (The same question arises with estimates of beta.)
9. Is the market risk premium before-tax or (as is normally assumed) after-tax? Can we properly allow for a changing tax system over time?

General

10. Are we right to concentrate entirely on market risk in using CAPM? Can we really ignore specific (unique) risk? What about (a) managers and (b) family-company shareholders, neither of whom are anything like fully diversified?
11. Most betas of listed companies seem to be between about 0.7 and 1.3 – in other words, fairly close to 1.0. Especially if you think the market risk premium is much lower than 8 per cent a year, is it really worth bothering with betas other than 1.0?
12. Many aspects of capital investment projects and valuing assets are likely to be more important than refining the supposed accuracy of the discount rate. So might it make sense to limit one's use of CAPM to seeing whether the industry concerned seems to be low, average or high risk? Maybe one could then similarly distinguish between (a) cost reduction; (b) expansion and (c) new product projects as low risk, average risk and high risk respectively.

The point of the above questions is not to denigrate the Capital Asset Pricing Model. But it would be absurd to pretend its results can be precisely accurate in practice. There are just too many dubious assumptions. Points 4, 5, 8 and 10 above seem especially worrying.

11.3. Cost of equity (Dividend Growth Model)

In principle we can value equity shares in the same way as risk-free securities. Thus we discount the expected future cash receipts from owning the shares, using the opportunity cost of equity capital. Instead of a regular fixed money annuity, we now have to deal with dividends which can fluctuate. A common simplifying assumption is that the latest annual net dividend per share will grow at a *constant* rate in future. This can be either in real terms or in money terms.

Dividend payments do *not* represent the whole cost of equity capital for a company. Equity capital still has an opportunity cost even for a company which pays no dividends (if it is trying to maximize shareholders' wealth): it is what the *shareholders* could otherwise have done with the money invested. Hence it is the discounting rate that shareholders (presumably) apply to the expected future dividends.

A shareholder's return from holding shares consists of two parts: dividends plus **capital gain** (or less capital loss). Yet Table 11.4 shows how the stock market can value a company's equity shares solely on the basis of expected future cash dividends.

It is true that an individual mortal shareholder (A) (or his estate) will ultimately sell his shares. But he will sell to some other shareholder (B), who will value the shares on the basis of future dividends plus ultimate sales proceeds. We can 'cancel out' the various intermediate purchases and sales, ending up with valuing the shares only on the basis of the stream of future dividends. We assume that shareholders A, B, C, D, etc. hold the shares for exactly ten years each. Clearly we could pursue the logic right through the alphabet.

Applying the present value model to share valuation is straightforward enough in theory, though of course in practice guessing the actual numbers is not easy.

If the latest annual net dividend per share is d, the expected (assumed constant) annual rate of growth in future net dividends per share is g, and the opportunity cost of equivalent-risk equity shares is k, then we find the present value per share (p) by discounting the expected future dividends for ever, as follows.

$$p = d(1 + g) + \left(\frac{d(1 + g)^2}{(1 + k)^2} + \frac{d(1 + g)^3}{(1 + k)^3} + \cdots + \frac{d(1 + g)^\infty}{(1 + k)^\infty} \right)$$

This simplifies[*] to:

$$p = \frac{d'}{k - g} \qquad \text{or} \qquad k = \frac{d'}{p} + g$$

In words: the cost of equity capital (k) is the expected current-year net dividend yield (d'/p) plus the annual (assumed constant) rate of growth (g) in net dividends per share. Because shareholders may have different tax positions, estimating the after-tax amount

---

[*] Multiply both sides of the equation shown by $\frac{(1 + k)}{(1 + g)}$.

Then from the resulting product, subtract the equation shown above. This gives

$$p\frac{(1 + k)}{(1 + g)} - p = d^0 - d\frac{(1 + g)^\infty}{(1 + k)^\infty}$$

Since $k > g$, the final term collapses to zero, which leaves:

$$p\frac{(1 + k)}{(1 + g)} - p = d^0$$

leading to $p(1 + k) - p(1 + g) = d^0(1 + g)$
hence $p(k - g) = d'$.

Table 11.4 Valuing shares solely on the basis of future dividends

Shareholder	Cost of purchase	Cash receipts from holding shares		Sales proceeds
		Dividends		
A	Value EOY 0	= Dividends EOY 1–10 +		Value EOY 10
B	Value EOY 10	= Dividends EOY 11–20 +		Value EOY 20
C	Value EOY 20	= Dividends EOY 21–30 +		Value EOY 30
D	Value EOY 30	= Dividends EOY 31–40 +		Value EOY 40
E	Value EOY 40	= ...		
	Value EOY 0	= Dividends EOY 1–40 ...		

of dividends can be difficult. But in practice guessing the value of g normally matters more than correctly adjusting for tax on d.

Example 11.3

Burnham Ltd. proposes to pay a net dividend this year on ordinary shares of 11p; the expected future growth rate in dividends per share is 10 per cent a year; and the opportunity cost of equity capital is reckoned to be 15 per cent a year. The dividend growth model would value Burnham Ltd's ordinary shares at 220p each.

$$\text{Value} = \frac{11}{0.15 \quad 0.10} = \frac{11}{0.05} = 220\text{p}$$

To determine the opportunity cost of equity capital we simply add the assumed constant growth rate (of 10 per cent a year in this case) to the net dividend yield (of 5 per cent a year), based on d' – the end-of-current-year dividend. In this case this gives an (after-tax) cost of equity capital of 15 per cent a year. Both k and g are only rough estimates, so the difference between them ($k - g$) may be subject to a very large margin of error.

11.4. Weighted average cost of capital

Overall cost of capital

A firm's cost of capital is the minimum return its assets must produce to justify raising the funds to acquire them. We have discussed how to estimate a company's after-tax cost of debt; and we have seen that the cost of equity is largely an opportunity cost whether one uses the Capital Asset Pricing Model or the Dividend Growth Model. Combining the cost of debt and the cost of equity gives the company's overall weighted average cost of capital (WACC). This is the basis for a discount rate to use as the hurdle rate in assessing capital investment projects.

As a rule it is best to separate two questions: (a) whether a project is worth investing in or not; and (b) if it is, how to finance it. A company may plan to finance a project by borrowing; but it still bases the project's minimum rate of return (the discount rate for

NPV purposes) on the *overall* weighted average cost of capital. In effect we think of using a *pool of funds* (both debt and equity) to finance all projects.

Example 11.4

A company has equity capital with a market value of £120 million and debt capital with a market value of £40 million. So equity has a 'weight' of 75 per cent and debt of 25 per cent. Using costs of 13 per cent for equity and 5 per cent for debt, the result is an overall weighted average cost of capital of 11.0 per cent $[(0.75 \times 15) + (0.25 \times 5)]$.

It is common to use the book value of debt as a proxy for its market value, if interest rates have not changed much since the debt was issued. It is less common to make that assumption about equity, because of problems with balance sheet amounts (especially in the UK). In principle using market values for both debt and equity is the right thing to do. Even so, using book values as the basis for weighting may not make much difference to the WACC estimate, unless the market value of equity is very different from its book value.

We must remember that nearly all the numbers are only estimates: the amount and timing of the incremental cash flows from a capital project; and the costs of debt and of equity (as well as their respective weightings). For this reason, it is probably not worth distinguishing between two kinds of equity capital – retained profits and new issues of equity shares – even though share issues would involve some extra costs. (Notice that the WACC is a weighted average of the *marginal* costs of debt and of equity!)

Adjusting WACC for risk

Rather than using WACC itself as the hurdle rate for all capital projects (the horizontal 13 per cent line in Figure 11.5), a company may choose to adjust the WACC upwards (= require a higher rate of return) for high-risk projects and to adjust the WACC downwards (= accept a lower required rate of return) for low-risk projects. Otherwise there would be a tendency to accept too many high-risk projects (such as H) and to reject too many low-risk projects (such as L).

How much to adjust WACC for risk is a matter of judgement. The cash flows for capital projects usually involve such fallible estimates that a difference of one or two percentage points in the discount rate is unlikely to be critical. (There is also a question about how to define – let alone measure – 'risk'.)

For a project with zero risk (if there could be such a thing), the relevant required rate of return would be the risk-free rate of return – say, 5 per cent. (*Not* 0 per cent, of course!) The WACC itself, say 13 per cent, would be a suitable required rate of return for a 'typical' project with 'average' risk.

A rough rule of thumb for other projects of varying risk might be as follows: for a project thought to have below-average risk, move halfway from 'average' to 'zero' risk (that is, to a required rate of return of 9 per cent – halfway between 13 per cent and 5 per

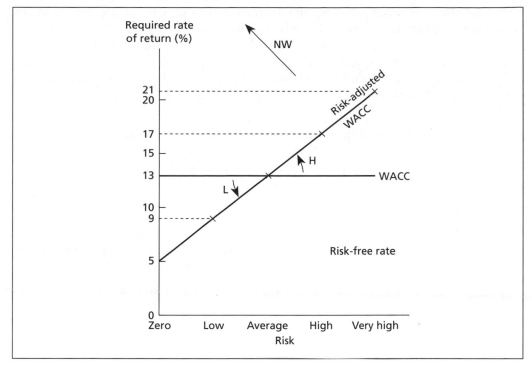

Figure 11.5 Adjusting WACC for risk

cent); for a project with an above-average level of risk, move as much *above* the WACC (to 17 per cent); and for a very high-risk project, move as far again above the WACC (to 21 per cent).

Of course managers are not merely trying to measure levels of risk and required return. They are also trying to *manage* the projects in order to 'move' them to the 'north-west' (on Figure 11.5) – either to the 'west' (by reducing the risk) or to the 'north' (by increasing the expected return) or both.

We saw earlier (Chapter 9) how lenders may seek to reduce their risk (by personal guarantees, by taking security or by loan covenants). Company managers, too, may seek to *reduce risk* by various means, such as: extensive market research; arranging long-term sales contracts; or dual sourcing. Managers may also try to *increase returns*, for example, by: expanding the volume of sales; increasing selling prices; or reducing costs without hurting quality. (These may be easier to say than to do.)

Asset betas

To calculate the weighted average cost of capital (WACC), we average the cost of equity and the cost of debt. For this purpose we may use a cost of equity capital based either on the capital asset pricing model (CAPM) or on the dividend growth model (see above).

The beta we have used so far to estimate the cost of equity by means of CAPM is a geared beta (**equity beta**). That is, it is based on the volatility of equity in a capital structure which (normally) contains both debt and equity. Another way of reaching a similar result is to use CAPM but with an ungeared, or asset beta. This reflects only the company's business risk rather than (as the equity beta does) *both* business risk and financial risk (gearing). (The betas in Figure 11.2 were asset betas.)

Example 11.5

Suppose a company has an equity beta of 1.4, debt represents 25 per cent of the total capital, and (to simplify) the cost of debt is the same as the risk-free rate of return, namely 4 per cent. Then the cost of equity capital will be 15.2 per cent: $[4.0 + 1.4(8.0)]$; and the WACC will be 12.4 per cent: $[(0.75 \times 15.2) + (0.25 \times 4.0)]$.

Another way to calculate the same WACC is as follows, using the asset beta approach. The overall asset beta should be a weighted average of the debt beta and the equity beta. In this case (to simplify) we are assuming a debt beta of zero (in other words, debt which is risk-free). So the expression:

$(0.25 \times$ debt beta$) + (0.75 \times$ equity beta$) =$ asset beta

simplifies to:

zero $+ (0.75 \times 1.4) = 1.05$

Now if the asset beta is 1.05, the relevant required rate of return is $4.0 + 1.05(8.0) = 12.4$ per cent. The same as before.

In practice the asset beta would be somewhat higher than this, since a company's debt beta would be somewhat above zero (not being risk-free).

Problems

Problem 11.1.

The nominal rate of interest on a five-year business loan is 12 per cent. What would the direct after-tax cost be for:

a. a large loss-making company?
b. a small profit-making company?
c. a sole trader subject to top-rate income tax?

What would the 'real' after-tax cost be in each case if inflation is running at 5 per cent a year?

Problem 11.2.

ABC plc has a beta of 1.2. If the risk-free rate of return is 4.0 per cent and the market risk premium is 8.0 per cent, what is ABC's cost of equity capital?

Problem 11.3.

DEF plc has a beta of 0.75. If the market risk premium is 6.0 per cent and DEF's cost of equity capital is 8.0 per cent, what is the risk-free rate of return?

Problem 11.4.

GHI plc has a cost of equity capital of 16.5 per cent. If the market risk premium is 8.0 per cent and the risk-free rate of return is 4.5 per cent, what is GHI's beta?

Problem 11.5.

JKL plc has a beta of 0.8, and a cost of equity capital of 8.8 per cent. The risk-free rate of return is 4.0 per cent. What is the market risk premium?

Problem 11.6.

MNO plc has a beta of 0.75. The risk-free rate of return is 4.0 per cent and the cost of equity capital is 10.0 per cent. How much does the cost of equity increase if the beta doubles?

Problem 11.7.

MD Enterprises plc expects to pay a net dividend this year of 6.0p per share; and the market expects the dividend to increase by 5 per cent a year. The company's cost of equity capital is estimated at 15 per cent a year. Using the dividend growth model, what would you expect the company's current market price per share to be?

Problem 11.8.

MD Enterprises plc has run into trouble. The company's policy is to pay out a constant proportion of its earnings in dividends each year; but earnings per share are now expected to grow by only 2 per cent a year for the foreseeable future. Instead of 6.0p per share, the company is now planning a dividend of only 4.0p per share this year. The prospects for the industry look gloomy, and the risk premium applicable to the company has increased, so that the cost of equity capital is now reckoned to be 20 per cent a year. What combined effect will all these changes have on the company's market price per share, as calculated using the dividend growth model in problem 11.7 above?

Problem 11.9.

PLQ plc paid a dividend of 6.0p per share last year. The dividend yield is 5.0 per cent and dividends are expected to grow in line with earnings at 8.0 per cent a year in future. What is the cost of equity capital?

Problem 11.10.

RST plc has a cost of equity capital of 14.4 per cent. The current dividend yield (based on last year's dividend) is 4.0 per cent. What is the (constant) annual growth rate expected in future?

Problem 11.11.

UVW plc expects to pay a dividend this year of 12.0p per share. The current share price is 240p. The cost of equity capital is twice the expected growth rate in dividends. Using the assumptions of the dividend growth model, what is the expected (constant) annual growth rate in earnings?

Problem 11.12.

XY plc has equity with a market value of £60 million and debt with a market value of £20 million. The cost of equity capital is 12.0 per cent and the cost of debt is 6.0 per cent. What is XY's weighted average cost of capital (WACC)?

Problem 11.13.

ZA plc has a WACC of 12.0 per cent. The cost of debt is 6.0 per cent and the cost of equity is 15.0 per cent. What are the weights of debt and equity respectively?

Problem 11.14.

BC plc has a WACC of 12.0 per cent. The cost of debt is 5.0 per cent. The debt/equity weights are 30/70. What is the cost of equity capital?

Problem 11.15.

DE plc has book values of debt and equity of £200m and £400m respectively. Assume the market value of debt is the same as the book value. The cost of debt is 6.0 per cent, and the cost of equity is 12.0 per cent. If the market value of equity is £600m, how much will the WACC be increased by using market value weights rather than book value weights?

CHAPTER 12

Capital structure

12.1. Gearing

How financial gearing works

Financial gearing (or leverage) means borrowing to finance part of a business, rather than using only equity capital (both issued share capital and retained profits).

Financial gearing (financial risk) refers to the sources of a company's finance; operational gearing (business risk) refers to the nature of the business and how a firm has used its funds. How a firm *invests* funds is probably far more important than its sources of finance. This is because most financial markets are more competitive, with better information, than most factor markets dealing in 'real' goods and services. So in general, financing decisions provide fewer chances of large profits or losses.

Operational gearing sometimes refers to the level of fixed expenses as a proportion of total expenses. Thus most of a school's expenses are fixed, whereas most of a street trader's vary with volume. Where most expenses are fixed, the amount of profit is very sensitive to the level of sales revenue. (The marginal cost of supplying one more student in a school is normally very small; so almost all that student's tuition fee represents profit!)

If the rate of return on assets financed by debt exceeds the cost of borrowing, the extra profit increases equity earnings. Conversely a company must legally pay debt interest even if its rate of return on assets is lower than the rate of interest on borrowing. Thus when profit is high, gearing will benefit shareholders, and vice versa.

Example 12.1

Brown Ltd. and Green Ltd. are similar except for their gearing. Total **capital employed** in each case is £10 million. Brown's debt ratio is 10 per cent, Green's is 50 per cent. The rate of debt interest payable is 10 per cent a year. In Year 1, the before-tax rate of return on capital employed is 30 per cent, in Year 2 only 5 per cent. As a result, as Table 12.1 shows, in Year 1 the return on equity for high-geared Green (37.5 per cent) is much higher than for low-geared Brown (24.2 per cent); whereas in Year 2 the return on equity for low-geared Brown (3.3 per cent) is better than for high-geared Green (0 per cent).

We have looked at two years' results, but Figure 12.1 plots after-tax return on equity (on the vertical axis) against any rate of before-tax return on capital employed (on the horizontal

Table 12.1 Brown and Green: return on equity in years 1 and 2 (£'000)

	Year 1		Year 2	
	Brown	Green	Brown	Green
Profit before interest & tax	3,000	3,000	500	500
Debt interest @ 10%	100	500	100	500
Profit before tax	2,900	2,500	400	0
Tax @ 25%	725	625	100	0
Profit after tax	2,175	1,875	300	0
Return on equity (%)	24.2	37.5	3.3	0
Interest cover (times)	30	6	5	1

axis). The after-tax return on equity is the same for both companies at $7\frac{1}{2}$ per cent. This is what we would expect: the 10 per cent rate of debt interest, less the tax rate of 25 per cent.

Gearing and WACC

Debt is cheaper than equity partly because it is lower-risk to the investor and partly because interest payments (unlike ordinary dividends) are normally allowed as expenses

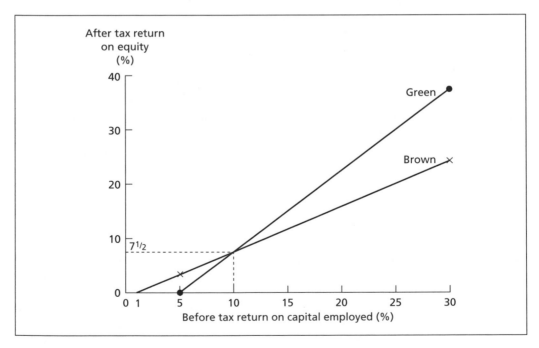

Figure 12.1 The effect of financial gearing

Table 12.2 WACC as gearing increases, under two assumptions

Debt ratio $(d/(d+e))$	0	20%	40%	60%	80%
(a) Costs of debt and equity stay the same					
Debt (cost 5%)	0.0	1.0	2.0	3.0	4.0
Equity (cost 13%)	13.0	10.4	7.8	5.2	2.6
WACC	**13.0**	**11.4**	**9.8**	**8.2**	**6.6**
(b) Costs of debt and equity increase as gearing rises					
Cost of debt	5.0	5.5	6.0	8.0	11.0
Cost of equity	13.0	13.5	14.0	16.0	19.0
Debt	0.0	1.1	2.4	4.8	8.8
Equity	13.0	10.8	8.4	6.4	3.8
WACC	**13.0**	**11.9**	**10.8**	**11.2**	**12.6**

for tax purposes. It might seem, therefore, that increasing the proportion of debt in a company's capital structure would be bound to reduce its overall weighted average cost of capital (WACC). If so, it would be best to have nearly all 'cheap' debt and very little 'expensive' equity capital. But this is not how the business world works.

There comes a time when the extra risks to a company of taking on more debt will increase the marginal cost of both debt and equity. (This is the indirect cost of debt mentioned earlier.) At some point the *average* cost of capital will actually start to increase and the firm's market value will begin to fall. Table 12.2 sets out an example.

The top part of Table 12.2 shows how WACC would change as the debt ratio increases if the cost of debt (5 per cent) and the cost of equity (13 per cent) were each to stay the same whatever the level of gearing. In that case, WACC would continue to fall across the whole range of possible gearing. The lower part of the table shows how WACC would change if the marginal costs both of debt and of equity started to rise as the debt ratio increases. The effect is, using hypothetical numbers, that when gearing rises beyond about 40 per cent, WACC actually starts *increasing*.

The traditional view of gearing is that there is an optimal range of **capital structure**. Over a wide range of moderate gearing, the overall average cost of capital is almost flat. Thus the WACC – and the firm's market value – is not very sensitive to small changes in gearing within that range. Outside the range, however, the company may have 'too much' debt or 'too little'. It can then increase its overall market value (debt plus equity capital) by adjusting its financial gearing (see below) and moving towards the optimal range.

Figure 12.2 shows this traditional view, both in terms of a U-shaped weighted average cost of capital and in terms of an inverted-U showing the firm's market value.

At what level of gearing is there 'too much' debt? It would vary for different industries. A company with high business risk (such as a car manufacturer) might not be able to bear much financial risk (gearing) on top; whereas a 'safe' company with low business

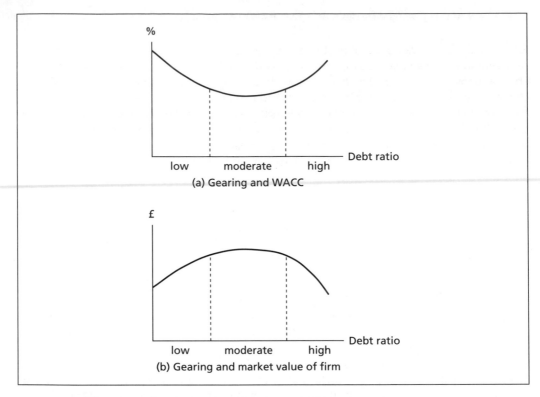

Figure 12.2 The effect of gearing on (a) WACC and (b) market value

risk (such as a utility) might be able to take on quite high levels of gearing without increasing WACC.

Another factor affecting the firm's market value may be the possible costs of **financial distress**. This includes liquidation costs, losses due to having to sell assets urgently at 'distress prices', diversion of management time, uncertainty about the firm's future affecting customers, employees, suppliers, and so on. As gearing rises, and the likelihood of financial distress increases, so the market value of the firm may fall to reflect this. It seems likely that the amounts involved may be fairly small as a rule.

If companies can borrow quite a lot before their WACC starts to rise, it may not make sense, from the shareholders' point of view, for firms to aim for the very highest credit rating.

12.2. Debt versus equity

Risk and return

Borrowing is normally cheaper after-tax than equity capital; but the risk to the borrowing company is higher. How then can firms choose between debt and equity?

Example 12.2

Rutherfords Ltd's current level of profit before interest and tax (PBIT) is £20 million a year; current debt interest payable is £3 million a year; and 30 million ordinary shares are outstanding. The company now needs £30 million of new capital to finance investment projects which are expected to increase profits (before interest and tax) by £5 million a year.

The choice is between (a) issuing 6 million ordinary shares at 500p net (compared with the current market price of 560p per share), or borrowing £30 million ten-year debentures at 8 per cent a year interest. On what basis should the company choose?

As a start, we can calculate what earnings per share (EPS) would amount to under each alternative. Table 12.3 shows that if PBIT really does increase by £5 million, the new EPS would rise to 42.8p if Rutherfords were to issue 6 million ordinary shares, and to 45.7p if the company borrows £30 million.

We can also see what is the 'cross-over' PBIT level (£x) at which EPS (in the first year) would be the same under the two methods of finance. For Rutherfords, simple algebra shows that the cross-over point comes at a PBIT level of £17.4 million:

$$\text{(debt)} \quad \frac{70\%(x - 5.4)}{30} = \frac{70\%(x - 3.0)}{36} \quad \text{(equity)}$$

$$36(x - 5.4) = 30(x - 3.0)$$

$$6x - 32.4 = 5x - 15.0$$

$$x = 17.4$$

Figure 12.3 shows that above the cross-over level of PBIT of £17.4 million, EPS will be higher with debt (due to the effect of gearing); whereas below it EPS will be higher with the equity issue.

It is also worth noticing at what PBIT level in each case EPS is zero. £5.4 million for debt and £3.0 million for equity. These, of course, are the respective amounts of debt interest payable. Until PBIT exceeds that level, EPS will be negative.

We know that by definition: MV = EPS × P/E. In words: the market price per share equals earnings per share multiplied by the price/earnings ratio. That helps us to see that we are not entitled to assume that the market value of each ordinary share need be higher

Table 12.3 Rutherfords Ltd. earnings per share calculations

£ million	Now	Increased capital		Break-even level	
		Equity	Debt	Equity	Debt
PBIT	20.0	25.0	25.0	17.4	17.4
Debt interest	3.0	3.0	5.4	3.0	5.4
Profit before tax	17.0	22.0	19.6	14.4	12.0
Tax @ 30%	5.1	6.6	5.88	4.32	3.6
Profit after tax	11.9	15.4	13.72	10.08	8.4
Ordinary shares (m)	30	36	30	36	30
EPS (pence)	**39.7**	**42.8**	**45.7**	**28.0**	**28.0**

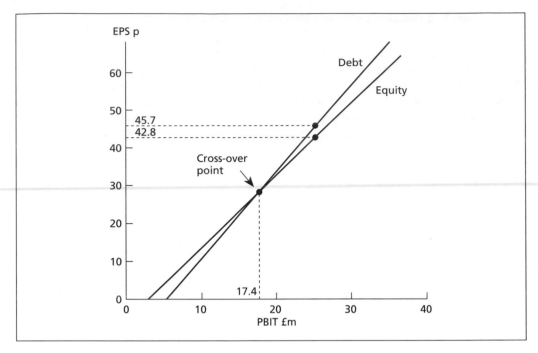

Figure 12.3 Rutherfords Ltd. EPS cross-over chart

if Rutherfords goes for debt, merely because the EPS would (probably) be higher. That would imply the *same* price/earnings multiple if the company borrows as if it issues new equity shares. But debt, being riskier for the company, might result in a lower price/earnings multiple than the equity issue. Hence it is possible for the financing alternative which produces a lower EPS actually to result in a higher market price per share.

Just how risky is it for Rutherfords to borrow another £30 million? It would increase the debt ratio from about 33 per cent to about 48 per cent (based on market values); and it would reduce interest cover from 6.7 times to 3.2 times. In both respects that would seem to be about the maximum comfortable level of debt. (You may wish to check where these numbers come from.)

The main problem, however, is not to calculate the numbers on certain assumptions. It is using commercial judgement to balance risks and returns. For example, how likely is PBIT in future to fall below the cross-over level of £17.4 million? How much would it matter if that did happen on occasion? What might be the impact of future inflation? What effect, in this case, might the increased risk from higher borrowing have on the price/earnings multiple (which is currently about 14)?

The pecking order theory

Another approach is the **pecking order** theory. According to this view, companies do not have any 'optimum' or 'target' debt ratio in mind. Instead, when they need money to

Table 12.4 Managers and shareholders under the pecking order theory

	Diversified shareholders	Managers
Order of preference:		
First	Debt	Retained profits
Second	Retained profits	Debt
Third	New issue of equity	New issue of equity

invest in profitable projects, managers prefer retained earnings to debt and debt to new issues of equity.

Table 12.4 suggests that shareholders, in contrast, might prefer debt to retained earnings as a rule. The implication is that often shareholders might prefer a company to have a higher debt ratio than managers are comfortable with. Under company law, though, shareholders cannot vote to increase dividends (and hence reduce retentions).

This may explain why companies in the same industry (with, presumably, similar business risks) may often end up with very different debt ratios. It may simply be happenstance. And the pecking order theory is probably not really inconsistent with the 'traditional' view of capital structure in the last section. Both views conclude that, over a wide range of moderate gearing, capital structure, or fine-tuning it, is really not an important issue.

Other relevant factors

Choosing about long-term finance is by no means solely a matter of numbers (many of which one can only guess). Other aspects of long-term finance may be of paramount importance.

Term

The choice between short-term and long-term borrowing depends mainly on comparing the relative costs and risks. To avoid uncertainty, a firm might try to 'match' the period of its borrowing to the period for which it needed the money. Thus it would finance long-term needs (say for a new plant expected to last for fifteen years) by long-term money (either long-term debt or equity), and short-term needs (say to finance high seasonal raw material stocks) by short-term sources. As a rule one might expect longer-term money to have a somewhat higher cost (see Chapter 2). Of course equity is *very* long-term money.

But a company may not be sure how much money it requires, nor for how long. Estimates of the amount and timing of capital project cash flows can be subject to very wide margins of error. It may often make sense to think of a company's needs as consisting of a long-term 'base load' which it can forecast with fair certainty, and a varying balance of short-term needs, depending on the nature of the business (see Figure 4.2).

Control

For **small and medium-sized enterprises**, the question of control of the equity capital is often critical. The controlling shareholders are often members of one or two families. They probably have limited surplus funds outside the business. Hence they may not wish their company to make a rights issue of new ordinary shares, since it would dilute their own equity interests and could mean them losing control.

'Control' may also refer to borrowing arrangements involving covenants or other restrictions (see Chapter 9) which owner/managers may dislike, especially if the restrictions become higher as the level of gearing gets higher. As a result, some companies may prefer to limit their rate of expansion to that which they can finance out of retained profits, even if that may mean shareholders foregoing larger potential profits from more aggressive financing.

Flexibility

Even in larger companies (where no small group of shareholders may own a major stake in the equity capital of UK companies, though it would often be otherwise in some other countries, such as Germany), managers will usually value flexibility – keeping their options open (see also Chapter 8). Thus they may not choose to borrow all the way up to some supposed 'optimum' level of gearing if that would rule out more borrowing for a number of years, or if it would make debt too expensive in time of crisis. Managers like to leave themselves elbow room to allow for the unexpected or even the unforeseeable. Even when the outlook seems fine, they often worry about rainy days ahead.

Making a loss, of course, reduces a company's total retained profits and thus the amount of its balance sheet equity. Paying ordinary dividends has the same result. A seemingly adequate level of gearing can soon become uncomfortably high through one or two years' losses, combined with further borrowing to finance current operations. So it is perhaps not surprising if managers sometimes seem to the outside observer to be rather cautious. In practice, some company managements (both of large and of smaller firms) seem on occasion to prefer lower risks to themselves rather than higher returns for diversified shareholders. In other words, they prefer managers (themselves) to sleep well rather than shareholders to eat well!

Adjusting capital structure

How a company invests funds determines its business risk; how it finances them determines its financial risk. A company can adjust its financial risk (gearing) by changing the proportions of debt and equity in its capital structure, as Figure 12.4 shows.

Equity (a) By retaining profits or paying out dividends;
(b) By issuing new shares or buying back existing ones in issue.
Debt By borrowing money or repaying existing debt.
Both By converting debt into equity.

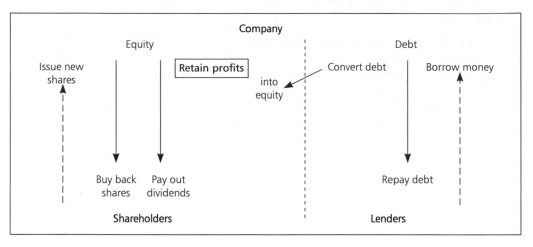

Figure 12.4 Events that change capital structure

In addition to the above, which all involve real cash flows (except the conversion of debt into equity), a UK company can change its balance sheet capital structure by revaluing fixed assets upwards. This has the effect of reducing gearing, as it increases the book amount of equity (by increasing the 'revaluation reserve'). Many countries, such as the US and Germany, do not permit this — a point to remember if trying to compare the accounts of companies in different countries.

12.3. Dividend policy

Do dividends matter?

Ordinary dividends are cash payments by a company to its shareholders out of after-tax profits. In a 'perfect' capital market, with no taxes or **transaction costs**, dividend policy should not affect shareholders' wealth. Dividends would transfer cash to shareholders, but the market value of the shares would precisely reflect any retained profits and dividend policy would not convey any information about future prospects. Any shareholders who wanted more cash than a company chose to pay in dividends could simply sell some of their shares, in effect declaring their own dividends.

Example 12.3

To begin with, Jane Smith owned 25 per cent of the shares in two identical companies, Adam plc and Bede plc. Adam paid out all its profits each year in dividends, while Bede retained all its profits to reinvest. (Thus the companies do not remain identical; but we ignore this for the sake of the example.) Smith kept her 25 per cent shareholding in Adam, which (with no retained profits) remained the same size. Each year Smith sold enough shares in Bede,

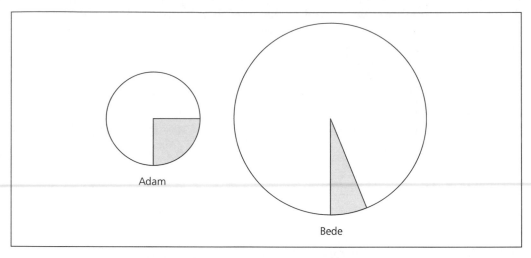

Figure 12.5 Smith's shareholdings in Adam and Bede after some years

which (by retaining all its profits) was growing larger, to provide the same amount of cash as Adam's dividends.

As Figure 12.5 shows, after some years Bede was much larger than Adam, but Smith's reducing share in Bede was worth exactly the same as her constant 25 per cent share in Adam. Since Smith had also received the same amount of cash from her shareholding (either in dividends or from the sale of some shares), the companies' different dividend policies had (in theory) had exactly the same effect on Smith's wealth. (In this presumed perfect market there were no taxes or transaction costs.)

In the real world the tax position of different shareholders can vary, from pension funds to higher-rate taxpayers. So it can be hard for companies to tell what dividend policy might be best for 'shareholders as a whole'. Transaction costs, too, matter in practice. A company which paid out 'too much' dividend one year would find it expensive to make a rights issue (a negative dividend!) the next year to compensate. (Lucas Industries plc used to do this regularly: over the 25 years 1969–94 it made four rights issues which, after allowing for inflation, almost exactly equalled the total real net dividends it had paid over the period!)

Taxes on shareholders' returns

A company aiming to maximize shareholders' wealth may need to allow for income tax on dividends and capital gains tax on any profit when shares are sold. For individual shareholders the marginal tax rate on dividends may vary from 10 per cent up to 40 per cent (on taxable income over £28,000 a year). Pension funds and insurance companies are liable only to the 10 per cent income tax on dividends.

Taxable capital gains bear the same marginal tax rate as dividend income as a rule, but shareholders may still prefer capital gains to dividends. There is a complex tapering arrangement which can reduce the taxable amount of capital gains after shares have been held for a number of years. And £7,100 of capital gains each year are exempt from tax. Moreover there is some delay in incurring capital gains tax, since it is payable only on realized gains not as gains accrue.

Choosing a policy

Most listed UK companies pay an interim and a larger final dividend each year. This contrasts with the American practice of equal quarterly dividends. At annual general meetings, shareholders may vote to reduce a proposed final dividend (though they rarely do), but cannot increase it. Thus they can increase but not reduce the amount of retained profits for a period. Shareholders might want larger dividends to prevent managers frittering away retained profits on unsuitable projects.

Most companies seem to decide on a dividend first, basing the current year's dividend on last year's payout. Dividends normally increase somewhat from year to year, partly to keep pace with inflation and also to reflect increased real earnings. Any profits left over (retained) are then available for investment. A different approach would be first to choose how much to invest, and how to finance it, and then to treat dividends as the residual. Dividends normally seem to follow a step-like pattern rather than varying in line with earnings (see Figure 12.6). Thus the absolute money amount of the dividend slightly increases each year, rather than the payout being a constant proportion of earnings.

The accounting standard FRS 3 requires companies to include in profits as '**exceptional**' items which accounts formerly excluded as '**extraordinary**'. As a result, reported earnings are now more likely to fluctuate from year to year. Where companies treat dividends almost as fixed amounts, retained profits can fluctuate more sharply even than

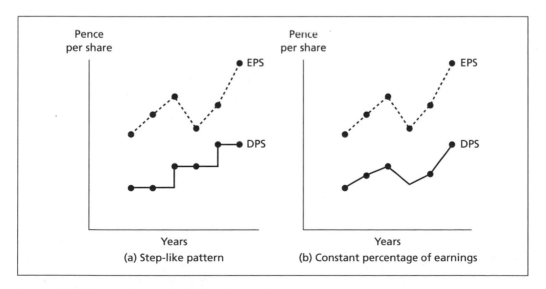

Figure 12.6 Two patterns of dividend payout

earnings. Indeed part of the function of post-FRS 3 dividend policy could be to provide stability for shareholders. Retained profits for a period will be negative where there are losses or where dividends exceed profits. But companies need *cumulative* retained profits in order legally to distribute dividends to shareholders.

If retained profits represent a volatile source of funds, companies could vary their investment spending. Or they could finance *all* worthwhile projects by borrowing or issuing more equity capital. Most companies are reluctant either to increase gearing or to issue more equity shares. They may therefore prefer to restrict regular dividends to a level where they can expect to finance all worthwhile investment projects out of retained profits (plus a pro rata increase in borrowing to maintain gearing). They might cover varying investment needs by surplus cash or by short-term changes in gearing.

Paying dividends reduces shareholders' funds, hence increases gearing. Indeed loan covenants may restrict maximum dividends payable in order not to let gearing increase too much. In principle a company which lacks cash could borrow to finance dividends, which would increase gearing even more (as debt replaced equity).

One can value shares on the basis of future dividends (Chapter 11), but in the end it is earnings that matter. Many companies try to keep their dividend payout ratio (or its reciprocal, the **dividend cover**) fairly constant. Dividends per share will then grow at much the same rate as earnings. (Indeed the so-called dividend growth model makes precisely this assumption.) If profits fluctuate from year to year, companies may have a dividend payout ratio target as an average over several years.

A loss-making company might not choose to omit or even reduce its dividend in a bad year. For managements can use dividend policy to communicate with shareholders about future prospects. (Managers normally know more than shareholders about their company's future prospects: this is called 'information asymmetry'.) A loss-making company might maintain its dividend as a **signal** that earnings would soon recover. In contrast, cutting the dividend could signify that a decline in earnings might take some time to reverse. For a similar reason managers may not want to increase dividends too much in a good year if that risks having to reduce dividends again later.

A company should tell shareholders clearly what its dividend policy actually *is* (and *why*) and stick to it. Any policy may suit some shareholders better than others from the point of view of tax. But shareholders can satisfy their own preferred habitat in this respect. Changing the dividend policy without warning might both disappoint shareholders who relied on the old policy and create needless uncertainty about the future.

In deciding on dividend policy directors should focus on the most important question: who can use the money best, company or shareholders? Thus 'mature' companies with few investment opportunities may tend to pay out a high proportion of their after-tax profits in dividends; while 'growth' companies with many good projects to invest in may prefer a much lower payout ratio.

Share buy-backs

Since 1982 UK companies have been able to buy back their own fully-paid ordinary shares. Like dividend payments, share buy-backs have the effect of reducing equity and increasing gearing. They also, of course, reduce the size of the company. Possible reasons for a company buying back its own shares include the following:

1. Buying out the estates of deceased shareholders.
2. Buying back employee scheme shares when the employee leaves.
3. Buying out dissident shareholders.
4. Offering investors an option to sell their shares back after a time.
5. Reducing capital, possibly to increase financial gearing.
6. Supporting the market for the shares (keeping the share price high).
7. Returning to shareholders funds which the company cannot use profitably.
8. Converting public companies back into private ones.

Only the last four reasons would be likely to apply to public companies. For private companies, the purchase price will normally be subject to capital gains tax in share-holders' hands, rather than income tax.

Section 162 of the Companies Act 1985 contains the legal rules. Companies which buy back their own shares must *cancel* them, not hold them 'in treasury' available for reissue, as in the United States. The company's Articles must authorize purchases of their own shares on the market; and an ordinary resolution must specify the maximum number of shares and a date within eighteen months when the power to purchase will expire.

In order to maintain a company's capital, the purchase monies must normally come either from distributable profits or from the proceeds of a fresh issue of shares for the purpose. Also the company must transfer certain amounts to a capital redemption reserve. But where its Articles expressly permit it, a private company may purchase its own shares out of capital.

Special dividends are somewhat similar to share buy-backs in many of their effects; but the tax consequences are different.

12.4. The corporate life cycle

This section explores the relationship between business risk and financial risk over a firm's life cycle. It also discusses changes in debt policy (capital structure) and in dividend policy over time. The approach is adapted from K.R. Ward, *Corporate Financial Strategy* (Butterworth-Heinemann, 1993).

Start-up

Most business start-ups involve high risk. There may be difficult technical problems to overcome. Even if the product 'works', can the firm make it for a low enough cost? And will enough customers want to buy it? Such high *business* risks suggest that it would be a mistake to pile much (if any) *financial* risk on top. Indeed most start-ups should probably finance themselves entirely with equity capital and have no interest-bearing debt at all.

In any event debt might be expensive, because it would carry a high-risk premium. Most new businesses make no taxable profit in the first year or two, implying they would have to pay any debt interest – with no tax shield – gross of tax. And since a start-up business probably has few tangible assets with much resale value if anything goes wrong, the costs of financial distress could be very high. Moreover, the high risk of complete failure means that a start-up business is quite likely to generate no net cash inflow from trading. In which case any debt at all, however little, could almost at once lead to severe financial distress.

Investors should not mind whether their returns come by way of dividends or capital gains. So it normally makes sense for a start-up business to pay no dividends in the first few years. (New companies may anyway often lack the post-tax profits legally needed to permit the payment of dividends.) Such a firm will probably have negative cash flows to begin with. Given a policy of zero borrowing, it might actually need to raise more equity capital to replace any cash dividends it did pay. And since transaction costs are mostly fixed, raising small amounts of equity capital is very expensive.

Growth

If a start-up business gets over the first hurdle and survives, the business risk will decline. But a successful new business will often be growing fast and thirsty for cash. It will probably still be best to keep debt low, and to proceed to raise new equity capital in one of three ways: retention of most or all of the profits; a rights issue to existing shareholders; or a launch of the business to the public. The third method will also enable the founding venture capitalists to realize some or all of their investment.

Heavy discretionary investment in technical research and in promoting the new product may restrict profits at this stage. In any event, capital allowances on investment in fixed assets (perhaps needed to expand production) may keep *taxable* profits very low or negative. Assuming that substantial business risks still remain, and possibly still lacking a tax shield on any debt interest, borrowing at this stage may continue to be expensive. But the costs of financial distress should be declining from their previous very high levels, as the business starts to acquire tangible fixed assets with some definite resale value.

Needing to finance rapid growth, the most obvious source of funds is internally generated cash. This implies that dividends should still be zero. But if the company is thinking of going public in the near future, it may wish to start paying a nominal dividend to build up a track record.

Maturity

Once the company reaches maturity, with the rapid growth period over, profits should become fairly steady. Dividends can now increase and represent a sizeable proportion of profits. Although the firm may need to replace existing fixed assets, in the absence of rapid inflation it should be able to do so mainly out of provisions for depreciation.

With the company now well established, business risk should be fairly low, enabling it to substitute debt for equity. This may even mean borrowing to increase dividend payments – in order to adjust the capital structure more quickly. (If there were no real growth, in principle the firm should be able to pay out all real profits in dividends.)

The potential conflict between managers and shareholders will be apparent. High dividends and fairly high debt ratios at this stage may help to maximize shareholders' wealth. But managers may be tempted to retain too much profit and use some of the funds to diversify in order to reduce their own personal risk. But shareholders would probably prefer to diversify themselves by holding a portfolio of different shares. It is not easy in practice for shareholders to put pressure on managers to increase the level of dividend payout (or indeed the debt ratio).

Decline

In the declining phase, managers should prolong the company's life as long as it can generate positive cash flows that exceed a reasonable rate of return on the net realizable value of the assets. Whether or not to replace fixed assets now becomes a genuine question, whereas earlier the main question may have been *when* to replace them (and with what modifications).

Internal cash flows will probably exceed reported profits, since depreciation expense may well exceed new investment in replacement fixed assets. (Thus the **net book value** of fixed assets will be falling.) Dividends paid may even exceed reported profits, thus running down the cumulative balance of profit retained in earlier years. (An offsetting influence may be the unwinding of deferred tax provisions from earlier years. They may have reduced reported profits in earlier years, but only now result in cash outflows.)

Levels of debt, too, should be high at this stage, since lenders may be able to assess accurately the realizable value of any assets against which they are lending. The main strategic problem towards the end of the company's life may be not with shareholders or lenders, but with the managers themselves. For managers are often reluctant to announce simply, 'Our work is done', and then retire gracefully!

Problems

Problem 12.1.

Laurel and Hardy.
Laurel plc and Hardy plc are similar companies except for their financial gearing. Each company's capital employed (debt plus equity) is £120 million. Laurel's debt ratio (debt/capital employed) is 15 per cent, Hardy's 60 per cent. The rate of debt interest is 10 per cent a year (before tax). The rate of corporation tax is 30 per cent. In Year 1, the Return on Capital Employed for each company is 25 per cent; in Year 2 it is only 7.5 per cent.

Required: Calculate the Return on Equity and the interest cover for Laurel and Hardy for Year 1 and Year 2.

At what level of Return on Capital Employed will the Return on Equity for the two companies be the same?

Problem 12.2.

Borg and Laver.
Borg plc and Laver plc, two companies in the same industry, are of similar size but have different levels of gearing. In Year 1 each company made an operating profit of £40 million, in Year 2 each company made £150 million. Each company has capital employed of £1,000 million (with 2,000 million ordinary shares in issue). Borg has a debt ratio of 5 per cent, Laver of 40 per cent. In each case the rate of debt interest is 15 per cent a year. Assume a corporation tax rate of 40 per cent.

Required: For each company in each year, calculate:

a. after-tax Return on Equity
b. earnings per share
c. interest cover
d. At what level of Return on Capital Employed will each company have the same rate of Return on Equity?

Problem 12.3.

Travis plc.
Travis plc has an operating profit of £150 million. Currently debt interest payable is £20 million a year, and there are 600 million ordinary shares in issue.

Travis is planning to raise an extra £300 million of capital to finance expansion, which is expected to increase operating profit by £50 million a year. Two alternatives are being considered:

a. Issue 120 million new ordinary shares @ 250p each (compared with the current market price of 300p); or
b. Borrow £300 million @ 12 per cent a year interest.

Required: For each alternative calculate earnings per share and interest cover. At what level of operating profit would earnings per share be the same under the alternative financing proposals?

Problem 12.4.

Andover Equipment plc.
Andover Equipment plc needs to raise £30 million of new capital to finance a major expansion which is expected to increase operating profit by £6.0 million a year. The company currently has 200 million ordinary shares in issue, and the current market price is 180p each. The balance sheet shows total debt of £90 million (with an average interest rate of 10 per cent a year) and shareholders' funds of £180 million.

Andover is considering two alternative ways to raise the new money. One is a 1 for 10 rights issue @ 150p, the other is to borrow £30 million @ 8 per cent a year for 10 years. (Ignore transaction costs.)

Annual operating profit (PBIT) is currently £54 million. Assume a tax rate of 30 per cent on profits.

Required:

a. Calculate the PBIT level at which earnings per share under the two financing alternatives will be the same.
b. Compare earnings per share (i) now, and (ii) expected after expansion under each of the financing alternatives.
c. Calculate interest cover (i) now, and (ii) expected after expansion under each of the financing alternatives.
d. Calculate debt ratio (i) now, and (ii) under each of the financing alternatives.

CHAPTER 13

Restructuring

13.1. Form of business

Sole trading

A 'sole trader' is simply a person in business on his or her own account. He or she might be a dentist, a taxi driver, a hairdresser or a management consultant.

Setting oneself up as a sole trader could hardly be simpler: there is almost no formality, so the process is very cheap. On the other hand, there is no distinction between personal assets and business assets; and it is the same with liabilities. Hence a sole trader is personally liable for all business debts without limit.

The death of a sole trader brings the business to an end; though no doubt an heir could try to carry on the same business under a different sole trading arrangement.

Any profits are taxed as personal income; though in practice there can be questions whether certain expenses are personal or business-related. The income tax rules require expenses to be 'wholly and exclusively' for the purposes of the business.

The sole trader is the sole owner; so his or her own wealth will limit the extent of the business, in addition to what others can be persuaded to lend the business. But others cannot put equity capital in and become joint owners – that would make them partners.

Partnerships

A partnership, like a sole trader, is a personal business arrangement – but between more than one person. Partnerships are common forms of business, either in small trading enterprises or in certain professions such as medicine and law. As with sole traders, each ordinary partner is personally liable without limit for all the firm's debts. (There may be exceptions for so-called 'limited' partners, but these are fairly unusual.)

Setting up a partnership is somewhat more complicated than starting up as a sole trader, since it involves more than one person. It is common – and desirable – to have a formal written agreement, though this is not essential. An oral agreement will suffice. Among other things, the partnership agreement will establish the basis for subscribing capital and for sharing profits and losses. 'Junior' partners may get a fixed money salary, perhaps plus a small share of any remaining profits, while the senior partners get a much larger share of profits.

The individual partners are liable to personal income tax on their share of any taxable profits, regardless of whether they have drawn any money out of the business or not. (They normally need to draw out enough to pay their personal tax bills.)

Absolute trust is essential for a partnership, since any partner can legally bind all his fellow-partners, whether or not they have specifically agreed to something in advance. As with a sole trader, death of any partner dissolves the firm; but the surviving partners can immediately set up a new firm (possibly under the same name) if they wish. In fact in firms with several partners there may be a continual coming of new partners and retiring of old ones, even though the business continues as recognizably the same to the outside world. (Death of a *limited* partner does not terminate a partnership.)

The unlimited nature of every partner's financial liability makes it difficult to raise large sums of capital, since the entire fortune of any wealthy partner would be at risk.

Limited companies

A limited company is formed by two documents: its Memorandum, which sets out its constitution (its name, objects, registered office and authorized share capital), and its Articles, which set out rules concerning election of directors, rights of shareholders, procedures for meetings, etc.

A limited company in law is a separate person which can perform legally binding acts in its own right, such as owning property, suing people, and so on. As a separate legal entity, a company's existence does not come to an end merely because of the death of one of its shareholders (there must be more than one). On a shareholder's death, his or her estate will transfer his or her shares to some other person, either by legacy or when the shares are sold.

There are two kinds of limited company: private and public. *Private* limited companies ('Ltd.') can have a maximum of fifty shareholders, though many have fewer than half a dozen. This arrangement may well suit a family business, which may want to grow beyond the size easily possible for a sole trader or partnership. At the same time, it is easy for a single family to retain control. Most limited companies are private and very small.

Public limited companies ('plc') have no limits on the number of shareholders. The stock exchange lists (quotes) their shares, and shareholders can easily transfer them to other people without the approval (or even the knowledge) of those running the business. (Many shareholdings nowadays are in 'nominee names', which means that as a rule nobody can tell the name of the ultimate beneficial owner.) Public limited companies can raise extra capital from members of the public if they wish, by issuing a prospectus, which is subject to fairly strict rules.

In the case of the largest companies, the household names (often household acronyms these days!), the directors probably own only a tiny fraction of the total number of shares. Hence the emphasis in this book on possible conflicts between managers and shareholders with respect to dividend policy, capital structure, etc.

The invention of limited companies about 150 years ago helped the UK become the world's leading commercial country. The great advantage of limited companies as a form of business was to encourage wealthy people to invest some of their resources in risky new enterprises without being liable (as they would be in a partnership) to the extent of their entire fortune. They could *limit* the maximum amount they could possibly lose in a venture.

Limited companies are subject to corporation tax on profits; and any dividends they pay to shareholders out of after-tax profits may be subject also to some personal income tax. On the other hand, smaller companies can pay their owner–managers a salary which will normally be a tax-deductible expense in computing the company's taxable profits.

Small private limited companies (like sole traders and partnerships) are not required to have a formal audit of their accounts. There are current proposals to raise the annual turnover limit for this exemption (from the Companies Act) from £350,000 up to £4.2 million. This may seem odd: surely audits are *useful* for most firms, among other things to encourage suppliers to extend credit and to reassure the Inland Revenue (who use accounts as the basis for taxing profits)? But the exemption simply means that those who don't think an audit is worthwhile don't need to have one. (General Motors had sales of over $500 million in 1919 when Alfred Sloan suggested it was time for the company to have an annual audit!)

13.2. Change of ownership

Privatization

During the fifteen years between 1981 and 1995 the British government privatized most of the state-owned and state-controlled 'nationalized industries', the largest being: coal, electricity, gas, rail, telecommunications and water. (British Petroleum was an example of a company in which the government held a significant shareholding but almost no control.) This was a major change, involving industries employing about two million workers and yielding sales proceeds of about £100 billion. Of the 100 largest UK companies in 1999, nearly one quarter had been in the state sector twenty years earlier.

The process of privatization involved splitting industries up (electricity generation and the railways were the most contentious in this respect); reforming some capital structures; strengthening boards of directors; and marketing the shares to the public. In some cases the government sold its shares in two or three separate tranches; but it turned out that the capital markets were able to absorb even very large numbers of shares with few problems. Another important aspect was setting up new systems of regulation – which, indeed, are still evolving years later.

The reasons for privatization were not entirely clear-cut and they may have varied somewhat over time. At least six different reasons can be identified:

1. to provide some competition instead of a government monopoly, and thus to improve the quality of service to customers;

2. to reduce the inefficiencies of these huge monopolies (which politicians could not resist meddling in), and thus to end the need for taxpayers to finance their very large losses ('losseering');
3. to de-politicize an important part of British industry for which industrial relations had long been a political struggle between the workers and the government of the day;
4. to end the need for governments to finance capital investment (which they find difficult, as political time-horizons tend to be short-term for electoral reasons);
5. to increase the number of private shareholders (though this was probably not an efficient way for small investors to establish a portfolio); and
6. to raise money for the government.

The government did face some dilemmas. Selling the industries as monopolies would probably have yielded larger proceeds for the 'owner' (though this was never the main purpose). The government generally avoided this temptation, with the significant exception of gas. In order to get a wide spread of small shareholders and make the issues a success, most of the businesses were sold too cheap (which became even more evident with hindsight). Further, if the purpose was to allow competition, the government needed to allow some flexibility in each industry's post-privatization structure. After all, an important argument in favour of competition is that nobody can tell in advance precisely *what* its outcome will be! (Hayek's 'competition as a discovery procedure'.) Hardly anyone realized in advance what huge savings would turn out to be possible in many state industries.

It may be worth briefly reviewing why industries were ever nationalized in the first place. An official study around 1980 listed six purposes of nationalization, which it said 'have not altered significantly over the last 50 years':

1. to promote greater efficiency (which may now sound ironic);
2. lack of private risk capital. The emphasis should be on the *riskiness* not on the *amount* of investment capital needed. Governments cannot create resources out of nothing: they can borrow, or tax, or have state industries charge monopoly prices. But in each case lenders, taxpayers and consumers – who actually provide the funds – could do so also for private enterprise. But governments may sometimes be willing and able to undertake some risks which a commercial business might refuse.
3. to regulate certain natural monopolies. This remains on the agenda.
4. to assist national economic planning. This is now out of fashion.
5. to obtain employees' legitimate rights. It is not clear what this means, nor why legal arrangements in the market system could not achieve as much.
6. to achieve the most equitable distribution of income. This political objective probably does not justify state ownership and control of industries. (If desired, there are other ways to achieve the aim.)

To these 'official' reasons, three more may be added:

7. for defence or security reasons;
8. to provide a social service, as with subsidizing railways – which still occurs;

9. to rescue 'lame ducks', such as Rolls Royce or British Steel. Also now out of fashion (though the British government has just offered BMW £150 million to invest heavily in its Longbridge plant).

In many countries important services, such as education, health and pensions, are still more or less state monopolies. The welfare state remains a sensitive topic; but at least one can now openly discuss whether it might be possible to involve free markets more. We must distinguish between taxpayers to some extent collectively *financing* a service as opposed to government actually *providing* it.

Management buy-outs

A holding company or group may wish to dispose of a business for one or more of the reasons for selling listed in Table 7.2 earlier. In particular, where a business appears to be under-performing or no longer fits in with the group's core focus, **management buy-outs** may be attractive. Senior managers themselves may initiate the process if they believe they could improve the business if given a free hand.

Precise details can vary widely. In general, a group of senior managers puts up an amount of equity capital, and venture capitalists and other lenders provide the bulk of the funds required, in the form of equity or debt or **mezzanine finance** (ranking before equity but after debt).

Because the new company is often highly geared, it is likely to be very risky. (MBOs are also sometimes called **leveraged buy-outs [LBOs]**.) Needing most of the cash flow to service the high debt puts pressure on the management team to perform. (This probably involves 'working smarter' rather than 'working harder'.) If things work out, the managers stand to make large capital gains from their equity stake. While the total amount of equity capital the managers put up may not be a large proportion of the total finance needed, for incentive purposes what matters is whether the amount each manager subscribes represents a significant proportion of his or her own personal wealth. (Notice that managers here bear significant downside risk – they stand to lose a lot if things go wrong – in contrast with most executive share option schemes where for the managers concerned there is only an upside.)

There is an obvious moral hazard for managers of a subsidiary business. While working for a larger group, they may be tempted to do less than their best, or provide less than complete and accurate information, in order to benefit themselves later by buying their controlling equity shares cheap. The danger may be even stronger if a management team plans to buy out the whole group (from its ultimate shareholders), rather than just a part of it (from a presumably knowledgeable group board of directors).

A variant of a management buy-out is a 'management buy-in' (MBI), where a management team from outside an enterprise offers to buy it. Venture capitalists back the team, just as in MBOs – indeed they may *select* the team. In such cases there is likely to be no moral hazard; but outsiders will not know the business as well as existing managers. Another variant is an employee buy-out (rather than just a management buy-out), such as occurred in an unusual early privatization of the National Freight Corporation.

De-mergers and spin-offs

From time to time a group may want to sell off one of its business units. This may be because someone has offered a high price (for example, Grand Metropolitan selling Inter-Continental Hotels to a Japanese group); or to avoid the need to finance heavy future investment (for example, British Aerospace selling Rover cars to BMW); or to dispose of a loss-making business with poor prospects under existing management. In such cases, another company in the same industry might well be prepared to offer a higher price than any alternative. Some of the early privatizations were trade sales of this sort; for example, the sale of British Rail Hotels.

With a **spin-off**, the holding company doesn't *sell* a subsidiary business to anyone: but merely distributes shares in it to the existing group shareholders, on a pro rata basis. Often this is a substantial business in its own right, which thereafter has its own stock market listing. Examples include Courtaulds Textiles (Courtaulds), Vodafone (Racal Electronics), Zeneca (Imperial Chemical Industries), and British American Tobacco (BAT Industries).

De-mergers may make sense where two businesses are not closely related and enjoy few if any economies of scale. A recent example is Tarmac splitting up its Heavy Building Materials and Construction Services divisions or Tomkins splitting off its food business. Conglomerates tend to be out of fashion at the moment; so some de-mergers may now be 'undoing' mergers of twenty or so years ago. Sometimes a hostile acquirer will sell off some of the businesses newly acquired: indeed it may be the prospect of this that supports the market values of some poorly-performing conglomerates.

13.3. Financial distress

Predicting trouble

A number of studies have tried to test whether financial ratios from published accounts can predict trouble ahead. This is an ambitious quest, since the main purpose of accounts is to report on the past.

The main types of ratio deal with profitability, liquidity, gearing, cash flow and turnover. Hence among likely ratios are the following:

1. profit to assets
2. current assets to current liabilities
3. working capital to total assets
4. total liabilities to total assets
5. cash flow to total debt
6. sales to assets.

Some approaches have used a number of ratios together. Such a combined indicator is sometimes called a **Z-score**. As well as choosing which ratios to use, one must also decide what weights to attach to each. (Do the weightings change over time?)

The same value of a ratio may imply a different chance of failure in different industries (and defining an industry may not be easy). There may also be reasons why larger companies are less likely to fail than small ones, even with the same ratios.

Several questions arise:

1. How does one define 'trouble' (or 'financial distress' or 'failure')?
2. Are there more useful signs of likely failure than financial ratios? Examples might be directors resigning, delay in publishing accounts, qualified audit reports.
3. How long before 'failure' does one need notice? Is *more* than one year required?
4. If the approach works, can it be used to take corrective action in time? (In which case it no longer works!)
5. Or is the approach self-fulfilling, in that any lender seeing a poor Z-score will refuse to extend loans?
6. The signal may not mean 'lend' rather than 'don't lend'. It may merely suggest conditions to impose before lending.

Finally, if markets are 'efficient', does the share price predict trouble for listed companies as well as any other indicator? This would not help in respect of unlisted companies, which may be just the sort of companies where advance warning signals would be most useful.

Being in difficulty

Defining precisely what 'financial distress' means is not easy. In a corporate context, it is by no means synonymous with winding-up. Many companies have survived financial distress, just as many people have managed to survive personal financial problems without going bankrupt. Table 13.1 outlines major categories of financial distress.

Given that a major reason for being in financial difficulty in the first place is poor management, an obvious way to overcome the problem is to allow more capable

Table 13.1 Types of financial distress

Survival
Acquirer takes over – and keeps going
Voluntary easement by creditors
Reorganization of capital structure
Administration

Winding-up
Acquirer takes over – and closes down
Members' voluntary winding-up
Creditors' voluntary winding-up
Compulsory winding-up by Court

managers to take over. So acquiring companies may often manage to make a success of (at least parts of) a business that was in trouble. This may be as a separate division of the new owning group, or perhaps merged with an existing business unit.

Sometimes creditors will agree to voluntary concessions, agreeing either to defer due repayment dates for loans or even to accept less than is legally owing in full settlement of claims. In each case the purpose is to avoid legal costs and allow the creditor to do better than would otherwise be likely.

Part of the process of surviving financial problems may involve reorganizing the firm's capital structure. For instance, firms sometimes recognize past losses by reducing the nominal amount of equity capital. This may enable them to raise *new* equity capital on which they can pay dividends almost straight away. There are strict legal safeguards, because otherwise there is a danger of equity shareholders gaining at the expense of creditors. Or creditors may be given equity in part satisfaction of the amounts owing to them.

The Insolvency Act 1985 introduced an 'administration' procedure which aimed to keep firms alive as going concerns. The Court appoints an insolvency practitioner as 'administrator' with power to manage the company on behalf of its creditors. If the process is successful, management may revert to the company's directors as appointed by shareholders. Part of the process may involve voluntary easement by creditors or reorganization of capital structure as noted above. If unsuccessful, in the end the company may have to be wound up.

When people are short of money, they tend to cut back on spending, even on things they would like. So with companies. If cash is short, a company may not be able to afford even a profitable investment. That may merely mean deferment for a few months; but it may mean losing the opportunity for ever. It may also be tempting to skimp on necessary maintenance, if one can 'get away with it' in the short term.

Another likely consequence is diversion of management time: getting suppliers to extend longer credit than normal, negotiating with bank managers about overdrafts, purchasing some supplies in smaller quantities than usual, persuading workers to accept uncompetitive levels of pay (or spending time on replacing workers and managers who leave as a result), and so on.

When a firm is in trouble, the interests of creditors and shareholders can diverge. (In normal times their interests may not be identical, but they don't usually cause managers, on behalf of shareholders, to act badly towards creditors. In the long run that would probably not pay.)

For example, suppose a company seems unlikely to be able to repay debt maturing in the near future. In which case, the creditors would not get repaid in full and shareholders would end up with nothing. Managers (on behalf of owners) might then be tempted to undertake very risky projects (even ones with negative expected net present values). If they succeed, against the odds, the firm will survive; and if not, the shareholders will (still) get nothing – but are no worse off. In effect the owners are betting with the creditors' money.

Similarly, managers, on behalf of owners, might be unwilling to invest even in *good* projects with positive net present values. Much of the profit might go to improve the chances of creditors being paid in full, with relatively little benefit going to the owners. This may be obvious if one looks at shareholders actually putting up more capital by way of a rights issue; but the principle remains the same when it comes to dividend policy. In times of trouble, shareholders might favour maximum dividends even if that reduces the ultimate chance of the firm surviving.

Winding-up (liquidation)

Acquisitions have been called 'a civilized alternative to bankruptcy'. Certainly in a large group individual business units can be quietly closed down behind the scenes and their assets sold off with little publicity. It is obviously impossible to know how frequently this occurs; but in a changing business environment, individual products do have 'lives', which eventually must somehow come to an end. Sometimes managers who have been involved with products for many years find it almost impossible to abandon them. New acquirers can be more ruthless, lacking any sentimental attachment.

Liquidation (or winding-up) is a legal process triggered by **insolvency** (failure to pay debts due). In outline it involves:

1. The appointment of a liquidator
2. Disposing of all the assets for cash
3. Sharing out the cash proceeds among creditors and (perhaps) shareholders, in order of legal priority.

Members of a company themselves can decide to wind it up (members' voluntary liquidation). Or creditors can take steps to do so (creditors' voluntary winding-up). Or the Court may make a compulsory winding-up order. The effect of a compulsory winding-up is to remove resources from the control of managements which have made losses or mismanaged their company's finances. Company liquidations other than members' voluntary liquidations were running at 24,000 a year at their peak in 1992. The current level is about half that.

Lack of profit, of course, is not the same thing as lack of cash. Not all firms which make losses go into liquidation: the higher the proportion of equity capital in the company's capital structure, the lower the chance of that. Indeed, most start-up companies lose money at first, which comes out of the initial equity capital.

When a company goes into liquidation, its assets do not all disappear in a puff of smoke! They are sold for cash, often for much less than their book amounts in the balance sheet (though sometimes for much more). The possibility of closing down unprofitable operations is an essential part of the market system. (It was a serious 'problem' with the nationalized industries that there seemed to be no possibility of any of them going bust, however hopeless.)

There is a priority order in which liquidators distribute assets on a winding-up, outlined in Table 13.2. All countries have a similar system, though the precise details can vary.

Table 13.2 Priority of distribution on liquidation

1. Costs of liquidation
2. Creditors secured by a fixed charge on property
3. 'Preferential' creditors:
   a. one year's taxes due to government
   b. wages of employees
4. Creditors secured by a floating charge
5. Unsecured creditors
6. Preference shareholders
7. Ordinary shareholders

CHAPTER 14

Valuing companies

14.1. Discounting future cash flows

The cash flows

In principle one can value a company in just the same way that one values a capital project (see Figure 5.4). That means estimating the amount and timing of the incremental cash flows, and then discounting at a suitable discount rate.

The 'cash flows' will be the operating cash flows, together with tax effects, as well as any investments in (or disposals of) working capital or fixed assets. It is normally best, as with other capital projects, to *exclude* financing charges, such as interest payments.

Often when one is trying to value a company (C), what we really want to value is C's equity capital. This may be an individual shareholder simply trying to decide whether to buy or sell shares in C; or a potential corporate acquirer of C (or, rather, of C's equity).

If we value C as a whole (that is, debt capital plus equity capital), then in order to get to the value of the equity we shall need to deduct the value of C's debt (see Chapter 9).

The discount rate

The discount rate to use in valuing a business is a rate which reflects the risks of that business. (If we are valuing the whole business, in CAPM terms that means using the *asset* beta, or WACC, *not* the cost of equity capital alone.)

Suppose Company A is trying to value Company B with a view to acquiring it. People sometimes ask: should Company A discount Company B's expected future cash flows (a) at Company A's own cost of capital, or (b) should it use Company B's cost of capital? The answer is: to value Company B you should use Company B's cost of capital. What matters is the riskiness of the *use* of funds, not of their source.

The easiest way, using the CAPM approach, is to add a suitable risk premium to the risk-free rate of return. The risk premium should reflect the estimated riskiness of Company B, let us say with an asset beta of 1.25. Figure 14.1 shows this, resulting in a real discount rate of 12 per cent.

There is an alternative way, which comes to the same thing in the end, for Company A (which, let us assume, has an asset beta of 0.75) to value Company B. That is for Company A to *start* from its own WACC (cost of capital), and then make a

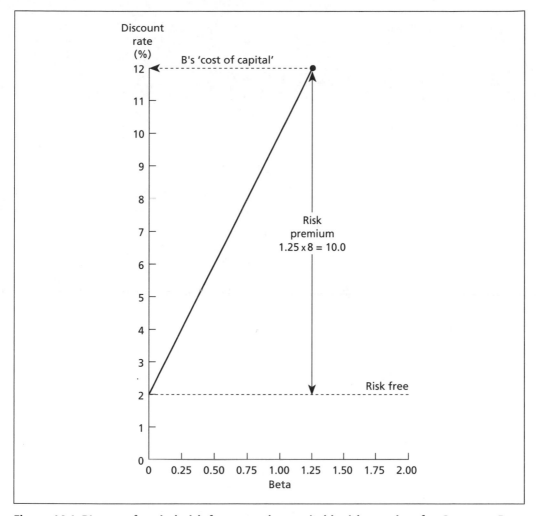

Figure 14.1 B's cost of capital: risk-free rate plus a suitable risk premium for Company B

'risk-adjustment' to allow for the (possible) difference in riskiness of the asset it is planning to acquire (and therefore needing to value). Figure 14.2 illustrates.

14.2. Terminal values

Horizon period

How many years' cash flows should we consider in valuing a company (F)? If we want to assume that F has an infinite life, the obvious answer is to make the valuation in two stages: (1) look at a number of years (perhaps ten) in some detail; and then (2)

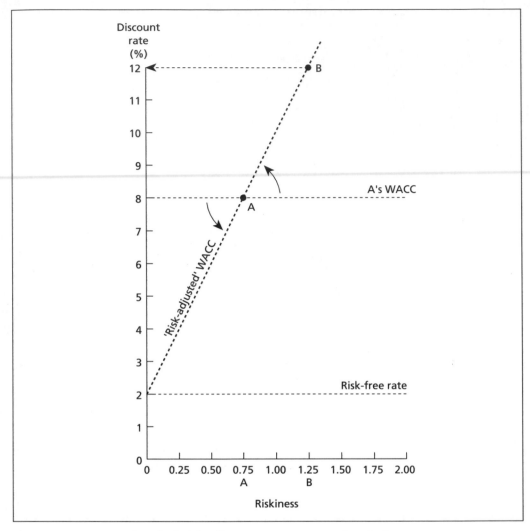

Figure 14.2 B's cost of capital: risk-adjustment to A's cost of capital

assume that beyond Year 10 F's cash flows amount to a 'perpetuity' (that is, with no growth in real terms).

If we were *not* to assume that Company F will last for ever, we must decide when it is to die. At high discount rates this may not matter much (see also Table 6.5). Table 14.1 shows the extra present value as one extends an annuity from 10 years to 25 years (and then to 40 years and to infinity) at three real discount rates: 5 per cent, 10 per cent and 15 per cent.

Normally, people don't find it worthwhile to try to project detailed cash flows beyond ten years, sometimes not even as far ahead as that. The question then becomes: what, if any, terminal value should we assume at the end of the horizon period? (Of course, by

Table 14.1 Present value of annuities (10, 25, 40, ∞ years) at various discount rates

Present values	10 years	25 years	40 years	∞ years
Discount rate:				
5 per cent	7.722	14.094	17.159	20.000
>previous PV:	0.0	6.372 (83%)	3.065 (39%)	2.841 (37%)
10 per cent	6.149	9.077	9.779	10.000
>previous PV:	0.0	2.932 (48%)	0.702 (11%)	0.221 (4%)
15 per cent	5.019	6.464	6.642	6.667
>previous PV:	0.0	1.445 (29%)	0.178 (3%)	0.025 (1%)

including any terminal value at all, strictly speaking we are implicitly extending the horizon.)

Valuation methods

One valuation method for terminal values is to assume constant annual cash inflows beyond a certain date, either for some years or for ever. These annuities (being constant amounts each year) will be in 'real' terms (of 'constant purchasing power'). That means we shall need to discount them using 'real' discount rates.

Another method is, at the horizon date, to abandon discounted cash flows and use some cruder method. Perhaps the most obvious is to use a price/earnings multiple (see below). (If we are assuming no real growth, we would expect to use a fairly low price/earnings multiple.)

Another alternative might be to try to value some or all of the assets separately. Or one might take the assumed book value of the equity at the horizon date: it is likely to be a conservative measure (which may be no bad thing).

Discounting the terminal value

When we have somehow managed to produce a terminal value as at the horizon date (let us suppose this is at the end of Year 5, to simplify the details), we still have one remaining point to bear in mind. Given that we want to establish the value (that is, the *present* − end of Year 0 − value) of the company, we must remember to *discount* the terminal value back from the horizon date into EOY 0 terms.

The discount rate to use for this exercise, of course, may well be different from the rate used to establish the EOY 5 terminal value itself (even if we used DCF − see above).

For instance, suppose we can estimate specific cash inflows for Company G for the first five years in money terms (that is, including any expected inflation), whereas the annuities beyond the horizon date may well be in 'real' terms. The discount rate needed to establish the *present value* of the terminal value will then need to be a *money* discount rate, not a real one, as Table 14.2 shows.

There is no doubt some danger of confusion unless one is very careful. One way to overcome this may be to 'label' the money amounts (as one does in Constant Purchasing

Table 14.2 Discounting terminal value back to EOY 0

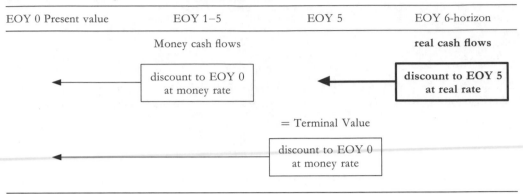

EOY 0 Present value	EOY 1–5	EOY 5	EOY 6-horizon

Power accounting), to denote whether they are 'current' pounds (c£) or Year 5 pounds (5£) or what.

14.3. Price/earnings multiples

Definitions

Simply, a price/earnings multiple (or ratio) is the market price of an ordinary share divided by the earnings per share. (In aggregate, this amounts to market capitalization of the equity divided by profit available for ordinary shareholders.)

For listed companies, the market price per share is the current market price. Thus the price/earnings ratio fluctuates from day to day. The 'earnings' for last year are fixed, but the market price changes.

In the UK we normally use *last year's* earnings for 'earnings per share'. (American analysts often use an estimate of current year ['prospective'] earnings.)

If one uses the bottom line earnings figure, including some items which will not recur, the earnings figure – hence the price/earnings ratio too – can fluctuate quite sharply. One might prefer to use a 'normalized' earnings figure, which was more stable, based on earnings before exceptional items; but this does require subjective judgement.

Analysts sometimes use **earnings yield** (earnings/market price), which, of course, is simply the reciprocal of the price/earnings multiple, as a basis for valuation.

As we saw in Chapter 11, the dividend growth model says the market price per share is equal to the expected current year's dividend divided by: the cost of equity capital less the expected constant rate of growth in dividends (and in earnings). The formula is:

$$P = \frac{d'}{k - g}$$

Table 14.3 Price/earnings multiples for given DPR (50%), *k* and *g*

real *k* =	8%	10%	12%	14%
real *g*				
0%	6	5	4	3.5
2%	8	6	5	4
4%	12.5	8	6	5
6%	25	12.5	8	6

If we divided both sides of this equation by the expected earnings for the current year, we get a prospective price/earnings multiple:

$$\frac{P}{e'} = \frac{d'/e'}{k - g}$$

In words, the expected dividend payout ratio this year divided by $(k - g)$.

The higher the dividend payout ratio, obviously, the lower the **retention ratio**. And, other things being equal, the lower the retention ratio, the lower the likely future growth rate. An obvious problem is that one may not expect the growth in future to be constant.

Using such a model makes it clear why the higher the growth rate (g) you expect, or the lower the riskiness (k varies with risk), the higher will be the price/earnings ratio. Since the value (price) of each share depends on $(k - g)$, it is highly sensitive to even small changes in either.

We can draw up a table showing what price/earnings multiple will result from this formula, for specific values of k and of g, on the assumption of a given dividend payout ratio. If, for example, we use a DPR of 50 per cent, the table – in 'real' terms – might look as shown in Table 14.3.

It will be noted that this table seems to produce rather low price/earnings ratios, by today's standards. It is only fair to say that some of the faster-growth companies might well have a retention ratio of more than 50 per cent (in other words, a dividend payout ratio of *less* than 50 per cent).

We should also note that the price/earnings multiple does not represent literally the 'number of years' future earnings' included in the price. The discounting process means that future earnings are worth *less* than the same amount of earnings this year. Thus a price/earnings multiple of 9, for instance, does *not* mean that we are looking only 9 years ahead. As we know, in principle our formula includes estimated future dividends *for ever*! Nothing short-termist about that!

For example, Table 14.4 shows – at various real interest rates – what the price/earnings multiple would be for a perpetuity (which by definition lasts for ever).

Using price/earnings multiples

With listed companies, we have a market price, and can calculate the price/earnings ratio by simply dividing that market price by earnings per share (either last year's or the current year's estimate).

Table 14.4 Price/earnings multiples for perpetuities

Real interest rate	Capitalization factor [= price/earnings multiple]
4%	25.0
6%	16.7
8%	12.5
10%	10.0
12%	8.3

With unlisted companies, however, by definition we don't have a market price in the same way. (There may be records of recent share deals to indicate what recent market prices have been; but there may not.)

We will, however, have an earnings per share figure. So it may be tempting to try to estimate the market value per share by applying to the earnings per share figure an 'appropriate' price/earnings multiple.

Doing this is not easy. As a start, we might try to find a listed company in the same industry, and preferably with similar growth prospects. We might then note the listed company's price/earnings multiple, reduce it somewhat, to allow for the 'extra risk' in the unlisted company; and use that as a rough guide to possible value per share in the unlisted company.

For instance, suppose Lower is a listed company and Upper is an unlisted one. Lower's shares are quoted at 150p, and last year's earnings per share was 10.0p. So Lower's price/earnings ratio, on the usual basis, is 15.0. Let us suppose Upper has slightly worse growth prospects than Lower; so that if everything else was the same, we might look for a price/earnings multiple for Upper of around 13 (rather than Lower's 15).

But since Upper is unquoted, we might feel that this adds a good deal to its riskiness (from an ordinary shareholder's point of view). So we might want to downgrade the provision price/earnings ratio of 13 even further, say to 11.0, to allow for this. Now suppose that Upper's earnings per share last year was 25p. Then we might reckon that a value per Upper share of about 265p [= 25 × 11] might be about right.

It should be apparent how many rather crude assumptions we have had to make to get this far. But it is already clear that price/earnings ratios are hardly very scientific, in that if a company made a loss last year (but still, of course, has a positive share price), its price/earnings ratio will be *negative*!

GLOSSARY

Accelerated depreciation Any depreciation method that produces larger deductions for depreciation in the early years of a fixed asset's life.

Accounting standards Rules on disclosure and measurement in accounts (Statements of Standard Accounting Practice = SSAPs up to 1990 and Financial Reporting Standards = FRSs since 1990). See Appendix 1 for topics covered.

Accounts Profit and loss account for a period, balance sheet as at end of period, and notes to the accounts, together with auditors' report and a cash flow statement.

Accounts payable (creditors) Amounts due to suppliers for goods or services purchased on credit.

Accounts receivable (debtors) Amounts due from customers for goods or services sold on credit.

Accruals concept Recognizing transactions in period to which they relate, rather than when cash passes.

Accrued charge Liability not yet invoiced.

Acid test ratio Liquid assets (cash + debtors) divided by current liabilities. Yardstick of ability to pay short-term debts.

Acquisition Purchase by one company of another.

Adjusted Present Value (APV) Net present value of an asset if financed solely by equity, plus or minus the present value of any financing side-effects.

Ageing schedule Total debtors analyzed to show how long invoices have remained unpaid.

Agency costs Costs of resolving conflicts of interest among shareholders, bondholders and managers. They include costs of providing incentives for managers to maximize shareholder wealth and then monitoring their behaviour, and costs of protecting bondholders from shareholders.

Alternative Investment Market (AIM) Lightly-regulated market for smaller companies, operated by London Stock Exchange.

American option Option which the purchaser may exercise at any time up to the expiry date.

Amortization (a) Depreciation, usually of intangible assets; (b) Repayment of a loan by instalments.

Annualized cost (AC) Discounted cash flow technique, which annualizes the initial investment, rather than capitalizing revenue.

Annuity Regular annual amount for a number of years. For present values, see Appendix B.

Arbitrage Buying in one market and selling in another to gain from price differences (which the process will reduce but, due to transaction costs, not eliminate).

Arbitrage Pricing Theory (APT) Multi-factor asset pricing theory which relates return on securities to various non-diversifiable risk factors. The expected return on any risky asset is a linear combination of these factors.

Arithmetic average The sum of the values observed divided by the total number of observations (also called the 'mean').

Asset Valuable resource which a business owns or controls.

Asset beta (or ungeared beta) Beta of a firm's total assets, rather than of its equity shares.

Asset turnover Annual sales revenue divided by net assets.

Associated company (or related company) Enterprise in which the company has a participating interest: (i) owns between 20 and 50 per cent of the equity shares, and (ii) influences management.

Asymmetric information Information not equally possessed by both parties to a relationship.

Audit External examination of financial accounts (and records and systems) by independent professional accountants, to report whether accounts give a true and fair view.

Authorized share capital The maximum amount of share capital which a company can legally issue, which shareholders can vote to change.

Average collection period The average number of days it takes to collect debts from credit customers.

Bad debt Debt reckoned to be uncollectable

Balance sheet Classified statement of financial position of a business, showing assets, liabilities, and shareholders' funds at a particular date.

Bank of England UK central bank.

Bank overdraft Amount owing to bank, repayable 'on demand'. Both the amount borrowed, and the rate of interest, may fluctuate.

Bankruptcy Legal process when someone is unable to pay due debts. Equivalent for companies is liquidation (winding-up).

Basis point One-hundredth of one per cent, applied to interest rates.

Bear Speculator expecting prices to fall, who may sell assets he does not own, hoping to buy back later at a lower price.

Beta Coefficient relating an investment's return to that of the whole market. Published betas usually refer to listed equity shares (see asset betas).

Bid premium The amount an acquirer offers above the pre-bid price.

Bond A long-term debt obligation of firms or governments.

Bonus issue (scrip issue) Issue of more shares pro rata to existing shareholders 'free' (i.e. in exchange for no cash or other assets).

Book value (BV) Balance sheet amount shown for an asset. Usually means not 'value' but 'cost less any amounts written off'.

Book value per share Shareholders' funds in balance sheet divided by number of equity shares in issue.

Budget Financial or quantitative statement for a period, agreed in advance, reflecting the policies to be pursued to attain agreed objectives.

Bull Speculator expecting prices to rise, who may buy assets (or options) hoping to sell them at a profit (rather than 'use' them).

Bullet payment When most or all of a loan is repaid at or near the final maturity date.

Business risk The volatility of a business's operating profits, due to the specific assets owned, regardless of their financing.

Call option The right, but not the obligation, to buy a fixed quantity of a defined asset at a stated exercise price on or before a given date.

Capital (a) Paid-up ordinary shares; (b) capital employed; (c) contrasted with 'revenue'.

Capital allowance (or writing-down allowance) Tax equivalent of (book) depreciation of (some) fixed assets, calculated according to Inland Revenue rules. For most equipment, 25 per cent on declining balance.

Capital Asset Pricing Model (CAPM) Theory about valuing assets. Key feature is distinction between two different kinds of risk: non-diversifiable market risk and unique (or specific) risk which shareholders owning a portfolio of shares can diversify away.

Capital budgeting Planning use of investment funds, usually including methods of evaluating capital investment projects.

Capital employed Shareholders' funds plus long-term liabilities (= net assets, = total assets less current liabilities.)

Capital expenditure Expenditure treated as an asset on the balance sheet, in contrast to 'revenue' expenditure written off as an expense in the profit and loss account.

Capital gain Part of the 'return' to shareholder from investment in securities, stemming from increase in market value, not from dividends or interest.

Capital gains tax (CGT) Tax at marginal income tax rate on personal gains exceeding £7,100 per year.

Capital Market Line (CML) The set of risk-return combinations available by combining the market portfolio with (risk-free) borrowing or lending.

Capital markets Financial markets which deal in long term finance, both debt and equity.

Capital rationing Limit on the amount of capital to invest in a period, either internal or external.

Capital structure Mix of various debt and equity securities comprising a firm's capital.

Capitalize Record expenditure as an asset, rather than write it off as an expense.

Cash discount Reduction in amount payable for goods sold on credit, offered in exchange for prompt settlement.

Cash flow Usually defined as 'retained profits plus depreciation' for a period.

Caveat emptor (Latin) 'Let the buyer beware.'

Collateral Asset serving as security for a loan.

Compound interest Interest earned both on initial principal and on interest earned in previous periods.

Compounding to horizon (CH) DCF method showing what interest rate will compound the initial investment to the same amount as the project itself is expected to produce, by the horizon date.

Conglomerate Diversified group of companies whose subsidiaries operate in unrelated areas.

Consistency Principle in accounting, and other statistics, of treating similar items in the same way, to allow meaningful comparisons.

Consolidated accounts (group accounts) Accounts for group of companies, 'consolidated' by combining the separate assets and liabilities of all subsidiaries with those of the holding (parent) company.

Constant purchasing power (CPP) accounting Method of inflation accounting which adjusts historical money costs of various dates by means of the retail prices index. (The 'C' once used to mean 'current'.)

Contribution Sales revenue less variable costs.

Control (a) In management accounting, planning, comparing actual performance with budget, explaining significant variances, and acting to improve things; (b) in financial management, in contrast to 'ownership'.

Convertible loan Loan convertible at holder's option into equity on pre-arranged terms.

Corporation tax (CT) Tax payable by companies on taxable profits. 30 per cent $> £1.5$ million, or 20 per cent $< £0.3$ million.

Cost Amount given up in exchange for goods or services received. May appear in accounts either as an asset or as an expense.

Cost of capital Usually $=$ WACC, i.e. risk-adjusted weighted average of the (marginal) after-tax costs of equity and debt. The required minimum rate of return for capital investment projects. May be either in money or in real terms.

Cost of goods sold (COGS) Costs identifiable with stocks, for example: raw materials and bought-in components, direct labour and production overheads.

Coupon rate Nominal rate of interest payable on fixed-interest securities.

Covenants Conditions attached to loan agreements restricting discretion re: dividends, working capital, etc.

Creditors (accounts payable) Amounts due to suppliers for goods or services purchased on credit.

Currency debasement Process of reducing purchasing power of currency, once by adding base metal to precious metal, in modern times by more sophisticated methods of fraud.

Current asset Cash or any asset, such as stocks or debtors, expected to turn into cash (or be consumed in the normal course of business) within twelve months from balance sheet date.

Current cost accounting (CCA) System of current value accounting which uses money as the unit of account (unlike CPP), but shows assets and expenses at current replacement cost instead of historical cost.

Current liabilities Amounts owing to others (such as trade creditors or tax) payable within twelve months from the balance sheet date. May split short-term interest-bearing finance from other creditors falling due within one year.

Current ratio Measure of liquidity, current assets divided by current liabilities. Rule of thumb: normally between 1½ and 2.

Current value May mean current replacement cost of asset, or net realizable value. Unlike historical cost, which is usually a definite known fact, current value can only be a hypothetical estimate.

Days' sales in debtors Debtors divided by daily sales (i.e. by annual sales revenue divided by 365). Ratio showing how much credit customers are taking. (Needs adjusting for VAT.)

Debenture Long-term liability (Latin: 'they are owed').

Debt Negotiated interest-bearing borrowing (as opposed to 'equity'). May include short-term as well as long-term finance.

Debt capacity Ability to borrow. The amount a firm can borrow up to the point where the firm's value no longer increases.

Debtors (accounts receivable) Amounts due from customers for goods or services sold on credit. May include prepayments.

Debt ratio Balance sheet measure of financial gearing. In UK often: debt/(debt + equity); in US often: debt/equity.

Decision tree Graphical representation of possible sequential decisions and outcomes.

Declining balance Depreciation method which charges each year a constant percentage of the declining net book value. Used by Inland Revenue for plant and equipment.

Deep discount bond Loan stock issued well below par (its redemption amount), so that much (or all) of the 'interest' yield comes by way of capital gain.

Default risk The chance that interest or principal will not be paid in full on the due date.

Deferred taxation Part of tax expense charged in accounts not payable for some time, due to timing differences between reported and taxable profits.

Depreciation Process of writing off the cost of a fixed asset, to spread the total net cost over its useful life and match against revenues.

Derivatives Financial instruments, such as options, 'derived' from underlying assets, such as equity shares. May also relate to foreign currencies and commodities.

Dilution Process which reduces a shareholder's equity interest when a company issues more shares to other shareholders (for example, on converting debt or exercising options).

Discount factor Multiplier needed to reduce future cash flows to present value.

Discount rate Interest rate used in making present value calculations.

Discounted cash flow (DCF) Technique for evaluating capital projects, using interest rate as 'exchange rate over time'. Main methods: NPV, IRR.

Discounted payback Payback period calculated using discounted (present value) amounts for cash inflows.

Disinvestment Reducing investment by selling or abandoning asset(s).

Diversification Adding or substituting investments with low or negative covariance with existing holdings, to help reduce total risk of portfolio.

Dividend Cash payable to ordinary (or preference) shareholders out of profits if declared by a company's directors. May be 'interim' or 'final'.

Dividend cover Profits for a year divided by dividends.

Dividend growth model (DGM) Share valuation model which assumes dividends grow at a constant rate in perpetuity.

Dividend payout ratio (DPR) Reciprocal of dividend cover: dividends proposed for a year divided by profits for the year.

Dividend yield (DY) Dividends per share for a year, divided by the market price.

Double-entry accounting System of recording business transactions based on two aspects: a 'source' of funds and a 'use' of funds.

Earnings per share (EPS) Profit after tax for a year (and after minority interests and preference dividends) divided by the average number of ordinary shares in issue.

Earnings yield (EY) EPS divided by the market price per share.

Earn-out Linking the purchase price of a company to future profits.

Economic value added (EVA) (= residual income) Profit for a period less interest (actual or notional) on total capital employed.

Efficient Market Hypothesis (EMH) Theory that security prices fully reflect available information.

Employee Share Ownership Plans (ESOP) Schemes designed, usually with tax advantages, to allow employees to build up shareholdings in their companies.

Equity Ordinary share capital and reserves; (ordinary) shareholder's funds.

Equity beta Coefficient relating an equity share's return to that of the whole market. (Contrasted with asset beta.)

European option Option which the purchaser may exercise only on the expiry date.

Ex ante In advance; before the event.

Exceptional items Items disclosed separately in profit and loss account, unusual on account of size or infrequency of occurrence.

Exchange controls Restrictions on freedom to convert foreign currency into domestic currency or vice versa, or to transfer funds to or from abroad.

Exercise price Strike price. Price at which the holder of an option can buy (for call) or sell (for put) the underlying asset.

Expected return Average of possible returns weighted by subjective estimate of probabilities.

Expected value Weighted average of subjective probabilities applied to all possible anticipated outcomes.

Expenditure (or cost) Amount spent: may be either revenue (expense) or capital (asset).

Expense Amount written off against profit in respect of goods or services consumed, or other loss.

Ex post Afterwards; after the event.

External finance Funds raised from 'outside' a company, such as borrowing or issuing new equity shares for cash. Contrasted with retained profits.

Extraordinary items Prior to FRS 3 (a) material; (b) not expected to recur frequently, and (c) derived from events or transactions 'outside the ordinary activities of the business'. FRS 3 now says almost everything is part of 'ordinary' activities, hence extraordinary items are now extremely rare.

Factor Company which buys trade debts at a discount for cash.

Final dividend Second dividend for a year, after interim dividend.

Finance lease Contract giving lessee use of an asset over most of its life providing in effect another way to finance its 'acquisition'.

Financial accounting External accounting leading to published accounts for the shareholders and other 'outsiders'.

Financial distress Events preceding and including bankruptcy, such as violating (or meeting only with difficulty) loan contracts.

Financial leverage Financial gearing. Extent to which firm relies on debt capital.

Financial objective (of a company) 'To maximize the wealth of the present ordinary shareholders.'

Financial risk Extra volatility of stream of equity earnings due to presence of debt (gearing) in capital structure.

Financial Services Authority (FSA) The main regulator of financial services in the UK.

Financial year The 12-month period for which a firm prepares accounts.

Finished goods Stocks of completed manufactured goods, held for sale.

First in, first out (FIFO) Method of valuing stock at cost, assuming most recent purchases remain in stock at the end of a period.

Fixed asset Resource, either tangible or intangible, with long life, which a firm intends to hold, not for sale in the ordinary course of business.

Flat yield Interest yield ignoring capital gain (or loss) on redemption. Annual interest divided by current market price.

Floating charge Charge which is not secured against specific assets, but which 'floats' over all (otherwise unsecured) assets, crystallizing only on occurrence of specified events.

Fully diluted EPS What EPS would be on exercise of all outstanding conversion rights and other options.

Gearing Leverage. Proportion of debt in capital structure is 'financial gearing'. Proportion of fixed costs to total operating expenses is 'business gearing'.

Geometric average The *n*th root of the product of *n* observations.

Gilt-edged securities UK government securities, regarded as 'risk-free' apart from the risk of inflation.

Going concern Assumption in accounting that a business entity will continue to operate for the foreseeable future.

Goodwill Excess of purchase price paid to acquire another company over the 'fair value' of the net separable assets acquired.

Group accounts (consolidated accounts) Accounts for a group of companies, 'consolidated' by combining the separate assets and liabilities of all subsidiaries with those of the holding (parent) company.

Guarantee Undertaking to be responsible for the debts of another (person or company) if the nominal debtor fails to pay in full.

Hire purchase (HP) System of paying for an asset by instalments.

Historical cost (HC) Accounting convention showing assets and expenses at actual past money cost (rather than, for example, at current value). CPP is an HC system, using constant purchasing power rather than money

Holding company (or parent company) Company owning more than 50 per cent of equity shares in subsidiaries, directly or indirectly; or controlling the composition of the board of directors.

Horizon Point in future beyond which explicit financial estimates are not made (though including a 'terminal value' makes them implicitly).

Horizontal merger Combination of firms making the same kind of product.

Hurdle rate (or criterion rate) Required rate of return on capital project.

Income bonds Bonds on which interest is legally payable only if earned in the period, though unpaid interest normally cumulates to be paid later when earnings permit.

Income tax Tax payable on personal incomes, such as dividends or trading profits of partnerships or sole traders. Basic rate is 20 per cent, higher rate 40 per cent on taxable incomes above £28,000.

Incremental cash flows Cash flows which occur as a result of action (such as investing in a capital project), but not otherwise. May include opportunity costs, such as foregone proceeds from selling an asset, so that it can be used in a project.

Index fund Investment fund designed to match the performance of a stock market index.

Index-linking (or indexation) Linking a money amount to the rate of inflation as measured by the RPI. Examples: government securities, pensions, tax thresholds, capital gains.

Inflation Rise in the general level of money prices, measured by the annual rate of increase in the retail prices index (RPI).

Inflation accounting Constant purchasing power (CPP) accounting. (Current cost accounting (CCA) is *not* a method of adjusting accounts for general inflation.)

Inflation premium Part of the nominal (money) rate of interest, depending on the expected future rate of inflation.

Initial Public Offering (IPO) Offering shares in a company's equity to the public for the first time.

Inland Revenue UK tax authority responsible for assessing and collecting taxes on income and profits.

Insiders Individuals held to have 'inside' knowledge of material events not yet made public, forbidden from dealing in relevant shares, or from passing on inside information to others.

Insolvency Inability to meet financial obligations.

Interest cover The number of times profit before interest and tax (PBIT) covers interest payable on loans. Sometimes calculated net of interest receivable.

Interest rate Annual rate of compensation for borrowing or lending (money) comprising: (a) pure time-preference; (b) inflation premium, and (c) risk premium.

Interim dividend First (of two or more) dividends payable in respect of a year's profits, the last being the final dividend.

Intermediaries Financial institutions which separate borrowing from lending and may alter the time-pattern of loans. They profit from economies of scale and specialization.

Internal finance Raising funds from 'within' a company, usually referring to retained profits (plus depreciation), or perhaps selling fixed assets.

Internal rate of return (IRR) Rate of discount which, when applied to a capital project's expected cash flows, produces a net present value of zero.

Inventories (stocks) Holdings of goods, either as raw materials or components, work-in-progress or finished goods, with a view to sale (perhaps after further processing) in the ordinary course of business.

Investment (real) Fixed capital formation, investment in fixed assets or stock.

Investment (financial) Acquisition of a security, often from an existing holder via the secondary market. Hence 'financial' investment need not imply 'real' investment.

Investment trust Company which holds a portfolio of securities.

Irredeemable loan Stock with no maturity date, whose annual interest is a 'perpetuity'. May be redeemable at issuer's option (not at holder's).

Junk bonds Low quality speculative bonds to which high risk premium attaches.

Last in, first out (LIFO) US method of valuing stock at cost, very rare in UK where it is not allowed for tax purposes. Assumes that most recent purchases have been used up in current period, leaving (much) earlier purchases in stock at end.

Lease Commitment (by the 'lessee') to pay rent to the owner ('lessor') in return for the use of an asset. May be 'financial' (long-term) or 'operating' (short-term).

Leverage Gearing. Extent to which firm relies on debt capital.

Leveraged Buy-Out (LBO) Acquisition in which a large proportion of the purchase price is debt financed with the remaining equity held by a small group of investors (possibly also managers – see Management Buy-Out).

Liability Amount owing to a creditor.

Limited company Form of business organization in which the liability of the owners (shareholders) for the company's debts is limited to the fully paid nominal amount of their share capital. Abbreviated to 'ltd' (or 'plc' [public limited company] for larger companies).

Liquid resources Cash in hand and at bank, plus short-term marketable securities.

Liquidation (winding-up) Legal process of ending a company's life, by selling all its assets for cash, paying off the creditors (if possible), and distributing any residual amount to the shareholders.

Liquidity The degree to which an asset can be sold quickly and easily without loss in value.

Listed company Company whose ordinary shares are listed ('quoted') on a stock exchange, as opposed to a private company.

Loan stock Long-term loan (to a company or government agency), often tradable on the stock exchange in the secondary market.

London InterBank Offered Rate (LIBOR) The rate of interest offered on loans to highly rated banks in London.

London International Financial Futures and Options Exchange (LIFFE) The main derivatives exchange in London.

Long-term liability (creditors: amounts falling due for payment after more than one year). Liability not due for settlement until more than twelve months after the balance sheet date.

Loss Negative profit, where expenses exceed sales revenue. Though not the aim, often the result of business (especially after allowing for (a) inflation and (b) interest on equity capital).

Management Buy-Out (MBO) Acquisition of a business by a team of its senior managers who themselves take an equity interest, but largely financed by venture capitalists, often mainly with debt.

Market capitalization Market 'value' of equity: price per share multiplied by number of shares in issue.

Market portfolio A theoretical portfolio which contains all listed securities. In practice a representative index (such as FTSE) is taken as a proxy.

Market risk The non-diversifiable part of the total risk attaching to investment, measured by beta.

Market-to-Book (M/B) ratio The ratio between market price per share and book value per share (or calculated in aggregate).

Matching principle The accounting principle according to which balance sheets carry forward expenditures as assets only if there are expected to be sufficient sales revenues (or disposal proceeds) in future against which to match them.

Matching the maturity Process of 'matching' the time period of assets and liabilities, to reduce risk.

Maturity Date at which a loan falls due for repayment (redemption).

Merger A combination of two or more formerly independent business entities into a single enterprise, meeting certain accounting criteria.

Mezzanine finance Unsecured debt or preference capital offering high return with high risk, ranking behind secured debt but ahead of equity.

Minority interests (MI) Equity interests of minority shareholders in subsidiary companies which are less than wholly owned.

Modern portfolio theory (MPT) Distinguishes non-diversifiable market risk from unique risk, which a properly diversified portfolio can eliminate.

Monetary asset/liability Asset receivable or liability payable in terms of money, as opposed to 'real' assets such as stocks or tangible fixed assets.

'Monetary loss/gain' In CPP accounting, the loss arising (in terms of constant purchasing power, not of money!) in times of inflation from holding cash or other monetary assets (or the gain from owing monetary liabilities). Not taxable.

Negative interest rate 'Real' interest rate, after-tax and net of inflation, which may be negative: (a) because, while the inflation premium is tax-deductible, the 'monetary gain' from inflation is not taxable; or (b) because the actual rate of inflation exceeds that anticipated in the inflation premium.

Net assets (or capital employed) Total assets less current liabilities (other than short-term interest-bearing finance) = fixed assets + operating working capital.

Net Asset Value (NAV) Total assets minus total debt = shareholders' funds. Thus NAV per share = book value per share.

Net book value (NBV) Cost (or valuation) of assets, less amounts written off.

Net current assets (working capital) Current assets less current liabilities.

Net dividend Amount of cash dividend payable to ordinary shareholders.

Net present value (NPV) Discounted estimated future cash inflows minus (discounted) cash outflow(s). If positive, indicates prima facie acceptability on financial grounds of capital project (using discount rate as hurdle rate).

Net Present Value of Growth Opportunities (NPVGO) sometimes explicitly valued separately.

Net realizable value (NRV) Net amount for which asset could currently be sold. If less than cost, used for valuing stocks.

Net terminal value (NTV) As for NPV, but with cash flows compounded to future horizon date instead of discounted back to present (value).

Nominal amount value (par value) Face value of security, unrelated to current market value. Usually refers to ordinary shares, with nominal value often of 25p each or £1 each, or to government securities per £100 of stock.

Offer for sale Method of selling ordinary shares to the public.

Operating lease Lease other than a financial lease, usually for a short period of time.

Opportunity cost The hypothetical revenue or other benefit that might have been obtained by the 'next best' alternative course which was forgone in favour of the course actually taken.

Option Right to buy or sell a security or other asset at a pre-stated price, within a certain period of time = 'derivative'. Or, more generally, simply the right (not the obligation) to choose to take a particular course of action in future.

Ordinary share capital Capital of a company, consisting of the amount called up on issued ordinary shares.

Owners' equity Ordinary shareholders' funds.

Partnership Form of enterprise with two or more partners (owners), each with unlimited personal liability to meet all the firm's debts in full.

Par value Nominal or face value of share or bond, unrelated to market value.

Payback Method of evaluating capital projects which measures how long before the initial investment is 'paid back' by later cash inflows. The method ignores cash inflows *after* payback, so does *not* measure profitability.

Pecking order Theory of financing priorities for managers: retained profits, then debt, finally new issue of equity.

Perpetuity Annuity payable for ever.

Placing Method of issuing shares to clients of brokers.

Portfolio Group of different investments held by a single owner, which diversifies away some of their 'unique' risk.

Post-project audit The process of comparing part or all of a capital project's outcome after the event with the *ex ante* forecast.

Preference share capital Form of share capital entitled to fixed rate of dividend (usually cumulative) if declared, and to repayment of a fixed sum on liquidation, with priority over ordinary shares.

Prepayment Expense paid in advance of the period to which it relates, shown on the balance sheet as a current asset, often combined with debtors.

Present value (PV) Discounted amount of future cash flows.

Price/earnings (P/E) ratio Market price per ordinary share divided by annual earnings per share (usually last year's, but may be estimate for current year).

Primary market Market for securities which raises new money from the public.

Principal (a) Capital amount of debt excluding interest; (b) Person acting on his own account, rather than as agent for another.

Privatization Selling off government holdings in businesses.

Profit Surplus of sales revenues over expenses usually for a period.

Profit and loss (P&L) account Accounting statement showing the result (profit or loss) of business operations for a period, usually one year.

Profit before interest and tax (PBIT) Operating profit before deducting costs of financing and tax.

Profit margin Operating profit (before interest and tax) as a percentage of sales revenue. Profit margin × net asset turnover = return on net assets.

Profitability index (PI) DCF method which divides PV of inflows by PV of investment outflows (instead of, like NPV method, deducting PV of investment outflows from PV of inflows). Ratio >1.0 signals 'go'. Sometimes multiplied by 100.

Project finance Method of finance whose repayments (and perhaps interest) are tied to a project's operating results.

Prospectus Advertisement to public about an issue of securities.

Prudence (conservatism) Convention of accountants to provide in full for all known losses in accounts, but to recognize sales revenue (and profit) only when 'reasonable certainty' exists. Sometimes clashes with matching principle.

Public limited company (plc) Modern UK name for large limited company.

Purchasing power (value) of money What money will buy in 'real' terms, usually measured by the 'basket of goods and services' comprising the constituent items in the retail prices index.

Purchasing power parity (PPP) theorem Theory that (in the 'long run') the relative exchange rates of currencies will vary in proportion to the relative rates of currency debasement.

Put option Right, but not obligation, to sell a fixed quantity of a defined asset at a stated price on or before a given date.

Q ratio Tobin's Q. Market value of firm's assets divided by their estimated replacement value.

Quick ratio Acid test ratio. Liquid assets divided by current liabilities.

Quoted company Listed company. Company whose shares are quoted (listed) on stock exchange.

Raw materials Input to manufacturing process, held for a time as stocks.

Real option Strategic or operational option to undertake different courses of action (as opposed to derivatives).

'Real' terms Amounts expressed after adjustments to allow for inflation.

Realization The concept in accounting that recognizes sales revenue (and therefore profit) only when it is 'realized' in cash, or in other assets the ultimate cash realization of which can be assessed with reasonable certainty.

Receiver Official managing a company's affairs, on behalf of debenture holders or others, often as a preliminary to liquidation.

Redemption Repayment of loan or preference share capital.

Redemption yield Yield on loan stock including element of capital gain (or loss) anticipated when the principal is repaid at par on maturity, in addition to the 'flat' yield of annual interest.

Reinvestment rate Assumption (explicit or implicit) about the rate of return a firm can earn on cash inflows 'reinvested' during a capital project's life.

Replacement cost Amount for which it is currently estimated that an asset held could be replaced.

Required rate of return (or hurdle rate, criterion rate) The rate of return needed for a capital project to be profitable, used as the discount rate for NPV.

Research and Development (R&D) Expenditure on research and development, often effectively an 'investment', but treated in accounts as a current expense.

Reserves Shareholders' funds other than paid-up share capital, including: share premium, revaluation reserves, cumulative retained profits. These represent past sources of funds; they may not be currently available in cash.

Residual income (RI) (or economic value added) Profit less a capital charge representing interest on total capital. May be before or after tax.

Residual value Net realizable value of fixed asset at the end of its useful life.

Retail prices index (RPI) Monthly government statistic measuring the weighted average of money prices of a representative 'basket of goods'. Based on January 1987 = 100.

Retained profits (retained earnings) Amount of profits earned by a company not paid out in dividends (either for current period or cumulatively).

Retention ratio Retained earnings for a period (normally a year) divided by the profit available for dividend in the period.

Return on capital employed (ROCE) (see return on net assets)

Return on equity Profit after tax divided by shareholders' funds.

Return on funds employed (ROFE) (see return on net assets)

Return on investment (ROI) (see return on net assets)

Return on the market (R_m) The expected return on the market portfolio.

Return on net assets (RONA) (or ROCE, ROFE, or ROI) Operating profit before interest and tax (PBIT) divided by net assets (= by total assets less current liabilities other than short-term interest-bearing finance).

Revaluation Process of including asset in accounts at estimated current value when higher than historical cost.

Revaluation reserve Increase in shareholders' funds needed to 'balance' the increase in net book value of assets due to revaluation.

Revenue (a) Sales revenue; (b) as contrasted with capital, relating to the profit and loss account rather than to the balance sheet or (c) 'The Revenue' = The Inland Revenue.

Rights issue Issue, usually of ordinary shares, to existing shareholders, to raise cash.

Risk Volatility about a mean (average) 'expected value'. More loosely, possibility of loss (either likelihood or extent). Sometimes treated as synonymous with uncertainty.

Risk premium Part of interest rate relating to perceived risk of investment. The risk premium on the whole market is sometimes estimated at 8.0 per cent a year.

Risk-free rate of return (R_f) Rate of return available on securities of (some) governments. May include an inflation premium.

Sale and leaseback Arrangement for a firm to sell certain assets to a financial company which then immediately leases them back to the firm for a defined period. Aims to raise cash for the firm (in effect by borrowing).

Sales revenue (turnover) A firm's gross trading income for a period.

Scrip Issue (bonus issue) Issue of more shares pro rata to existing shareholders 'free' (i.e. in exchange for no cash or other assets).

Secondary market Market for securities in which existing holders can sell, and buy, without involving the original issuer.

Secured loan Liability 'secured' on an asset, with lender having legal right to the proceeds from the sale of that asset on liquidation, up to the amount of the liability.

Security (or collateral) Legal charge on asset(s) by lender. In the event of default, the lender is entitled to priority of repayment out of the proceeds of disposal of the charged asset(s).

Security (share) Any stocks or shares, usually listed.

Selling short Selling assets not owned, in the hope of buying back later after the market price has fallen.

Semi-strong efficiency Theory that stock market prices fully reflect all publicly available information.

Sensitivity analysis Method of seeing how much difference it makes to alter key variables. Allowing for interdependence is tricky.

Share Partial ownership of ordinary (or preference) capital of company (= US 'stock').

Share premium Excess of issue price over nominal (par) value of shares.

Share split Process of dividing share capital into more shares of smaller nominal amount each. Reduces market price per share pro rata, without affecting the total market value.

Shareholders Usually refers to ordinary shareholders, who own company in proportion to number of shares held (but may also mean preference shareholders).

Shareholders' funds (capital and reserves) Amount shown in company (and group) balance sheets as attributable to ordinary shareholders.

Short-termism Alleged failure to take a 'sufficiently' long-term view.

Signalling Some financial decisions are taken as 'signals' from managers to financial markets (e.g. dividend changes or gearing changes), reflecting asymmetric information.

Small and Medium Enterprises (SMEs) Firms other than large (precise definition is elusive). May have special financing problems (e.g. less than efficient capital markets).

Solvency Ability to settle liabilities when due.

Specific risk (unique risk; diversifiable risk) Part of total risk, which can be diversified away by holding a suitable portfolio.

Speculator Anyone who acts on a view about the uncertain future. Sometimes used pejoratively by governments.

Spin-off Distribution by a parent company to its shareholders of shares in a subsidiary.

Stag Bull of new issues.

Stewardship Original basis for financial accounting, to account regularly to dispersed shareholders. Partly intended for protection of steward.

Stock (US) Share.

Stocks (inventories) Holdings of goods, either as raw materials or components, work-in-progress or finished goods, with a view to sale (perhaps after further processing) in the ordinary course of business.

Stock turnover Annual cost of goods sold divided by value of stocks held.

Straight-line depreciation Method of writing off net cost of fixed asset in equal instalments over its estimated useful life.

Subsidiary Company most or all of whose equity shares are owned by another (its 'holding' or 'parent' company).

Sunk cost A cost that has already been incurred, which should not be treated as incremental in making decisions about the future (but see 'opportunity cost').

Synergy What is hoped on merger to make $2 + 2 = 5$. Often elusive.

Taxable profit Differs from 'profit before tax' in accounts: (a) by deducting writing-down allowances instead of (book) depreciation; (b) by any accounting expenses disallowed by tax authorities; and (c) by any timing differences.

Taxation In company accounts means UK corporation tax plus any foreign tax on profits earned abroad. Excludes other taxes.

Technical analysis Chartism. Method of security analysis that seeks to detect and interpret patterns in past security prices.

Tender method Method of issuing shares to the public, leaving the price to be settled by demand for the shares.

Term loan Loan, probably from a bank, for a fixed period of time, often between one and five years.

Term structure of interest rates The pattern of interest rates covering different periods of time, for example, from three months to twenty-five years. Normally upward-sloping.

Terminal value Amount (expected to be) recoverable at the end of a capital project's life.

Time preference Ratio between someone's valuation of a good now and the same person's valuation of an otherwise identical good at some future date.

Trade credit Normal business arrangement to buy and sell goods 'on credit', that is, not settling in cash until some time later.

Transaction cost The cost of undertaking a transaction, for example, taxes, commissions, administrative costs, and so on.

True and fair view, a Aim of financial accounts, implying the use of generally accepted accounting concepts and conventions.

Turnover (sales revenue) A firm's gross trading income for a period.

Uncertainty Lack of knowledge about the future. Differs from 'risk' which implies known probabilities of all possible outcomes.

Underwriter Person or firm agreeing, for a fee, to meet the financial consequences of a risk, for example, on new share issues.

Ungeared beta = asset beta. Beta of a firm's total assets (rather than of its equity shares only).

Unique risk Specific risk, diversifiable risk.

Unit of account The numeraire in accounting. Normally the monetary unit (as in HMC or CCA); but in times of rapid inflation CPP accounting proposes an alternative: the 'constant purchasing power' unit.

Unit trust Financial enterprise holding a range of securities; hence may be a suitable vehicle for a small unit-holder to spread his risks.

Unlisted company Company whose shares are not listed (quoted) on the stock exchange. Hence shareholders may find it hard to sell their shares.

Value Added Tax Indirect expenditure tax, usually excluded from published sales revenue (turnover) figures.

Vertical format Modern form of accounts, showing net assets and capital employed underneath each other in the balance sheet; and deducting expenses seriatim from sales revenue in profit and loss account.

Vertical merger Combination of two (or more) businesses engaged in different stages of production process in same industry; for example, a brewery buying pubs, or a tyre manufacturer buying a rubber plantation.

Warrant Call option issued by a company.

Wealth Well-offness, expressed in terms of money, normally related to ultimately marketable assets.

Weighted average cost of capital (WACC) Average of the after-tax (marginal) costs of various kinds of finance (debt, equity, etc.) 'weighted' by their market value (or by their book value).

Winding-up Liquidation. Legal process of ending company's life, by selling all its assets for cash ('liquidating' them), paying off the creditors to the extent possible, and distributing any residual amount to the shareholders.

Working capital Net current assets. Excess of current assets over current liabilities. May be negative.

Write off To charge as an expense in the profit and loss account (or, rarely, against reserves).

Writer of an option The seller of an option contract.

Writing-down allowance (wda) = Capital allowance. Tax equivalent of (book) depreciation of (some) fixed assets, calculated according to Inland Revenue rules. For most equipment, 25 per cent on declining balance.

Yield Rate of return on investment (usually security). Interest or dividend for a year, divided by the current market place.

Z-score Coefficient measuring likelihood of financial distress.

Zero coupon bond A bond that pays no regular interest, but is issued at a (deep) discount and redeemable at par.

ACRONYMS

AC	Annualized Cost
AIM	Alternative Investment Market
APR	Annual Percentage Rate
APT	Arbitrage Pricing Theory
APV	Adjusted Present Value
BV	Book Value
CAPM	Capital Asset Pricing Model
CCA	Current Cost Accounting
CGT	Capital Gains Tax
CH	Compounding to Horizon
CML	Capital Market Line
COGS	Cost Of Goods Sold
CPP	Constant Purchasing Power
CT	Corporation Tax
DCF	Discounted Cash Flow
DGM	Dividend Growth Model
DPR	Dividend Payout Ratio
DTR	Double Tax Relief
DY	Dividend Yield
EMH	Efficient Market Hypothesis
EMU	Economic and Monetary Union
EOY	End Of Year
EPS	Earnings Per Share
ERM	Exchange Rate Mechanism
ESOP	Employee Share Option Plan
EVA	Economic Value Added
EY	Earnings Yield
FIFO	First In First Out
FRS	Financial Reporting Standard
FSA	Financial Services Agency
FTSE	Financial Times Stock Exchange (index)
FX	Foreign eXchange

HC	Historical Cost
HMC	Historical Money Cost
HP	Hire Purchase
IAS	International Accounting Standards
IPO	Initial Public Offering
IRR	Internal Rate of Return
LBO	Leveraged Buy Out
LIFFE	London International Financial Futures and options Exchange
LIFO	Last In First Out
Ltd.	Limited
MBI	Management Buy In
MBO	Management Buy Out
MI	Minority Interests
MPT	Modern Portfolio Theory
NBV	Net Book Value
NPV	Net Present Value
NPVGO	Net Present Value of Growth Options
NRV	Net Realizable Value
NTV	Net Terminal Value
PBIT	Profit Before Interest and Tax
P/E	Price/Earnings ratio (or multiple)
PI	Profitability Index
P & L	Profit & Loss
PLC	Public Limited Company (or plc)
PPP	Purchasing Power Parity
PV	Present Value
Q	(Tobin's) Q ratio
R & D	Research & Development
R_f	Risk-free
RI	Residual Income
R_m	Return on the market
ROCE	Return On Capital Employed
ROFE	Return On Funds Employed
ROI	Return On Investment
RONA	Return On Net Assets
RPI	Retail Prices Index

SEAQ	Stock Exchange Automated Quotations
SME	Small and Medium Enterprises
SSAP	Statement of Standard Accounting Practice
VAT	Value Added Tax
WACC	Weighted Average Cost of Capital
wda	writing-down allowance
WIP	Work In Progress

UK accounting standards at 30 June 1999

SSAPs (Statements of Standard Accounting Practice)

2. Accounting policies
4. Government grants
5. Value Added Tax
8. Taxation
9. Stocks and long-term contracts
13. Research and development
15. Deferred taxation
17. Post-balance sheet events
19. Investment properties
20. Foreign currency translation
21. Leases and Hire Purchase contracts
24. Pension costs
25. Segmental reporting

FRSs (Financial Reporting Standards)

1. Cash flow statements
2. Subsidiary undertakings
3. Reporting financial performance
4. Capital instruments
5. Reporting the substance of transactions
6. Acquisitions and mergers
7. Fair value in Acquisition accounting
8. Related party disclosures
9. Associates and joint ventures
10. Goodwill and intangible assets
11. Impairment of fixed assets
12. Provisions and contingencies
13. Derivatives: disclosures
14. Earnings per share

15. Tangible fixed assets

* FRS for Smaller Enterprises (FRSSE).

25 Statements of Standard Accounting Practice were issued between 1970 and 1990 by the Accounting Standards Committee, of which 13 are still outstanding. Since 1990 the Accounting Standards Board has issued 15 numbered FRSs (plus one revision), plus FRSSE plus a draft of its Statement of Principles for Financial Reporting.

APPENDIX 2

Present value tables

Table A Present value of £1

Years Hence	1%	2%	4%	6%	8%	10%	12%	14%	15%	16%	18%	20%	22%	24%	25%	26%	28%	30%	35%	40%	45%	50%
1	0.990	0.980	0.962	0.943	0.926	0.909	0.893	0.877	0.870	0.862	0.847	0.833	0.820	0.806	0.800	0.794	0.781	0.769	0.741	0.714	0.690	0.667
2	0.980	0.961	0.925	0.890	0.857	0.826	0.797	0.769	0.756	0.743	0.718	0.694	0.672	0.650	0.640	0.630	0.610	0.592	0.549	0.510	0.476	0.444
3	0.971	0.942	0.889	0.840	0.794	0.751	0.712	0.675	0.658	0.641	0.609	0.579	0.551	0.524	0.512	0.500	0.477	0.455	0.406	0.364	0.328	0.296
4	0.961	0.924	0.855	0.792	0.735	0.683	0.636	0.592	0.572	0.552	0.516	0.482	0.451	0.423	0.410	0.397	0.373	0.350	0.301	0.260	0.226	0.198
5	0.951	0.906	0.822	0.747	0.681	0.621	0.567	0.519	0.497	0.476	0.437	0.402	0.370	0.341	0.328	0.317	0.291	0.269	0.233	0.186	0.156	0.132
6	0.942	0.888	0.790	0.705	0.630	0.564	0.507	0.456	0.432	0.410	0.370	0.335	0.303	0.275	0.262	0.250	0.227	0.207	0.165	0.133	0.108	0.088
7	0.933	0.871	0.760	0.665	0.583	0.513	0.452	0.400	0.376	0.354	0.314	0.279	0.249	0.222	0.210	0.198	0.178	0.159	0.122	0.095	0.074	0.059
8	0.923	0.853	0.731	0.627	0.540	0.467	0.404	0.351	0.327	0.305	0.266	0.233	0.204	0.179	0.168	0.157	0.139	0.123	0.091	0.068	0.051	0.039
9	0.914	0.837	0.703	0.592	0.500	0.424	0.361	0.308	0.284	0.263	0.225	0.194	0.167	0.144	0.134	0.125	0.108	0.094	0.067	0.048	0.035	0.026
10	0.905	0.820	0.676	0.558	0.463	0.386	0.322	0.270	0.247	0.227	0.191	0.162	0.137	0.116	0.107	0.099	0.085	0.073	0.050	0.035	0.024	0.017
11	0.896	0.804	0.650	0.527	0.429	0.350	0.287	0.237	0.215	0.195	0.162	0.135	0.112	0.094	0.086	0.079	0.066	0.056	0.037	0.025	0.017	0.012
12	0.887	0.788	0.625	0.497	0.397	0.319	0.257	0.208	0.187	0.168	0.137	0.112	0.092	0.076	0.069	0.062	0.052	0.043	0.027	0.018	0.012	0.008
13	0.879	0.773	0.601	0.469	0.368	0.290	0.229	0.182	0.163	0.145	0.116	0.093	0.075	0.061	0.055	0.050	0.040	0.033	0.020	0.013	0.008	0.005
14	0.870	0.758	0.577	0.442	0.340	0.263	0.205	0.160	0.141	0.125	0.099	0.078	0.062	0.049	0.044	0.039	0.032	0.025	0.015	0.009	0.006	0.003
15	0.861	0.743	0.555	0.417	0.315	0.239	0.183	0.140	0.123	0.108	0.084	0.065	0.051	0.040	0.035	0.031	0.025	0.020	0.011	0.006	0.004	0.002
16	0.853	0.728	0.534	0.394	0.292	0.218	0.163	0.123	0.107	0.093	0.071	0.054	0.042	0.032	0.028	0.025	0.019	0.015	0.008	0.005	0.003	
17	0.844	0.714	0.513	0.371	0.270	0.198	0.146	0.108	0.093	0.080	0.060	0.045	0.034	0.026	0.023	0.020	0.015	0.012	0.006	0.003	0.002	
18	0.836	0.700	0.494	0.350	0.250	0.180	0.130	0.095	0.081	0.069	0.051	0.038	0.028	0.021	0.018	0.016	0.012	0.009	0.005	0.002	0.001	
19	0.828	0.686	0.475	0.331	0.232	0.164	0.116	0.083	0.070	0.060	0.043	0.031	0.023	0.017	0.014	0.012	0.009	0.007	0.003	0.002	0.001	
20	0.820	0.673	0.456	0.312	0.215	0.149	0.104	0.073	0.061	0.051	0.037	0.026	0.019	0.014	0.012	0.010	0.007	0.005	0.002	0.001	0.001	
21	0.811	0.660	0.439	0.294	0.199	0.135	0.093	0.064	0.053	0.044	0.031	0.022	0.015	0.011	0.009	0.008	0.006	0.004	0.002	0.001		
22	0.803	0.647	0.422	0.278	0.184	0.123	0.083	0.056	0.046	0.038	0.026	0.018	0.013	0.009	0.007	0.006	0.004	0.003	0.001	0.001		
23	0.795	0.634	0.406	0.262	0.170	0.112	0.074	0.049	0.040	0.033	0.022	0.015	0.010	0.007	0.006	0.005	0.003	0.002	0.001			
24	0.788	0.622	0.390	0.247	0.158	0.102	0.066	0.043	0.035	0.028	0.019	0.013	0.008	0.006	0.005	0.004	0.003	0.002	0.001			
25	0.780	0.610	0.375	0.233	0.146	0.092	0.059	0.038	0.030	0.024	0.016	0.010	0.007	0.005	0.004	0.003	0.002	0.001	0.001			
26	0.772	0.598	0.361	0.220	0.135	0.084	0.053	0.033	0.026	0.021	0.014	0.009	0.006	0.004	0.003	0.002	0.002	0.001				
27	0.764	0.586	0.347	0.207	0.125	0.076	0.047	0.029	0.023	0.018	0.011	0.007	0.005	0.003	0.002	0.002	0.001	0.001				
28	0.757	0.574	0.333	0.196	0.116	0.069	0.042	0.026	0.020	0.016	0.010	0.006	0.004	0.002	0.002	0.002	0.001	0.001				
29	0.749	0.563	0.321	0.185	0.107	0.063	0.037	0.022	0.017	0.014	0.008	0.005	0.003	0.002	0.002	0.001	0.001	0.001				
30	0.742	0.552	0.308	0.174	0.099	0.057	0.033	0.020	0.015	0.012	0.007	0.004	0.003	0.002	0.001	0.001	0.001					
40	0.672	0.453	0.208	0.097	0.046	0.022	0.011	0.005	0.004	0.003	0.001	0.001										
50	0.608	0.372	0.141	0.054	0.021	0.009	0.003	0.001	0.001	0.001												

Table B Present value of £1 received annually for N years

Years Hence	1%	2%	4%	6%	8%	10%	12%	14%	15%	16%	18%	20%	22%	24%	25%	26%	28%	30%	35%	40%	45%	50%
1	0.990	0.980	0.962	0.943	0.926	0.909	0.893	0.877	0.870	0.862	0.847	0.833	0.820	0.806	0.800	0.749	0.781	0.769	0.741	0.714	0.690	0.667
2	1.970	1.942	1.886	1.833	1.783	1.736	1.690	1.647	1.626	1.605	1.566	1.528	1.492	1.457	1.440	1.424	1.392	1.361	1.289	1.224	1.165	1.111
3	2.941	2.884	2.773	2.673	2.577	2.487	2.402	2.322	2.283	2.246	2.174	2.106	2.042	1.981	1.952	1.923	1.868	1.816	1.696	1.589	1.493	1.407
4	3.902	3.808	3.630	3.465	3.312	3.170	3.037	2.914	2.855	2.798	2.690	2.589	2.494	2.404	2.362	2.320	2.241	2.166	1.997	1.849	1.720	1.605
5	4.853	4.713	4.452	4.212	3.993	3.791	3.605	3.433	3.352	3.274	3.127	2.991	2.864	2.745	2.689	2.635	2.532	2.436	2.220	2.035	1.876	1.737
6	5.795	5.601	5.242	4.917	4.623	4.355	4.111	3.889	3.784	3.685	3.498	3.326	3.167	3.020	2.951	2.885	2.759	2.643	2.385	2.168	1.983	1.824
7	6.728	6.472	6.002	5.582	5.206	4.868	4.564	4.288	4.160	4.039	3.812	3.605	3.416	3.242	3.161	3.083	2.937	2.802	2.508	2.263	2.057	1.883
8	7.652	7.325	6.733	6.210	5.747	5.335	4.968	4.639	4.487	4.344	4.078	3.837	3.619	3.421	3.329	3.241	3.076	2.925	2.598	2.331	2.108	1.922
9	8.566	8.162	7.435	6.802	6.247	5.759	5.328	4.946	4.772	4.608	4.303	4.031	3.786	3.566	3.463	3.366	3.184	3.019	2.665	2.379	2.144	1.948
10	9.471	8.983	8.111	7.360	6.710	6.145	5.650	5.216	5.019	4.833	4.494	4.192	3.923	3.682	3.571	3.465	3.269	3.092	2.715	2.414	2.168	1.965
11	10.368	9.787	8.760	7.887	7.139	6.495	5.937	5.453	5.234	5.029	4.656	4.327	4.035	3.776	3.656	3.544	3.335	3.147	2.757	2.438	2.185	1.977
12	11.255	10.573	9.385	8.384	7.536	6.814	6.194	5.660	5.421	5.197	4.793	4.439	4.127	3.851	3.725	3.606	3.387	3.190	2.779	2.456	2.196	1.985
13	12.134	11.343	9.986	8.853	7.904	7.103	6.424	5.842	5.583	5.342	4.910	4.533	4.203	3.912	3.780	3.656	3.427	3.223	2.799	2.468	2.204	1.990
14	13.004	12.106	10.563	9.295	8.244	7.367	6.628	6.002	5.724	5.468	5.008	4.611	4.265	3.962	3.824	3.695	3.459	3.249	2.814	2.477	2.210	1.993
15	13.865	12.849	11.118	9.712	8.559	7.606	6.811	6.142	5.847	5.575	5.092	4.675	4.315	4.001	3.859	3.726	3.483	3.268	2.825	2.484	2.214	1.995
16	14.718	13.578	11.652	10.106	8.851	7.824	6.974	6.265	5.954	5.669	5.162	4.730	4.357	4.033	3.887	3.751	3.503	3.283	2.834	2.489	2.216	1.997
17	15.562	14.292	12.166	10.477	9.122	8.022	7.120	6.373	6.047	5.749	5.222	4.775	4.391	4.059	3.910	3.771	3.518	3.295	2.840	2.492	2.218	1.998
18	16.398	14.992	12.659	10.828	9.372	8.201	7.250	6.467	6.128	5.818	5.273	4.812	4.419	4.080	3.928	3.786	3.529	3.304	2.844	2.494	2.219	1.999
19	17.226	15.678	13.134	11.158	9.604	8.365	7.366	6.550	6.198	5.877	5.316	4.844	4.442	4.097	3.942	3.799	3.539	3.311	2.848	2.496	2.220	1.999
20	18.046	16.351	13.590	11.470	9.818	8.514	7.469	6.623	6.259	5.929	5.353	4.870	4.460	4.110	3.954	3.808	3.546	3.316	2.850	2.497	2.221	1.999
21	18.857	17.011	14.029	11.764	10.017	8.649	7.562	6.687	6.312	5.973	5.384	4.891	4.476	4.121	3.963	3.816	3.551	3.320	2.852	2.498	2.221	2.000
22	19.660	17.654	14.451	12.042	10.201	8.772	7.645	6.743	6.359	6.011	5.410	4.909	4.488	4.130	3.970	3.822	3.556	3.323	2.853	2.498	2.222	2.000
23	20.456	18.292	14.857	12.303	10.371	8.883	7.718	6.792	6.399	6.044	5.432	4.925	4.495	4.137	3.976	3.827	3.559	3.325	2.854	2.499	2.222	2.000
24	21.243	18.914	15.247	12.550	10.529	8.985	7.784	6.835	6.434	6.073	5.451	4.937	4.507	4.143	3.981	3.831	3.562	3.327	2.855	2.499	2.222	2.000
25	22.023	19.523	15.622	12.783	10.675	9.077	7.843	6.873	6.464	6.097	5.467	4.948	4.514	4.147	3.985	3.834	3.564	3.329	2.856	2.499	2.222	2.000
26	22.795	20.121	15.983	13.003	10.810	9.161	7.896	6.906	6.491	6.118	5.480	4.956	4.520	4.151	3.988	3.837	3.566	3.330	2.856	2.500	2.222	2.000
27	23.560	20.709	16.330	13.211	10.935	9.237	7.943	6.935	6.514	6.136	5.492	4.964	4.524	4.154	3.990	3.839	3.567	3.331	2.856	2.500	2.222	2.000
28	24.316	21.281	16.663	13.406	11.051	9.307	7.984	6.961	6.534	6.152	5.502	4.970	4.523	4.157	3.992	3.840	3.568	3.331	2.857	2.500	2.222	2.000
29	25.066	21.844	16.984	13.591	11.154	9.370	8.022	6.983	6.551	6.166	5.510	4.975	4.531	4.159	3.994	3.841	3.569	3.332	2.857	2.500	2.222	2.000
30	25.808	22.396	17.292	13.765	11.254	9.427	8.065	7.003	6.566	6.177	5.517	4.979	4.534	4.160	3.995	3.842	3.569	3.332	2.857	2.500	2.222	2.000
40	32.835	27.355	19.793	15.046	11.925	9.779	8.244	7.105	6.642	6.234	5.548	4.997	4.544	4.166	3.999	3.846	3.571	3.333	2.857	2.500	2.222	2.000
50	39.196	31.424	21.482	15.762	12.234	9.915	8.304	7.133	6.661	6.246	5.554	4.999	4.545	4.167	4.000	3.846	3.571	3.333	2.857	2.500	2.222	2.000

REFERENCES

Brealey, Richard A. and Myers, Stewart C. (1996) *Principles of Corporate Finance*, McGraw Hill, 5th ed., 1996, p. 161.

Buckley, Adrian A. (1996) *International Capital Budgeting*, Prentice Hall, 1996, p. 81.

Ho, S.S.M. and Pike, R.H. (1991) *Risk analysis in capital budgeting contexts: simple or sophisticated?* Accounting and Business Research, no. 83, Summer 1991, pp. 227–38.

Pike, R.H. (1992) *Capital Budgeting Survey: an update*, Bradford University Discussion Paper.

Siegel, Jeremy J. (1998) *Risk and return: start with the building blocks* in *Mastering Finance*, FT Pitman, 1998, p. 9.

Van Horne, James C. (1998) *Financial Management and Policy*, Prentice Hall, 11th ed., 1998, p. 73.

BIBLIOGRAPHY

Arnold, Glen, *Corporate Financial Management*, Pitman Publishing, 1998.

Buckley, A., *Multinational Finance*, Prentice Hall, 3rd ed., 1999.

Buckley, A., *International Capital Budgeting*, Prentice Hall, 1995.

Chew, Donald H., ed., *The New Corporate Finance: Where Theory Meets Practice*, Irwin McGraw Hill, 2nd ed., 1999.

Chew, Donald H., ed., *Discussing the Revolution in Corporate Finance*, Blackwell, 1998.

Copeland, T., Koller, T, and Murrin, J., *Valuation: Measuring and Managing the Value of Companies*, John Wiley, 2nd ed., 1995.

Davies, Mike, Paterson, Ron and Wilson, Allister: *UK GAAP: Generally Accepted Accounting Practice in the United Kingdom*, Macmillan for Ernst & Young, 6th ed., 1999.

Financial Times: *Mastering Finance*, Pitman, 1998.

Grundy, Tony and Ward, Keith, eds, *Strategic Business Finance*, Kogan Page, 1996.

Hull, John C., *Options, Futures, and Other Derivatives*, Prentice Hall, 3rd ed., 1997.

Reid, Walter and Myddelton, D.R., *The Meaning of Company Accounts*, Gower, 6th ed., 1996.

Rutterford, Janette, ed., *Financial Strategy: Adding Stakeholder Value*, John Wiley, 1998.

Stern, Joel and Chew, Donald H., eds.: *The Revolution in Corporate Finance*, Blackwell, 3rd ed., 1998.

Sudarsanam, P., *The Essence of Mergers and Acquisitions,* Prentice Hall, 1995.

Ward, Keith, *Corporate Financial Strategy*, Butterworth-Heinemann, 1993.

Ward, Keith, *Strategic Issues in Finance*, Butterworth-Heinemann, 1994.

ANSWERS TO PROBLEMS

Chapter 1. Introduction

Problem 1.1.   Bulldog plc

a. Return on net assets   = PBIT/(Net assets + short-term borrowing)
                            = 30/(195 + 15)   = **14.3%**

b. Profit margin   = PBIT/Turnover
                            = 30/190   = **15.8%**

c. Net asset turnover   = Turnover/(Net assets + short-term borrowing)
                            = 190/210   = **0.90**

d. Residual income   = Profit after tax 18.0 − Capital charge 14.4
                              [= 12% × 120]   **Residual income = +3.6**

Problem 1.2.

a. Stock turnover   = Cost of sales/Stock = 130/20   = **6.5 times**

   NB. We use cost of sales (if available), rather than sales turnover.

b. Days' sales in debtors = Debtors × 365/Turnover = (50 × 365)/190
                                                                              = **96.1 days**

c. Current ratio   = Current assets/Current liabilities
                            = 80/60   = **1.33**

d. Acid test ratio   = Liquid assets/Current liabilities
                            = 60/60   = **1.00**

Problem 1.3.

a. Debt ratio   = (long-term debt + short-term debt)/(equity + total debt)
                            = (75 + 15)/(120 + 90) = 90/210   = **42.9%**

b. Interest cover   = PBIT/Interest payable = 30/6   = **5.0 times**

Problem 1.4.

a. Dividend payout ratio   = Dividends/Profit after tax
                            = 12/18   = **66.7%**

b. Dividend cover   = PAT (earnings)/Dividends
                            = 18/12   = **1.50**

c. Dividend yield   = Dividend per share*/Market price per share
                            = 15*/270   = **5.6%**

* Dividends/Number of shares = 12/80 = 15.0p.

Problem 1.5.

a. Earnings per share	= Earnings (PAT)/Number of shares	
	= 18/80	= **22.5p**
b. Earnings yield	= eps/market price = 22.5/270	= **8.3%**
c. Price/earnings ratio	= Market price/eps	
	= 270/22.5	= **12.0**

Chapter 2. Interest rates

Problem 2.1.

Approximately, 4.5 per cent a year inflation premium.
Precisely, 4.369 per cent [1.075/1.030 = 1.04369]

Problem 2.2.

a. Probably no change (if people trust the indexing)
b. Increase, as the inflation premium increases.

Problem 2.3.

It depends on the maximum level of interest rate legally chargeable. It might be too high to have any effect! Assuming otherwise, the higher risks, who would be charged the highest risk premiums, would be affected, while lower-risk borrowers would not. Historically, this is what actually happened.

Problem 2.4.

If people expected *deflation* (negative inflation), then the 'inflation premium' would itself be negative; and might exceed the positive amount of pure time-preference.

Problem 2.5.

If the inflation premium charged *ex ante* turned out to be much less than the amount of inflation actually experienced. (This happened in the UK in the mid-1970s.)

Chapter 3. Cash

Problem 3.1.

a. Profit   £'000

Sales	450
Cost of sales	250
Gross profit	200
'Depreciation'	20
Net profit	180

b. Cash flow: profit + depreciation = $180 + 20 = £200,000$.

c. End-of-June cash balance: nil. Shareholders' funds £380,000 is balanced by debtors £300,000 plus equipment £80,000. The company is 'better off' by the extent of the profit. This is not necessarily yet reflected in cash.

Problem 3.2.

a. £20,000 is the only answer there is any basis for in the numbers ($= £200,000/10$); but (i) possible end-of-life salvage value could be used to reduce it; and (ii) it is possible to use 'accelerated' rather than 'straight-line' depreciation.

b. £30,000 post-depreciation profits a year.

c. £15,000 pre-depreciation profits would leave a post-depreciation *loss* of £5,000 a year. The 'correct' answer is that it would *not* change the answer to (a): we charge depreciation to find out what profit or loss the business has made, not according to what we think it can 'afford'! (In practice, one must admit, some business people might let their judgement be affected.)

d. (i) Depreciation would become £40,000 for the first five years, nil for years 6 to 10.

  (ii) post-depreciation profits would become £10,000 for the first five years and £50,000 for years 6 to 10.

 (iii) There would be no effect on cash flow! (Note too that the tax depreciation allowance would not be affected by a change in the estimated life.)

Problem 3.3.   Spanner Ltd

The exercise is fairly straightforward. It is worth getting it completed, so that the overall correspondence between cash and profit in the long run is established.

a. See Table A.3.1 (below).

b. Maximum need is £3,000,000 at the end of the fifth quarter. It is important to note the *timing* as well as the *amount* of this need.

c. Overall profit expected is £600,000 (7.5 per cent), which equals the net cash at the end.

Notes on layout:

1. It is usually desirable to have a 'total' column on the right. This can be very useful in checking the accuracy of the arithmetic.

2. Two separate rows are necessary at the foot of the table:
  (i) a net total for each period (column), reflecting either a cash inflow or a cash out-flow. (It is convenient to use a plus (+) sign to represent a cash inflow, and a minus (−) sign to represent a cash outflow.)
  (ii) a cumulative total to date.

Table A.3.1.   Spanner Ltd

	1	2	3	4	5	6	7	8	9	Total
Receipts										
Progress		700	700	700	700	700	700	700		4,900
Final									3,100	3,100
M/c sold									200	200
									3,300	8,200
Payments										
M/c	1,200									1,200
Labour	300	300	300	300	400	400	400	400		2,800
Materials		500	500	500	500					2,000
Other	200	200	200	200	200	200	200	200		1,600
	1,700	1,000	1,000	1,000	1,100	600	600	600		7,600
Balance										
Qtr.	−1,700	−300	−300	−300	−400	+100	+100	+100	+3,300	+600
Cum:	−1,700	−2,000	−2,300	−2,600	−3,000	−2,900	−2,800	−2,700	+600	

Problem 3.4.

Table A.3.2.   Gordon Bennett's bank overdraft July to January

Month	Bank overdraft (£)
August	5,200
September	16,800
October	21,200
November	26,400
December	24,400
January	18,800

Problem 3.5.

a. Table A.3.3.   Mrs. Congreve's cumulative bank balance

Month	Bank balance ($)
January	+ 670
February	+ 140
March	− 90
April	− 320
May	+ 50
June	+ 420

b. Overall loss for six months: $1,580. But the business is now making $370 per month profit (=$4,440 per year).

Problem 3.6.

A profitable firm can run out of cash by:

a. spending money on fixed assets (not yet charged as expenses), or
b. by heavy investment in stocks (not yet sold), or
c. by paying out all its profits in dividends to shareholders, or
d. by failing to collect cash from its customers, or
e. by repaying loans before there is sufficient equity capital.

A cash-rich firm may be unprofitable if:

a. it simply raises too much capital (equity or debt) to start with, or
b. it fails to pay its creditors, or
c. depreciation is a significant item of expense (and perhaps fixed assets are acquired by long-term leases).

Chapter 4. Working capital

Problem 4.1.

a. 2 weeks + 1.5 months = 2.0 + 6.5 weeks = 8.5 weeks @ £500 per week = £4,250.
   (Or simply £1,000 + £3,250 = £4,250.)
b. 2 weeks + 0.5 months = 2.0 + 2.17 weeks = 4.17 weeks @ £500 per week = £2,083.
   (Or simply £1,000 + £1,083 = £2,083.)
c. Investment in debtors saved: £4,250 − £2,083 = £2,167 @ 12 per cent a year = £260 per year.

Problem 4.2.

a. Current ratio: $(80 + 60 + 40)/120 = 180/120 = 1.50$.
b. Acid test ratio: $(60 + 40)/120 = 100/120 = 0.83$.
c. Working capital: $180 − 120 = £60,000$.

Problem 4.3.

a. $40/150 \times 365 = 97.3$ days.
b. $31 + 30 + 31 + (5/20 \times 30) = 92 + 7.5$ days $= 99.5$ days.
   The three full months outstanding are: Dec. 8, Nov. 12, Oct. 15; plus one quarter of Sept.
c. $31 + 30 + (5/12 \times 31) = 61 + 12.9$ days $= 73.9$ days.
   The two full months outstanding are: Dec. 20, Nov. 15, plus 5/12ths of Oct.

Problem 4.4.

	b	c
a. Overdue	32/40 = 80%	20/40 = 50%
b. 1 month + overdue	20/40 = 50%	5/40 = 12%
c. 2 months + overdue	5/40 = 12%	0/40 = 0%

Problem 4.5.

Debtors	$48/180 \times 12$ months	=	3.2 months
Finished goods	$25/120 \times 12$ months	=	2.5 months
Work in progress	$15/\ 90 \times 12$ months	=	2.0 months
Raw materials	$15/\ 60 \times 12$ months	=	3.0 months
Creditors	$18/\ 60 \times 12$ months	=	*3.6 months*
	7.1 months	=	213 days

Problem 4.6.

One can

a. arrange long-term funds to finance the maximum need, and have surplus cash at other times of year. This is less risky, but perhaps also less profitable (due to the low 'risk-free' rate of return earned on the surplus cash). Or
b. one can arrange long-term funds to finance only the minimum need, and then have to borrow short-term to finance the extra working capital requirement at other times of year. This is more risky, but perhaps also more profitable (since one only finances the amount actually needed).

Problem 4.7.

Some of the current liabilities may not actually be payable within the next one or two months (for example: corporation tax, dividends proposed, and perhaps bank overdrafts). And (or) some of the current assets may turn into cash very quickly, as may *future* sales (as in Tesco's case in the chapter). Using aggregates is a short-cut approximate way to assess liquidity; but ideally one should look at expected cash receipts and cash payments month by month. If a deficit of cash is expected, there may be sources of finance (such as increasing the bank overdraft) available.

Problem 4.8.

Literally having *zero* bad debts, if sales are made on credit, implies an extremely strict attitude to extending credit. Assuming a reasonable contribution on marginal extra sales, it seems likely that on balance it would pay to extend more credit, to include some rather less creditworthy customers (one or two of whom eventually would fail to pay in full). The increase (from zero) in bad debt expense would be more than offset by the additional contribution earned; thus the effect would be to increase profit.

Chapter 5. Capital project appraisal

Problem 5.1.

a. 14.87% (5 years); 7.18% (10 years).
   The Rule of 72 says: 'Divide 72 by the number n of years to find what interest rate will double an amount in n years.' This would give the answers: $72/5 = 14.4$ years; $72/10 = 7.2$ years. From seven years onwards, the Rule of 72 answer is within one-tenth of a percentage point of the correct answer.
b. Nearly quadrupling in 13 years implies an average rate of inflation of about 11% a year between 1974 and 1987.
c. The increase from 100 to 165 over 12 years since 1987 implies an average rate of inflation of about 4.25% a year.

Problem 5.2.

a. £550 × 0.909 = £500.
b. £1728 × 0.579 = £1,000.
c. £251 × 0.797 = £200.
d. £2000 × 0.500 = £1,000.

Problem 5.3.

a. £200 × 4.968 = £994.
b. £200 × 7.469 = £1,494.
c. £200 × 8.304 = £1,661.
d. The present value of the £200 annuity from Years 21 to 50, at a discount rate of 12 per cent a year, is only £167!
e. A *perpetuity* of £200 a year (for ever) would be worth £200 × 8.333 = £1,667. This can also be calculated as: £200/0.12 = £1,667.

Problem 5.4.

a. £3,000 × 4.870 = £14,610.
b. £2,000 × 7.469 = £14,938.
c. £1,000 × 14.877 = £14,877.

From Appendix 2, a guess between 2% and 4% for 20 years would be:
£1,000 × (16.351 + 13.590)/2 = £1,000 × 14.971 = £14,971.

All the answers are pretty close; but one would prefer (b) strictly; but (c) using the approximation.

Problem 5.5.

(b) would be better at *any* positive discount rate. (b) gives £200 a year more than (a) for Years 1 to 5, but £500 a year less for Years 6 and 7.

Problem 5.6.

9.33%.
Aiming for a factor of 410/1000 = 0.410:
8% = 0.463; 10% = 0.386.
8% + (53/77 × 2) = 8% + 106/77 = 8% + 1.38 = 9.38%.
Or 10% − (24/77 × 2) = 10% − 48/77 = 10% − 0.62 = 9.38%.

Problem 5.7.

a. 13.12%.
   Aiming for a factor of 5400/1000 = 5.400:
   12% = 5.650; 14% = 5.216.
   12% + (250/434 × 2) = 12% + 500/434 = 12% + 1.15% = 13.15%.
   Or 14% − (184/434 × 2) = 14% − 368/434 = 14% − 0.85 = 13.15%.
b. £1,288 = £5,400/4.192.

Problem 5.8.

a. +£1,200 × (3.605 − 2.106) = +£1,200 × 1.499 = +£1,799.
b. −£4,000 × (5.019 − 3.352) = −£4,000 × 1.667 = −£6,668.
c. + £800 × (4.968 − 2.402*) = + £800 × 2.566 = +£2,053.
d. +£5,000 × (6.661 − 6.566) = +£5,000 × 0.095 = + £475.

* The 'beginning of Year 4' = 'the end of Year 3'.

Problem 5.9.

Using a 4 per cent discount rate:

a. £997 × 4.452 = £4,439 − £4,200 = + £239.
b. £571 × 8.111 = £4,631 − £4,200 = + £431.
c. £366 × 13.590 = £4,974 − £4,200 = + £774.
d. £266 × 21.482 = £5,714 − £4,200 = +£1,514.

   This makes it clear that a change in interest rates affects the *longer-life* projects most.
Using an 8 per cent discount rate:

a. £997 × 3.993 = £3,981 − £4,200 = −£219
b. £571 × 6.710 = £3,831 − £4,200 = −£369
c. £366 × 9.818 = £3,593 − £4,200 = −£607
d. £266 × 12.234 = £3,254 − £4,200 = −£946

   It should be obvious why all the projects have a positive net present value when discounted at 4 per cent and a negative net present value when discounted at 8 per cent.

Problem 5.10.

a. Project J = +£142. Project H = +£139.
   So Project J has a higher NPV, by only £3.

Project H:

EOY $1 + £500 \times 0.870$	$=$	$+ £435$	
EOY $2 + £400 \times 0.756$	$=$	$+ £302$	
EOY $3 + £350 \times 0.658$	$=$	$+ £230$	
EOY $4 + £300 \times 0.572$	$=$	$+ £172$	
		$+£1139$	

Less: EOY 0	$-£1000$
Net present value:	$+£139$

Project J:

EOY $1-4 + £400 \times 2.855$	$=$	$+£1142$
Less: EOY 0		$-£1000$
Net present value:		$+£142$

b. Project H: $2 + 100/350 = 2.29$ years
   Project J: $2 + 200/400 = 2.50$ years.
c. Project H: $3 + 33/172 = 3.19$ years
   Project J: 3 years @ $15\% = 2.283 \times £400 = £913 + 87/229^* = 3.38$ years.

* PV of Year 4 cash inflow is $0.572 \times £400 = £229$.

Problem 5.11. Project T

a. Net Terminal Value: NTV

EOY $0 -200 \times (1.15)^5$	$= \times 2.011 =$	-402.2	
EOY $1 + 70 \times (1.15)^4$	$= \times 1.749 =$	$+122.4$	
EOY $2 + 70 \times (1.15)^3$	$= \times 1.521 =$	$+106.5$	
EOY $3 + 70 \times (1.15)^2$	$= \times 1.323 =$	$+ 92.6$	
EOY $4 + 70 \times (1.15)^1$	$= \times 1.150 =$	$+ 80.5$	
EOY $5 + 70 \times (1.15)^0$	$= \times 1.000 =$	$+ 70.0$	
Terminal Value:		$+472.0$	
Net Terminal Value:		$+69.8$	

Since the NTV is positive, yes it *is* worth investing.

b. Net Present Value: NPV

EOY 0	$-200 \times 1.000 =$	-200.0
EOY 1	$+ 70 \times 0.870 =$	$+ 60.9$
EOY 2	$+ 70 \times 0.756 =$	$+ 52.9$
EOY 3	$+ 70 \times 0.658 =$	$+ 46.1$
EOY 4	$+ 70 \times 0.572 =$	$+ 40.0$
EOY 5	$+ 70 \times 0.497 =$	$+ 34.8$
Present value:	$+ 70 \times 3.353 =$	$+234.7$
Net Present Value:		$+ 34.7$

Since the NPV is positive, yes it *is* worth investing.

Since we are looking at an annuity of £70,000 (for five years), we could use the cumulative discount factor for 15% for five years (namely, 3.353), instead of calculating the present value of each £70,000 year by year, as we have done above.

c. *Internal Rate of Return*

200/70 = 2.857. Hence IRR = 22.1%.

For 5 years, 22% factor = 2.864; 24% factor = 2.745.

So IRR = 22% + (7/119 × 2) = 22% + 0.12% = 22.1%.

d. *NTV = NPV*

NTV = 69.8 × 0.497 = NPV 34.7

NPV = 34.7 × 2.011 = NTV 69.8

So we see that Net Terminal Value and Net Present Value are precisely equivalent in terms of logic. The only difference between the two methods of course, is that Net Terminal Value compares cash inflows and outflows at the 'terminal' date, whereas Net Present Value compares cash inflows and outflows in 'present value' terms, that is, at End of Year 0.

Problem 5.12.

a. Cash saving £20,000 less depreciation £10,000 = Profit up by £10,000.

b. 10/50 = 20.0 per cent a year accounting rate of return on (initial) investment.

10/25 = 40.0 per cent a year accounting rate of return on (average) investment.

10/20 = 50.0 per cent a year rate of return on (average EOY) investment.

This shows that defining 'investment' can be tricky!

c. Annual net cash inflow = £20,000 labour savings.

Or annual profit £10,000 plus (add back) depreciation £10,000 = £20,000 cash inflow.

d. Payback period = 50/20 = 2.5 years.

e. PV EOY 1–5 = +20 × 3.352 = +£67,040 − £50,000 = NPV + £17,040.

f. IRR 5 years, 2.500 factor needed. 28% = 2.532; 30% = 2.436.

IRR = 28% + (32/96 × 2) = 28% + 64/96 = 28.67%.

Or IRR = 30% − (64/96 × 2) = 30% − 128/96 = 28.67%.

Chapter 6. More on capital projects

Problem 6.1. Stephen Collier

a. Cash expenses are £60,000 − £10,000 S/L depreciation = £50,000 a year. So for each of years 1 to 5, the net cash inflows are £30,000 (that is, £80,000 sales less £50,000 cash expenses). The £12,000 investment in stocks is assumed to be recoverable at the end of the project, that is EOY 5.

Net Present Value:

EOY		cash flow £'000	discount factor		present value £
0	Fixed assets	−50	1.000	=	−50,000
0	Stocks	−12	1.000	=	−12,000
1–5	Net inflows	+30	2.991	=	+89,730
5	Stocks	+12	0.402	=	+ 4,824
	Net Present Value:			=	+32,554

b. Conclusion: YES, invest in the project.

c. *Internal Rate of Return*

   With such a large positive net present value, the IRR must be a lot higher than 20 per cent. $62/30 = 2.067$, implying an IRR above 40 per cent (even ignoring the recovery of stocks). First trying 45 per cent (centre below), we get NPV $= -£3,848$; so we try 40 per cent (right below), and get NPV $= +£1,282$. By interpolation we then calculate IRR $= 41.3\%$.

EOY	Cash flow £'000	45% discount rate £	40% discount rate £
0	−62	× 1.000 = −62,000	× 1.000 = −62,000
1–5	+30	× 1.876 = +56,280	× 2.035 = +61,050
5	+12	× 0.156 = + 1,872	× 0.186 = + 2,232
Net Present Value:		− 3,848	+1,282

So IRR $= 40\% + (1282/5130 \times 5) = 40\% + 6410/5130 = 41.3\%$.
Or IRR $= 45\% - (3848/5130 \times 5) = 45\% - 19240/5130 = 41.3\%$.

Problem 6.2. Stephen Collier (after tax)

Notes.

1. The £2,000 sales proceeds would be subject to 30 per cent tax, so the after-tax cash inflow would be £1,400.
2. The net operating cash inflows in each of years 1 to 5 (£30,000) would also be subject to 30 per cent tax, leaving £21,000 a year after-tax.
3. There is no tax allowance on the investment in stocks, so the after-tax amount is £12,000 – the same as the before-tax amount.

4. Tax writing-down allowances @ 25% declining balance would be:

		50,000			
Year 1	25%	12,500 37,500	@ 30%	=	3,750
Year 2	25%	9,375 28,125	@ 30%	=	2,813
Year 3	25%	7,031 21,094	@ 30%	=	2,109
Year 4	25%	5,274	@ 30%	=	1,582
Year 5	Balance	15,820 15,000	@ 30%	=	4,746

a.

EOY		Cash flows £	Discount factor		Present value £
0	Sale	+ 1,400	×1.000	=	+ 1,400
0	New FA	−50,000	×1.000	=	−50,000
0	Stocks	−12,000	×1.000	=	−12,000 −60,600
1–5	Operations	+21,000	×3.352	=	+70,392
1	Tax WDA	+ 3,750	×0.870	=	+ 3,262
2	Tax WDA	+ 2,813	×0.756	=	+ 2,127
3	Tax WDA	+ 2,109	×0.658	=	+ 1,384
4	Tax WDA	+ 1,582	×0.572	=	+ 905
5	Tax WDA	+ 4,746	×0.497	=	+ 2,359
5	Stocks	+12,000	×0.497	=	+ 5,964
Net Present Value:				=	+25,793

b. Conclusion: YES, invest in the project.

c. *Internal Rate of Return*

For IRR, the first guess might be 25% (based on 60.6/21.0 = 2.89, allowing something for the tax WDAs and the recovery of stocks). This comes to an NPV of +£7,891, so it is clearly much too low. Then try 30%, still a bit too low; then 35%. The final estimate is 31.0%.

EOY	Cash flow	25 per cent	30 per cent	35 per cent
0	−60,600	1.000 − 60,600	1.000 − 60,600	1.000 − 60,600
1–5	+21,000	2.689 + 56,469	2.436 + 51,156	2.220 + 46,620
1	+ 3,750	0.800 + 3,000	0.769 + 2,884	0.741 + 2,779
2	+ 2,813	0.640 + 1,800	0.592 + 1,665	0.549 + 1,544
3	+ 2,109	0.512 + 1,080	0.455 + 960	0.406 + 856
4	+ 1,582	0.410 + 649	0.350 + 554	0.301 + 476
5	+16,746	0.328 + 5,493	0.269 + 4,505	0.223 + 3,734
NPV		+ 7,891	+ 1,124	− 4,591

The final estimate of IRR is then 31.0%:

30% + (1124/5715 × 5) = 30% + 5620/5715 = 31.0%
Or: 35% − (4591/5715 × 5) = 35% − 22955/5715 = 31.0%.

d. *Profitability Index*

86,393/60,600 = 1.43. [Or 143, if you multiply by 100.]

e. How low could the annual operating cash inflows be, and the project still be profitable?

@ 15% the net cash inflows of £21,000 a year after-tax × 3.352 = 70,392 PV. This could be £25,792 less, that is: £44,600.

£44,600/3.352 = £13,305 after-tax, or £13, 305/.7 = £19,008 before-tax.

Proof: Reduction of £10,992 a year before-tax = Reduction of £7,964 a year after-tax. 7,694 × 3.352 = 25,790 (the NPV @ 15%).

Problem 6.3. Park Products (German machine)

Tax writing-down allowances

Cost	60,000			
Year 1 @ 25%	15,000	@ 30%	=	4,500
	45,000			
Year 2 @ 25%	11,250	@ 30%	=	3,375
	33,750			
Year 3 @ 25%	8,438	@ 30%	=	2,531
	25,312			
Year 4 @ 25%	6,328	@ 30%	=	1,899
Year 5 balance	18,984	@ 30%	=	5,695
				18,000

EOY	Cash flow	Discount factor		Present value
0	−60,000	×1.000	=	−60,000
1–5	+14,000	×3.352	=	+46,928
1	+ 4,500	×0.870	=	+ 3,915
2	+ 3,375	×0.756	=	+ 2,552
3	+ 2,531	×0.658	=	+ 1,665
4	+ 1,899	×0.572	=	+ 1,086
5	+ 5,695	×0.497	=	+ 2,830
5	+ 3,500	×0.497	=	+ 1,740
Net Present Value:				+ 716

On the numbers above, the answer is YES, by a small margin. But clearly many of the numbers are only estimates.

Problem 6.4. Park Products Ltd. (Japanese machine)

EOY		Cash flow	Discount factor		Present value
0	Sale of G	+25,000	×1.000	=	+25,000
0	Tax on loss	+10,500	×1.000	=	+10,500
0	Purchase J	−60,000	×1.000	=	−60,000
					−24,500
1–5	Savings	+8,400	×3.352	=	+28,157
1–5	Tax WDAs (as before)			=	+12,048
	Net Present Value:				+15,705

a. On the numbers, Machine J should be acquired.
b. When Colin Park decided to buy Machine G, obviously he didn't know about machine J. Whether he *ought* to have known is hard to say. Perhaps at least he ought to have been aware of the *possibility* of a better Japanese machine, as he arranged to visit Tokyo only one month later.

Chapter 7. Mergers and acquisitions

Problem 7.1. David and Goliath

	Group balance sheet £ million
Fixed assets, net	400
Goodwill	50
Working capital	300
	750
Long-term debt	130
Shareholders' funds	
Issued £1 ordinary shares	180
Share premium	90
Retained profit	350
	750

Goodwill is the £120 million paid (30 million shares @ 400p each) less the £70 million book value of equity (= fair value) in David Ltd. Of the £120 million acquisition price (in shares in Goliath), £30 million represents nominal issued shares (@ £1 each) and the share premium of £90 million is the 30 million shares @ 300p each 'premium' over the nominal amount of £1 per share.

Problem 7.2.   Hollyhock plc

	£ million
Incremental cash flows:	
Existing	+4.0
Extra	+2.0
	+6.0
Less: to re-invest	−2.5
= Net inflow	+3.5

End of Year 0:	
Sale of surplus assets	+1.0
Capital investment	−5.0
= Net outflow	−4.0

a. EOY 1–10 @ 12% = 5.650 × +£3.5   =   +£19.78 million
    Less: EOY 0 net investment   =   −£ 4.00 million
    Maximum price: =   £15.78 million

b. EOY 1–15 @ 12% = 6.811 × +£3.5   =   +£23.84 million
    Less: EOY 0 net investment   =   −£ 4.00 million
    Maximum price   =   £19.84 million

    Or: £15.78 million + £3.5 (6.811 − 5.650)
=   £15.78 million + £3.5 × 1.161
=   £15.78 million + £4.06 million = £19.84 million.

Problem 7.3.   Beach Products

	Now £m	Equity £m	Debt £m
Capital structure			
Equity	90	140	90
Debt	30	30	80
	120	170	170
P&L summary			
PBIT	25	35	35
Interest	3	3	9
Profit before tax	22.0	32.0	26.0
Taxation @ 30 per cent	6.6	9.6	7.8
Profit after tax	15.4	22.4	18.2
Number of equity shares	10m	14m	10m
a. Debt ratio:	3/12	3/17	8/17
	25.0%	17.6%	47.1%
b. Interest cover	25/3	35/3	35/9
	8.3	11.7	3.9

c. Earnings per share   15.4/10   22.4/14   18.2/10
                                     1.54   1.60   1.82

Problem 7.4.   Peverill Plastics

a. EOY	Invest	Cash flow	+Extra	=	Total @ 10%	=	PV
0	−10				−10 × 1.000	=	−10.00
1	− 3	+ 8	+4	=	+ 9 × 0.909	=	+ 8.18
2	− 3	+ 9	+4	=	+10 × 0.826	=	+ 8.26
3	− 3	+10	+4	=	+11 × 0.751	=	+ 8.26
4	− 3	+11	+4	=	+12 × 0.683	=	+ 8.20
5	− *	+12	+4	=	+16* × 0.621	=	+ 9.94
Net present value:							+32.84

* Possibly include EOY 5: $-3 \times 0.621 = -1.86$ pv.

b. The maximum price that Peverill should pay for Middlesex is £32.83 million. If the £3 million investment at EOY 5 is included, that maximum price is reduced to £30.97 million.

c. Other possible methods of valuation include: price/earnings multiple or asset values.

Chapter 9. Borrowing

Problem 9.1.

The value of a perpetuity is a/r where a is the annual interest payment and r is the annual rate of interest.

Thus if $a =$ £6 and $r = 0.12$, $a/r = 6/0.12 =$ £50.
Then $6/50 = 12$ per cent.

a. If the current rate of interest falls from 12 to 10 per cent (r becomes 0.10), then a/r becomes $6/0.10 =$ £60. So the perpetuity's value *increases* from £50 to £60 if the interest rate falls from 12 to 10 per cent.

b. If the interest rate rises to 15 per cent, a/r become $6/0.15 =$ £40. So the perpetuity's value *falls* from £50 to £40 if the interest rate rises from 12 to 15 per cent.

Problem 9.2.

a. If a is 4 per cent and the value of a perpetuity is 60, then we have to solve the equation: $4/r = 60$. So $r = 4/60 = 6.67$ per cent.

b.   (i) If r is 5 per cent, then the value of the perpetuity is $4/0.05 = 80$.
     (ii) If r is 3 per cent, then the value of the perpetuity is $4/0.03 = 133$.

Evidently, if r were exactly 4 per cent, then the perpetuity would stand at par ($= 100$).

Problem 9.3.

The yield on an index-linked government bond comprises the risk free rate of pure time-preference – with no risk premium (because government bonds are supposed to be 'risk-free') and with no inflation premium (because the bond is 'index-linked' against inflation). Thus a change in the expected rate of inflation should not make any difference to the yield on an index-linked government bond. The same would be true if negative inflation (deflation) were expected: it should make no difference.

Of course, changes in the expected future rate of inflation *would* make a difference to the nominal yield on risk-free government stocks that were *not* index-linked.

Problem 9.4.

a. The value of a perpetuity is a/r where a is the annual interest payment and r is the annual rate of interest.

So if the composite rate of interest rises from 9 per cent $(2 + 3 + 4)$ to 10 per cent $(2 + 2 + 6)$, the value of a perpetuity paying £3.24 million per year $(= £36.0$ million @ 9 per cent) would *fall* from £36.0 million to $£3.24/0.10 = £32.4$ million.

b. If Dodgy's debt were redeemable 16 years after it had been borrowed, that means the debt is redeemable (one year later) in a further 15 years' time. So the value of the debt is £33.24 million, as follows:

EOY 1–15   £3.24 million × 7.606 = £24.64 million
EOY 15   £36.00 million × 0.239 = £8.60 million
                                     £33.24 million

Chapter 10. Ordinary share capital

Problem 10.1.

	a	b	c
Profit after tax (£'000)	20	60	100
Preference dividend	20	20	20
Profit for ordinary	0	40	80
Ordinary dividend (50%)	0	20	40
Ordinary dividend per share (pence)	0	5.0	10.0

Problem 10.2.   Nancy King

a. 240m (@ 330p = £792m) + 360m (@ 50p = £180m) = 600m (@ 162p = £972m).
b. 240m (@ 330p = £792m) + 60m (@ 300p = £180m) = 300m (@ 324p = £972m).

Value of rights:
a. 112p (162p − 50p) per *new* share; or 168p per old share.
b. 24p (324p − 300p) per *new* share; or 6p per old share.

	(a) 3 for 2 @ 50p		(b) 1 for 4 @ 300	
	OK	CB	OK	CB
Opening holding:				
2000 shares @ 330p	£6,600	£6,600	£6,600	£6,600
Buy 3000 shares @ 50p	£1,500			
Buy 500 shares @ 300p			£1,500	
Sell 2000 rights @ 168p		(£3,360)		
Sell 2000 rights @ 6p				(£120)
Closing holding:				
a. OK. 5000 shares @ 162p	£8,100			
CB. 2000 shares @ 162p		£3,240		
b. OK. 2500 shares @ 324p			£8,100	
CB. 2000 shares @ 324p				£6,480

Problem 10.3. Knight, Terry and Lincoln

£ million	Start	Knight	Terry	Lincoln
Issued £1 shares	120	140	160	150
Share premium	–	10	–	30
Retained profits	70	70	30	70
Shareholders' funds	190	220	190	250
Net change (total)	–	+30	–	+60
Market value	288	318	288	348
Number of shares (m)	*120*	*140*	*160*	*150*
= Market price per share (p)	240	227	180	232

Problem 10.4. George Shackle

a. Families sell $1/3 \times 24$m shares   =   8 million shares
   Company sells £21*m @ 150p each   =   14 million shares
                                       =   22 million shares

  * £20m net needed + £1m expenses.

b. 60m + 14m = 74m shares in issue
   74m @ 176p (= 160p + 10%) = £130.24m.

c. Earnings per share = 10p.
   So price/earnings ratio = 160/10 = 16.0 times.

Chapter 11. Cost of capital

Problem 11.1.

a. Large loss-making company: 12.0% *and* 12.0% − 5.0% = 7.0% real.
b. Small profitable company: 12.0% × (100 − 20)% = 9.6% *and* 4.6% real.
c. Sole trader 12.0% × (100 − 40)% = 7.2% *and* 2.2% real.

Problem 11.2.

ABC: 4.0 + 1.2(8.0) = **13.6.**

Problem 11.3.

DEF: **3.5** + 0.75(6.0) = 8.0.

Problem 11.4.

GHI: 4.5 + **1.5**(8.0) = 16.5.

Problem 11.5.

JKL: 4.0 + 0.8(**6.0**) = 8.8.

Problem 11.6.

MNO: 4.0 + 0.75(**8.0**) = 10.0;
hence when beta doubles: 4.0 + 1.5(8.0) = 16.0.
so *increase* is 0.75 × 8.0 = 6.0.

Problem 11.7.

6.0/(0.15 − 0.05) = 6.0/0.10 = 60p.

Problem 11.8.

4.0/(0.20 − 0.02) = 4.0/0.18 = 22p.

Problem 11.9.

PLQ: $k = d'/p + g$ = 5.4 + 8.0 = 13.4 per cent cost of equity.

Problem 11.10.

RST: 14.4 = 4.0%(100 + g) + g = 4.0 + 1.04g
hence 14.4 − 4.0 = 1.04g = 10.4
hence g = 10.0 per cent.

Problem 11.11.

UVW: 240 = 12/0.05
hence k − g = 0.05; which equals 2g − g = g.
hence g = 5.0 per cent.

Problem 11.12.

XY: equity £60m $= 3/4$; debt £20m $= 1/4$.
hence WACC $= (3/4 \times 12) + (1/4 \times 6) = 9 + 1.5 = 10.5$ per cent.

Problem 11.13.

ZA: Let debt fraction be x, and equity fraction $(1 - x)$.
Then $(x \times 6 \text{ debt cost}) + [(1 - x) \times 15 \text{ equity cost}] = 12$ WACC
$6x + 15 - 15x = 12$
$3 = 9x$
$1/3 = x$
So the debt fraction is $1/3$ and the equity fraction $2/3$.
Proof: $(1/3 \times 6) + (2/3 \times 15) = 2 + 10 = 12$.

Problem 11.14.

BC: The weights are debt 0.3 and equity 0.7.
Cost of debt is 5 and cost of equity unknown (say z)
Then $(0.3 \times 5) + (0.7 \times z) = 12.0$
Hence $0.7z = 12.0 - 1.5 = 10.5$
Hence $z = 15.0$.

Problem 11.15.

DE: Book values are: debt £200m and equity £400m.
Hence book value weights are: debt $1/3$ and equity $2/3$.
Cost of debt is 6%, cost of equity is 12%.
Hence WACC based on book value weights is: $(1/3 \times 6) + (2/3 \times 12) = 2 + 8 = 10.0$.
Market values are: debt £200m (assumed) and equity £600m.
Hence market value weights are: debt $1/4$ and equity $3/4$.
Hence WACC based on market value weights is: $(1/4 \times 6) + (3/4 \times 12) = 1.5 + 9 = 10.5$.
Hence WACC increases by 0.5 per cent using market value rather than book value weights.

Chapter 12. Capital structure

Problem 12.1. Laurel and Hardy

£ million	Year 1		Year 2	
	Laurel	Hardy	Laurel	Hardy
PBIT	30.00	30.00	9.00	9.00
Interest	1.80	7.20	1.80	7.20
Profit before tax	28.20	22.80	7.20	1.80
Tax @ 30 per cent	8.46	6.84	2.16	0.54
Profit after tax	19.74	15.96	5.04	1.26
Equity capital	102	48	102	48
Return on equity %	19.4	33.3	4.9	2.6
Interest cover	16.7	4.2	5.0	1.25

ROE will be the same when $[L] \, 0.7(x - 1.8)/102 = [H] \, 0.7(x - 7.2)/48$
when $48x - 86.4 = 102x - 734.4$
when $648 = 54x$
when $x = £12$ million.

Thus when ROCE is 10.0 per cent, ROE is 7.0 per cent for each company.

Problem 12.2. Borg and Laver

£ million	Year 1		Year 2	
	Borg	Laver*	Borg	Laver
PBIT	40	40	150	150
Interest	7.5	60	7.5	60
Profit before tax	32.5	*20*	142.5	90
Tax @ 40%	13.0	*8*	57.0	36
Profit after tax	19.5	*12*	85.5	54
Equity capital	950	600	950	600
a. Return on equity %	2.1	*2.0*	9.0	9.0
b. Earnings per share	0.98p	*0.60p*	4.28p	2.70p
Number of shares	2000	2000	2000	2000
c. Interest cover	5.3	0.67	20.0	2.5

d. Return on equity is the same in Year 2 at 9.0% (when ROCE is 15.0%).

* NB. Italics represent negative amounts for Laver in Year 1.

Problem 12.3. Travis plc

£ million	Now	With increased capital	
		Equity	Debt
PBIT	150	200	200
Interest	20	20	56
Profit before tax	130	180	144
Tax @ 40%	52	72	57.6
Profit after tax	78	108	86.4
Number of shares (m)	600	720	600
Earnings per share (p)	13.0	15.0	14.4
Interest cover	7.5	10.0	3.6

The cross-over level of EPS comes at a PBIT of £236 million:

$$[F] \ 0.6(x - 20)/720 = 0.6(x - 56)/600 \ [D]$$
$$5x \quad - 100 = 6x - 336$$
$$x \quad = 236.$$

Problem 12.4. Andover Equipment plc

a.
Equity		Debt
$0.70(x - 9.0)/220$	$=$	$0.70(x - 11.4)/200$
$10x - 90$	$=$	$11x - 125.4$
35.4	$=$	x

£ million	Now	After expansion		Same EPS	
		Equity	Debt	Equity	Debt
PBIT	54.0	60.0	60.0	35.4	35.4
Interest	9.0	9.0	11.4	9.0	11.4
Profit before tax	45.0	51.0	48.60	26.40	24.00
Tax @ 30%	13.5	15.3	14.58	7.92	7.20
Profit after tax	31.5	35.7	34.02	18.48	16.80
Number of shares (m)	200	220	200	220	200
Earnings per share (p)	15.75	16.23	17.01	**8.40**	**8.40**
c. Interest cover	6.0	6.7	5.3	3.9	3.1
d. debt ratio (mv)	$90^+/360^+$	$90^+/390^+$	$120^+/390^+$		
	$25^+\%$	$23^+\%$	$31^+\%$		
debt ratio (bv)	90/270	90/300	120/300		
	33%	30%	40%		

INDEX

Note: Page references in *italics* refer to Figures; those in **bold** refer to Tables